PRIVATIZATION AND
THE PUBLIC GOOD

PRIVATIZATION AND THE PUBLIC GOOD

Public Universities in the Balance

For Karen Schultz —
A scholar who understands the greater good
in a higher education and a great friend
to William & Mary.

Matthew T. Lambert

Matthew T. Lambert

HARVARD EDUCATION PRESS

CAMBRIDGE, MASSACHUSETTS

Library of Congress Control Number 2014936901

Paperback ISBN 978-1-61250-731-6
Library Edition 978-1-61250-732-3

Published by Harvard Education Press,
an imprint of the Harvard Education Publishing Group

Harvard Education Press
8 Story Street
Cambridge, MA 02138

Cover Design: Saizon Design
Cover Photo: © PictureNet/Corbis

The typefaces used in this book are Adobe Garamond Pro and ITC Legacy.

For my three joys,
the loves of my life—
Karen, William,
and Harrison

CONTENTS

FOREWORD

The tension between public and private purposes is endemic to American history and to its most important social institutions. Some scholars have interpreted American history as a perennial struggle between public and private interests, between values derived primarily from democratic ideals and those identified with free-market capitalism, with alternating eras in which these value sets were ascendant.

Higher education has not been insulated from these tensions. The post–World War II higher education system was developed during a time of public policy initiatives and public sector expansiveness. Whether measured in terms of increased college participation and educational attainment or the growth and quality of colleges and universities, American higher education is recognized as one of the national successes of the second half of the twentieth century. The epoch of public purpose that spawned this achievement has given way to a period of privatism that Michael Sandel has characterized as "market triumphalism" in American society. Private interests and deference to markets have supplanted normative public purposes and shared societal goals in the substance and language of public policy discourse. Fiscal stringency in the public sector has been both a cause and a consequence of this shift.

The role of higher education in American society has been shaped by market forces, by public policy reflecting broad societal goals, and by the values of educators. Higher education is expected to produce public and private benefits. To some international observers, our "system" of colleges and universities has long been substantially market-driven, because it encompasses public and private institutions, and is significantly influenced by decisions of students and by competition among institutions for students, faculty, resources, and status.

The unique privatization challenge currently confronting American higher education differs from the rebalancing of public and academic influences that is undertaken by higher education leaders in every era. The national political ethos has shifted toward preferences for private interests and markets as instruments for achieving the common good. Trust in government has eroded. Perceptions that the public sector is ineffective and inefficient, that Americans are overtaxed, and that the role of government in American life should contract have been widely embraced. Ironically, as these attitudes were gaining traction, most states were adding more functions by assuming greater responsibilities for supporting public schools and health care, even while reducing taxes in some instances. The consequences are long-term state structural deficits exacerbated by recessions over the last quarter-century, and recurrent fiscal crises as states seek to meet constitutional requirements for balanced budgets. Another repercussion is intensified competition for limited state resources. For public colleges and universities, this political and financial environment has brought incremental and episodic but relentless declines in state appropriations. The cumulative effect is that public higher education is now dependent as never before on alternative sources of revenue, principally tuition (substantially funded by student debt), private fundraising, research support from the private sector, and income from patents.

Matthew Lambert's Privatization and the Public Good provides our most comprehensive and definitive examination of the evolution of privatization and its significance for the future. Lambert's analysis extends far beyond the narrow financial issues raised in most discussions of higher education's "broken business model" to the broader implications for the missions and functions of public colleges and universities. How has the character of public higher education changed in response to the privatized funding model? What are the implications for the public purposes of public colleges and universities and for their role in a democratic society? Can core public missions that society depends upon more than ever—particularly access to affordable, high quality education and training—be preserved and enhanced in the privatized financial environment with its powerful incentives to "follow the money"?

While Lambert's findings are applicable across the fifty states and more than four thousand institutions of higher education, this book's principal focus is on three states and their public flagship research universities. This is appropriate because while privatization and the issues it raises are important for all of public higher education, the flagship universities have been the locus of the tensions and conflicts that have played out most explicitly and intensely over the last three decades. Generally, the flagship institutions have more access to private and federal revenue sources and greater capacity to raise tuition. Lambert's other focus is state government and politics. Historically, the states have been the principal funding source for most public colleges and universities, and state dollars have been provided primarily to support core public missions, particularly access, affordability, and instructional quality.

The case studies of Virginia, North Carolina, and California incorporate the perspectives of higher education leaders, state legislators, and other public officials and make it clear that the preservation of the public missions of colleges and universities is an intensely political as well as a financial and educational issue. The privatization scenarios and the responses have evolved in different ways in each state. Lambert provides rich and insightful documentation of states and universities grappling with privatization and its ramifications in the context of very different histories, traditions, and politics.

Lambert offers no formulaic solution. As his book shows, each state will need to develop its private-public model and its own political consensus. However these scenarios play out, he insists that the overarching commonalities are issues of public purpose and that the missions of public colleges and universities are more than the sum or size of their revenue streams. He finds grounds for guarded optimism in the experiences of the states—optimism that states and higher education institutions can develop new social contracts for the twenty-first century around well-articulated public purposes supported by hybrid public-private funding models. Even those who may not share his optimism will benefit from this multidimensional reframing of privatization and his call for explicit public discourse around higher education's public agenda and how it is to be funded.

I am persuaded by Lambert's analysis in this book. I believe there are several wild cards, some wholly or partly within the control of public higher education and some external, that will determine the effectiveness of our states and their public colleges and universities in assuring the vitality of their public purposes:

- In an increasingly contentious and polarized political world, will governors and legislatures emerge who can be the public stewards of the public missions of colleges and universities, lead public coalitions in support of a public agenda, and help create public accountability that stimulates, supports, and rewards responsiveness to public purposes?

- Will colleges and universities and their governing boards find and select presidents with the passion, commitment, and skill for stewardship of public purposes in the face of overwhelming pressures to focus
  on revenues?
- Will political and academic leaders continue to prefer the incremental
  drifts toward privatization to the clear articulation of public purposes
  and the explicit development of policies to support them?
- Can public trust in colleges and universities and their commitment
  to serving the public be raised to levels that enable state and academic
  leaders to develop and sustain new social contracts around public
  purposes?

To his credit, Matthew Lambert has considered all these issues. His call
is for public discourse that begins first with principles—public purposes and
institutional missions. *Privatization and the Public Good* makes the case for
the importance and urgency of that discourse and provides an essential re-
source for those willing to engage in it.

Patrick M. Callan
President, Higher Education Policy Institute

Frogs Boiling in the Water

WHEN I WAS an undergraduate student at the College of William & Mary during a state budget crisis in the 1990s, I was invited to the campus student center to write letters to the governor and state legislators, encouraging them to restore and then increase funding for the university's budget. I can recall vividly the overhead projector glowing brightly in the slightly darkened room, providing a template for us to follow in declaring all the things we would have to do without if funding were not restored. "Please help us to keep Professor _____ *(fill in the name of your favorite professor)* from leaving the university . . . don't force us to endure larger classes . . . several of my friends had to leave because of the rise in tuition . . . what will become of this great university?" Apocalyptic appeals to legislators seemed necessary at a time when state funding was so central to the budget and it had been cut so severely; almost no one at the time thought the trend would be permanent and worsening.

My letters, in retrospect, look eerily similar to the World Wildlife Fund appeals to "Save the Whales"; most faculty would probably prefer to be compared to dolphins, but the danger was real and immediate. I am nearly certain that the free pizza was the predominant reason I joined the effort initially, but over time I began to wonder whether the fate of my university and those of other public institutions in the state really depended on hungry students like me writing form letters to legislators. What did these people in the state capitol really know about students, colleges, and universities, or the

effects of what *they* were doing to *us*? My first introduction to higher education politics left me less than satisfied. Bigger questions about the broader
system of higher education would have to wait for graduate school. After four
slices of pizza and five letters, I was ready to move on and get back to Philosophy and Psychology.

Politics has always been a rough-and-tumble world. During the past several decades, however—as retired state legislators, policy makers, and institutional leaders told me time and again during our interviews—the mostly
respectful world of state politics and higher education public policy has de-
volved into talking past one another. The distance between the two political
parties has grown wider on many issues, while term limits and frequent turnover in statehouses have reduced collegiality among lawmakers. The foundational relationships and deep knowledge of issues that are central to political
deal making and good public policy seem more elusive than ever.

When asked what has changed most significantly in the legislature over
the past two decades, one retired college president pondered the question for
just a moment before saying, "There is no one in the legislature today who
has higher education in his heart." Responding to the same question, a long-
serving state legislator put it even more starkly, "We used to fight all day but
then have dinner together at night, always working to solve problems; now
we just don't talk to one another."

In addition to the challenges in the political sphere, there is less communication between college and university presidents and public officials. Public
higher education is alternately referred to by outsiders as being "profligate"
and by insiders as being in a "state of austerity."[1] Beyond mere differences
in terminology, legislators and higher education leaders often appear to be
speaking different languages about the same enterprise.[2] I found myself wondering whether leaders of colleges and universities and legislators and governors really understood—or even listened to—one another. There was no
agreement on the problem, so solutions seemed out of reach.

Beyond a broad discussion of concepts such as access, affordability, and
economic development in state capitols, there is rarely any thoughtful dialogue about the goals that states have for higher education. A national agenda
for higher education is even more elusive. Lacking, too, is an understanding
of what legislators believe they are "buying" when they fund higher education or how institutions can renew their trust in higher education. Considering the pressures of privatization and the calls for increased autonomy and
funding that face most states and many institutions today (not to mention

the federal government's budget problems), the timing may be perfect for states and institutions to collaborate on new models and solutions.

Perhaps because, when I began writing this book, I was teaching college students who were studying to be foreign service officers and diplomats, I tried my hand at the ancient art of diplomacy—particularly shuttle diplomacy. And so I set out to understand what is happening in public higher education not only by talking with college and university leaders, but also by spending countless hours with governors, state legislators, policy makers, federal officials, and the innumerable others who have a vested interest in the future of higher education outside the academy.

This is the story of public higher education in a rapidly globalizing world, told by those in state capitols as well as college campuses. For better or worse, higher education—particularly public higher education—is experiencing a "new normal," driven by the forces of globalization, economic turmoil, and changing demographics in the United States and around the world. Historically, higher education was viewed as a public good that benefited all in society, not just the enrolled student, and so taxpayers were willing to generously fund a system of public higher education. Today, however, there is a fundamental rethinking of whether higher education is and should be a public good or merely a private benefit to the individual.

Gordon Davies, reflecting on his twenty years leading Virginia's system of public higher education, noted in his memoir that "education is not a trivial business, a private good, or a discretionary expenditure. It is a deeply ethical undertaking at which we must succeed if we are to survive as a free people."[3] Privatization has been knocking at the door for more than two decades and is here to stay, but we must approach and conceive of higher education as a public good and seek to maintain its role in society as such. Democracy depends upon it.

Privatization: Not a Dirty Word

I am sitting in the small waiting area outside the state senator's office in California, and the receptionist barely notices me as he answers five phone calls from constituents in ten minutes. In state government, every voice can be heard, regardless of how large or small the issue may seem. The receptionist dutifully writes down the name of the constituents and whether they are for or against a particular measure, almost as if taking a poll to see which way the senator should vote. Today, whatever the issue du jour, the citizens appear to be in favor of it and want to be certain the senator is, too. "I will be sure to let him know you support the bill, ma'am. Thank you for calling."

The shabby and mismatched office furniture and fake wood paneling on the walls remind me of the 1970s. I am comforted, at least, that tax dollars don't appear to be going toward chic design and upscale furnishings. After perusing the senator's pamphlets and newsletters about his legislation introduced and passed in the last session, I scan the room for more clues. I am struck by just how many awards state legislators receive from organizations I have never heard of—many of them representing particular interests in the state, from agriculture to manufacturing to law enforcement to the Chamber of Commerce and everything in between. Most of these organizations have presented the senator with a plaque noting his commitment to furthering their cause or supporting their goals in some way—just one manifestation of the many competing interests for tax dollars in the state.

From the senator's inner chamber, another assistant emerges. "Dr. Lambert? Senator Smedley will see you now."[4]

"Thank you. Senator, it's a pleasure to meet you—thank you for taking the time to talk with me."

Standing behind the desk, his jacket draped over the chair, and without looking up from his BlackBerry for more than a quick glance over his bifocals to glare at his assistant, the senator asks, "Remind me what exactly you are here to talk about?"

I begin to explain that I am interested in the forces of privatization in public higher education. He interrupts me abruptly.

"I see. Well, in that case, let me just begin, young man, by making one thing abundantly clear to you. The public universities in this state will never, ever be private. Privatization is not a part of our vocabulary. Got it?"

State government is not the most glamorous venue of public service, but it is in many ways the bedrock of our system of democracy. The future of public higher education depends on these elected officials and their perception of the value of higher education. Over the course of nearly one hundred fifty interviews with current and former state legislators, governors, members of Congress, and policy makers, I became convinced that all hope is not lost for public higher education, but that the time for a renewed conversation is now.

In meeting after meeting with elected officials, I found myself explaining what I meant by *privatization* and asking the person across the desk to talk openly about what has happened to the colleges and universities in a state facing the same funding issues as most of the other forty-nine. Further,

I asked these lawmakers how higher education is seen relative to the many other pressing issues facing them each day. Generally, after ten minutes of back and forth, we were finally able to talk about the true substance of the significant changes in public higher education. Once we agreed on the problem, we were able to have a real conversation about what has happened, what they personally see and want to see in higher education, and how we move toward real change.

I often elicited the same visceral reaction to the word *privatization* from leaders of colleges and universities, who have learned the political lesson that using the "p" word is taboo. Every meeting with a president or chancellor began with them telling me, "I don't use the word because it makes for bad politics." One even went so far as to say, "Just look at Biddy Martin (former chancellor of the University of Wisconsin–Madison) and Richard Lariviere (former president of the University of Oregon). Both got fired for pushing for privatization."[5] Here, too, once we came to some agreement on the terms of the debate and what was meant by the broader definition of privatization, we made real progress in understanding the significant challenges in public higher education.

Privatization is manifested in many forms and definitions, and, as elected officials and university presidents made evident, it is a highly charged term. As Mark Twain once quipped, "the difference between the almost right word and the right word is really a large matter—it's the difference between the lightning bug and the lightning." While privatization may offend some, upset some, and excite still others, it is the right word to describe what has happened and is happening in public higher education.

Most often, in discussions of privatization, there is an emphasis on market orientation or the introduction of capitalism, typically resulting in increased philanthropic support, higher tuition, and more avenues for revenue, such as auxiliary services and executive education.[6] Because every state has different circumstances, the combination of some or all of these factors affects different states and institutions in different ways. The five main themes that are consistent across various privatization proposals in higher education are tuition control, autonomy with regard to management and governance, regulatory flexibility, performance contracting, and some form of vouchers.[7] I discuss each of these themes in greater depth in the chapters that follow.

Privatization often results in increased autonomy for institutions, allowing for greater flexibility and less bureaucracy in areas such as tuition and enrollment control, contracting, human resources, and capital projects, and it is frequently accompanied by additional accountability requirements and performance measures. Each of these factors and the related outcomes require deep examination for us to understand the balancing of an institution's public mission and the competitive market in which that institution exists.

While more prevalent in the United States, the privatization trend is not a uniquely American phenomenon. The privatization of higher education is occurring around the globe, and some of the trends, including higher tuition and increased autonomy, are similar to those in the United States. Increasingly, nations are finding it challenging to support both massification—broad-based access for more students—and high-quality, world-class institutions. Globalization has changed societies, and institutions of higher education follow the trends of society. Economies are no longer limited by state or national boundaries, and neither is knowledge, and so public institutions are pushing the limits of their missions, which have been historically tied to the local community or the state.[8]

Privatization is not and perhaps never will be true privatization in the sense of public entities being handed over fully to private control. Many elements of higher education institutions (including housing and dining, bookstores, fundraising, and even professional schools) may be fully privatized, and these examples will be discussed in this book, but it's unlikely that the entire institution will shift from "public" to "private" control. However, over the past twenty years, American colleges and universities have been forced to reimagine the definition of *public*. Rising enrollment and tuition, increasing costs and services, and decreasing state funding have led to a crossroads where higher education is being challenged and stretched today, and many are questioning it as a public good.

James Duderstadt, president emeritus of the University of Michigan, has described great public universities as "privately supported public universities" and famously described the evolution of the university from "state-supported to state-assisted to state-related to state-located to state-molested."[9] Sometimes language can make all the difference in illuminating an argument, and that is why privatization, at times, evokes emotionally charged reactions. In the political environment in which public colleges and universities exist, such descriptions do not earn more friends in the state capitol.

Privatization describes the forces changing public higher education rapidly in an era of globalization—the balancing act between the old way of envisioning a public university as the "people's university," funded by and solely accountable to the state, and the new public-private partnership that is funded by and accountable to multiple stakeholders. What remains to be seen is how privatization will affect state and national goals for democratic and civic education, economic development, research, health care, and even national security.

Frogs Boiling in the Water

One of the joys—if I can call it that—of spending innumerable hours with legislators and governors is learning to decode, decipher, and translate talking points, political language, and demagoguery into core concerns and viable solutions. Politicians are nothing if not colorful, and the analogies and metaphors they have for colleges and universities range from children ("sometimes adolescent, sometimes mature, but always needy") to certain members of the animal kingdom ("long arms and short memories") to Chicken Little ("the sky is falling!"). Their words help to tell the story of a rapidly changing system of higher education.

The most apt description of the current state of higher education, however, came from a legislator who described the problem as the one of the fabled frog in boiling water. As the story goes, if you put a frog into a pot of boiling water, he will jump out immediately. But if you put the frog into the pot of water and then turn on the heat, he won't realize it is boiling until it is too late. Though the story of the frog is more myth than science, that slow simmering to a boil is the essential challenge in public higher education. The changes in higher education have been so incremental over decades that very few outside the academy (or sometimes even within it) realize that the water is boiling today.

The problems confronting universities today are the result of a generational neglect by the states and citizens, a reluctance to change and a dearth of creativity within institutions, and a gradual shift in the perception of higher education from public good to private benefit. Slow erosion of support for public higher education and a lack of agreement about its problems have led to stalemate and a slow but steady change.

The country today needs a spirited public dialogue, at both the state and federal levels, about higher education public policy. We need such a dialogue to reestablish some consensus and trust as the country looks to an uncertain future and as institutions—particularly public colleges and universities—seek to fulfill their mission in the years ahead.

Since the earliest days of our republic, education has been considered synonymous with democracy, and we have been a people focused on the larger public good. There will often be disagreements about the best way to use public dollars and what defines the public good, but a vigorous dialogue about higher education public policy can help build consensus and strengthen the bonds among institutional leaders, state and federal officials, and the publics they serve. The challenges facing public colleges and universities are complex, but universities and states can work together to achieve a new, mutually beneficial model of privatization—the public-private partnership—where both the aspirations of the institution and its service to the public good can thrive.

As Thomas Jefferson said two centuries ago, education should be held sacred among all public entities because it not only "contribute[s] to the improvement of the country" but also helps ensure its "preservation."

CHAPTER ONE

Public Good or Private Benefit

Education is not a trivial business, a private good, or a discretionary expenditure. It is a deeply ethical undertaking at which we must succeed if we are to survive as a free people.

—Gordon Davies[1]

PUBLIC HIGHER EDUCATION is in crisis—and it has been for some time. The problem is, no one can agree on the problem, and when there is no agreement on the problem, it is nearly impossible to develop solutions.

After two centuries of extraordinary public higher education in the United States that was both well funded and high quality, the relationship between public colleges and universities and the public who created them is under strain. This firm covenant has been stretched, but not yet broken, by decades of incremental neglect—singular actions that have pushed one of America's greatest industries (higher education is a multibillion-dollar enterprise and an economic engine, after all) to a critical crossroads. But these institutions, after centuries of national and global dominance, have also been pulled by their own ambitions and self-interested actions. There is plenty of blame to be shared among state legislators and governors, Washington lawmakers and bureaucrats, college and university faculty and administrators, students and parents, and the citizenry more broadly.

Historic public commitments to access and finance are in jeopardy, and policies guiding state and federal governments are eroding. More than two decades of economic expansion and contraction have left academic institutions unsure which new turn the roller coaster will take. State and federal coffers are not just empty, governments are also burdened by debt obligations and underfunded mandates. At the same time, increased demand for education in an era of globalization is pressuring colleges and universities to serve more students and improve learning outcomes. To say that public colleges and universities are squeezed would be to understate the current situation.

This crisis is about money, to be certain, but it is not solely based upon a new or challenged financial model. Significant changes in mission, uneven quality and learning, insufficient access and unacceptable rates of completion, and a lack of coherent state or national policy linking the work of the university to the needs of the society are all contributing factors.

The perennial questions of who pays for, who should pay for, what is the value of, and who benefits from higher education are being asked in state capitols, on college campuses, and at kitchen tables across the country.[2] In many corners of the country and around the globe, privatization has emerged as a solution to—as well as a potential source of new problems for—the historic model of "public" or "state" colleges and universities. Clear distinctions must be made in this new world between mission and funding, where changes to the financial model need not necessarily change the mission of public higher education.

Privatization of public higher education—seen in increasing institutional autonomy, higher tuition, diminishing appropriations, alternative revenue sources (such as philanthropy and new business ventures), and modified governance relationships—has forced both public universities and the public to look for new solutions to preserve the nation's system of higher education.

A Tale of Two Pities

> *It was the best of times, it was the worst of times, it was the age of wisdom, it was the age of foolishness . . . it was the season of Light, it was the season of Darkness, it was the spring of hope, it was the winter of despair, we had everything before us, we had nothing before us . . . in short, the period was so far like the present period, that some of its noisiest authorities insisted on its being received, for good or for evil, in the superlative degree of comparison only.*
>
> —Charles Dickens, *A Tale of Two Cities*

Charles Dickens would have been prophetic had his description of the best and worst times been applied to the current state of higher education in the United States. Over the past few decades, we have heard a chorus of critics argue that higher education is in crisis or even on the verge of extinction ("universities are going the way of newspapers").[3] One critic has even gone so far as to suggest that within fifty years, there will only be ten institutions in the whole world that deliver higher education. Note the word *institutions*, indicating this critic's belief that new entities and organizations that did not exist five or ten years ago may replace today's colleges and universities.[4]

Conversely, others have asserted that higher education is now entering the most exciting era in its history. In a sort of golden age, technology has the potential both to improve traditional classroom learning and to provide access to millions of students around the globe. *MOOCs—massive open online courses*—are just one example of the potential for technology to transform learning for the twenty-first century and, perhaps, slash the cost of education and even shorten the time to complete a degree.

In addition to its parallels to the state of American higher education today, Dickens's classic opening also illustrates the debate between public officials—governors, legislators, and policy makers—and the leaders of public colleges and universities. Each side sees itself as the "Light" and the other side as something close to the "Darkness."[5]

The growing chasm between higher education and the public is alarming.[6] Presidents and chancellors see a diminishing commitment from the state coupled with shackling regulations that force them to pursue alternative revenue sources, increased tuition, and new forms of autonomy to secure the university's best interests. These institutional leaders point to the fact that, in many states, educational appropriations have shrunk from 50 percent or more of total budgets a few decades ago to less than 10 percent today.[7] While the proportion of operational funding most institutions receive from appropriations has declined, national appropriations for higher education have increased over time (as shown in figure 1.1). With their ever-increasing costs, rising tuition, and little perceived accountability, legislators, governors, and the citizens they serve believe public colleges and universities are failing at what it means to be *public*: accessible, affordable, and inherently connected to the needs of the people. Students and their families are often caught in the middle of this tug-of-war.

Ironically, while the schism between the public and their public institutions seems large and growing, in reality there is widespread praise, appreciation, admiration, trust, and affection for our nation's higher educational

FIGURE 1.1   Total U.S. educational appropriations for higher education (in constant 2012 dollars)

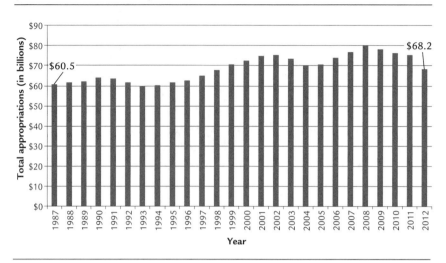

Source: SHEEO

Note: Constant 2012 dollars adjusted by SHEEO Higher Education Cost Adjustment (HECA). Educational appropriations include ARRA funds.

institutions. Students from around the globe flock to public and private institutions in the United States because American higher education is still seen as the "gold standard"—you just wouldn't know it by following the newspapers, blogs, or television news. The rhetoric of the twenty-four-hour news cycle generally focuses on increasing costs, skyrocketing tuition, productivity and efficiency (or lack thereof), plummeting state support, and piercing questions about what college students are learning and what they should be gaining from their education—jobs or love of learning.

Some of the noisiest actors become more muted, calm, and reasonable as you delve deeply into the complexities of higher education. The "crisis" in public higher education is not new, but it is far more complex than ever before, and it requires a reminder that the winter of despair can also be viewed as the spring of hope. Dickens's words ring truer today than ever before, perhaps because he was right: these are the best of times and the worst of times—for colleges and universities.

Is Higher Education a Public Good or a Private Benefit?

At the height of the Great Recession, the president of Pennsylvania State University was notified that the governor was proposing a 50 percent cut in the state's appropriation to the institution. Outraged, the president called a press conference the very next morning and stepped solemnly to the microphone. He began his prepared remarks by saying, "Abraham Lincoln is weeping today."[8] Clearly, something of significance is threatened when the sixteenth president, who during the darkest hours of the Civil War signed the Morrill Act of 1862 and expanded public education dramatically, has been brought to tears. What is at stake is of tremendous and widespread significance—the future of public colleges and universities, and the value of these institutions to current and future generations in democratic society.

Postsecondary education in the United States is distinct from that of most nations in its breadth, its diversity, and the scale of its institutions, all of which offer greater access for more citizens. Throughout the nineteenth and twentieth centuries, higher education in the United States, together with primary and secondary education, was viewed as a public good that benefited society overall. An educated population was considered critical to maintain a democratic system, and higher education was also seen as an engine of economic growth. Since the Second World War, higher education has served as a central and primary force for the betterment of society and the growth of the vast middle class.[9]

There was, in essence, a social compact between the state's citizens and the public universities. This compact supported public funding for higher education, even though only a small portion of the population directly benefited.[10] It was manifested in private institutions that received significant public support, both directly and from the tax laws' encouragement of philanthropy, as well as in public institutions that represented the public's desire for excellence in higher education.

Economists describe *public goods* as those consumed by all of us; they are typically subsidized or funded by government because they are rarely produced in large enough quantities by the private marketplace.[11] Culture, national defense, and parks are three examples of public goods where, in general, the government is ably equipped to support broad interests of the people. In his 1962 book *Capitalism and Freedom,* Milton Friedman—who rarely argued for government intervention—wrote that the "positive externalities" associated with public education justify government support to maintain a stable and democratic society with a "minimum degree of literacy and knowledge on the part of most citizens and . . . widespread acceptance of some common set of values." Further, Friedman noted "the gain from the education of a child accrues not only to the child or to his parents but also to other members of the society."[12]

The relationship between public universities and the state has long been a delicate one, requiring a nuanced understanding of the perspectives of institutional leaders and of the individuals and agencies focused on a public agenda. Any examination of the relationship between public universities and the state requires an understanding of the "essential and legitimate role of the state" and the vast differences among the states.[13] The state context is, in many ways, the most central yet least discussed element of privatization at public colleges and universities.

Though the first institutions of higher learning in the United States were both private and religiously affiliated until the end of the eighteenth century, public higher education has been a critical component of the nation's diverse system of higher education for over two hundred years.[14] The teaching, research, and service at public colleges and universities is central to the larger system of higher education in the United States. Total enrollment across the more than 4,000 public and private institutions of higher education in the United States is over 28 million students; but the majority of these students—20 million and growing—go to one of the more than 1,600 public colleges and universities.[15]

From community colleges to comprehensive colleges and universities, land-grant research universities to elite "public ivys," the landscape of public higher education has broad reach and varied missions in a country that has always featured a hybrid of public and private education.[16] These public institutions—especially community colleges and comprehensive colleges and universities—will have to take on the greatest responsibility if we are to achieve the national goals for access and completion.

Over the past several decades, public higher education has seen dramatic fluctuations in funding from the state at the same time that enrollments have increased. As a result, tuition has risen dramatically and has largely filled the gap created by decreasing state appropriations and the overall increase in costs. Figure 1.2 shows the interplay of rising enrollment, decreasing state appropriations, and increasing tuition. This "wave chart" is evidence of the up-and-down cycle that institutions and states have faced over the past twenty-five years. Shifting the burden from the taxpayers to the students

FIGURE 1.2   United States public FTE student enrollment, net tuition, and educational appropriations per FTE student, 1987–2012 (in constant 2012 dollars)

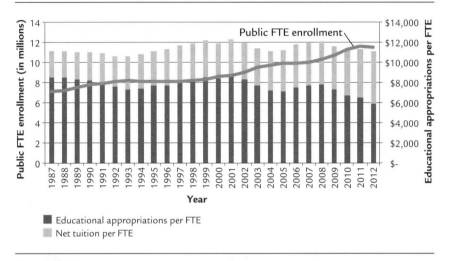

Source: SHEEO

Note: Constant 2012 dollars adjusted by SHEEO Higher Education Cost Adjustment (HECA). Educational appropriations include ARRA funds.

has had significant implications (higher student debt, longer time to degree, lower completion rates, etc.), but the solutions proposed have rarely been more creative than increasing tuition to fill the gap; that is, until more recently, when other elements of privatization have offered intriguing new solutions to the fluctuations in the states' fortunes and focus on higher education.

In addition to teaching the majority of students in the United States, public colleges and universities have been incubators for the entrepreneurship and innovation that has been a key economic driver for much of the last century; these institutions have been talent magnets for their states. Further, among all research universities, public research universities conduct 60 percent of all federally funded university-based research.[17] States, in addition to the federal government and private industry, also fund a significant amount of sponsored research at public research universities outside of capital and operating appropriations.

Even though many states have seen decreases in state appropriations for higher education, and university administrators commonly talk about "disinvestment" in higher education, the trend overall in the past three decades has been one of significant investment. But the investment has not been as significant as it was relative to other spending priorities in the two decades following World War II—and likely never will be again. State legislators across the country are responsible for providing more than $87 billion to support higher education, up from $31 billion in 1986.[18] These elected officials represent the people's desire to invest—or disinvest—in higher education. Since World War II, public higher education has also served as the ladder of opportunity in America—with relatively affordable and accessible institutions, subsidized by state appropriations—and been viewed as a benefit to all in the state, not just to those who attend the institutions. However, as public colleges and universities have moved down the path of privatization, regardless of the rationale or circumstances, there have been increasing questions about the societal benefits as opposed to the direct individual benefits. In other words, is higher education a public good or a private benefit?

In higher education public policy, privatization is often viewed as an agenda being pushed by a college or university seeking to gain more freedom, but forces at the institutional, state, and federal levels are leading to the shifts at these institutions. Indeed, colleges and universities are advocating for greater autonomy to set their enrollment mix and tuition level, and to compete in the marketplace, but many legislators and governors are pushing them to identify alternative revenue sources, to become more efficient, and to operate differently than the rest of government. At the same time, public universities are being pulled toward national and international prominence, which requires significant emphasis on research and decreasing the traditional focus on teaching as the primary domain of the university.

The divergence among institutional leaders, legislators, and the public in perceptions, interests, and motivations about higher education leaves many wondering whether the public nature of these universities can be preserved as privatization moves forward, and what effect the changes will have on the students, the institutions, the states, and the nation overall.[19] Echoing Abraham Lincoln's speech about a "house divided," Christopher Newfield suggests, "As the middle class cuts public education, it cuts the conditions of its own existence."[20] The national debates regarding public priorities, taxes, and higher education are inextricably intertwined. The valuation of higher education as a public good or a private benefit will carry great significance in the years ahead as an educated citizenry becomes increasingly important.

These debates are not new—states across the country have been experiencing varying degrees of privatization for two decades (or longer, in some states). The effects of privatization are only just beginning to force a new conversation about public higher education, a conversation focused less on revenues and autonomy and more on how public universities can continue to serve an important role in our states and in the nation. Such a conversation will require us to redefine what it means to be a public university.

Thomas Jefferson, who founded—or "fathered," to use his own word—the University of Virginia, would certainly have reason to join Lincoln in weeping, but UVA stands as evidence that public colleges and universities have endured changes for centuries. As just one example, UVA has seen declining appropriations from the state for decades and was among the first public universities to engage in serious—and successful—private fundraising. Virginia has long seen a semiautonomous relationship between its public universities and the state, but that autonomy has been used to strengthen the public mission.

Teresa Sullivan, the current president of UVA (who was fired and then rehired within days during the summer of 2012), told me that she is "in the same position as Thomas Jefferson was in 1825"; that is, she has to make a case each year to the legislature, and she has to prove the institution's worth to its many investors, constituents, and stakeholders. But privatization is about more than just money. "So let us stop talking about money as what is the difference between public and private institutions," she told me. "What makes this institution public is public mission. It is in our DNA. It is what Mr. Jefferson designed us to be." Jefferson founded UVA with almost equal parts public and private funding, stating his desire to ensure the university "would remain, be respected and preserved through the ages."[21] Privatization was alive and well in the 1800s. Virginia and its flagship university are discussed in great depth in chapter 5.

Indeed, two centuries before Thomas Jefferson's university became a model of the public-private partnership, the country's first institution of higher learning—Harvard College—was funded partially through income from the Charlestown ferry, and the president was paid directly from the public treasury.[22] The hybrid or privatized model may feel new, but it has in fact been the standard in American higher education. Today, though, the lines are less clear than ever between public and private. But privatization does not mean the end of public higher education's connection to the public good.

We have an opportunity right now to reset the relationship between public higher education and the public. We need deeper conversations with the leaders of state and federal government. We need to understand what they are thinking, what questions they have, and how we can advance together the collective public agenda for higher education in the nation. While privatization in the broadest sense may be one way to reset this relationship, not everyone agrees that this is the best word to describe what is happening. Some of those who oppose the term *privatization* have proposed *public-private partnership, hybridization, voucherization,* or *nationalization,* where, in essence, the "public" that these institutions serve shifts from the local and state constituents to include national and global stakeholders.[23]

But *privatization* is merely a descriptor for what is happening; no matter what word you use, the drivers and outcomes are the same, and the importance of higher education only increases with the rush of globalization.

More Than Just Money

Much of the public discussion and scholarly literature about privatization focuses on autonomy and finance—two areas that I examine closely in this book—but neglects the history and mission of public colleges and universities within the states and society more broadly. As a result of my research, I developed a different way of assessing the layered foundations of privatization—beginning with the history and mission of a state and a particular institution, then the vision and focus of the institution, then autonomy and finance, followed by an institution's students, and concluding with the role of the leadership. When we jump too quickly to issues of autonomy and finance, it is easy to overlook the historical tethering between public colleges and universities and the states in which they were born and raised.

Shortly after the passage of California's "Master Plan" legislation (discussed in chapter 7), Clark Kerr, described by many as the father of higher education in that state, wrote in his classic book, *The Uses of the University*, about the origins of the university as "a single community—a community of masters and students." Over time, however, the university evolved into what he described as a "multiversity." It is "a new type of institution, it is not really private and it is not really public; it is neither entirely of the world nor entirely apart from it. It is unique." Public colleges and universities came to serve a vital role in the state beyond their own boundaries. Put simply, "the university served the entire state."[24]

Half a century before Clark Kerr's work with the California Master Plan, University of Wisconsin–Madison President Charles Van Hise spoke in 1904 about the "Wisconsin Idea." Van Hise described his vision for a university with broad reach: "I shall never be content until the beneficent influence of the University reaches every home in the state." Further, he boldly declared that "the boundaries of campus are the boundaries of the state."[25] Such a commitment to the public good was the very definition of public higher education for most of the last two centuries, with significant funding from the federal and state governments and a strong connection to the home state.

As made clear in the Wisconsin Idea—and, more broadly, in the Morrill Act that created land-grant universities—public higher education existed to serve the state and society. In addition to educating the population, colleges and universities served as economic engines fueling job creation and innovation. The value of public higher education was defined in terms of its ability to create new technologies and train the work force, as well as the various forms of development—personal, cultural, social, and economic—at its core.[26]

For these reasons, the state context—history, mission, and culture—is vitally important to any understanding of the forces of privatization. Finance, while critically important to the operation and survival of public colleges and universities, cannot tell the entire story. Robert Berdahl notes that "even if the state role in financing higher education were to diminish markedly, all institutions—public and private—would still have to function in a context of state law and state sovereignty."[27] Beyond state law and practical ownership, the people of the state often feel significant psychological ownership and pride in their public colleges and universities and view the connection as more than just financial.

Clearly, the divide between state government and public colleges and universities has grown over time as finances have become scarcer, but this divide is also about much more than money. Berdahl astutely noted four decades ago that "many academics are trying to protect too much, and many persons in state government are trying to claim too much."[28] Privatization is much deeper than just autonomy, finance, and regulation. It requires a clear understanding of the significant history of public colleges and universities as creatures of the state. These institutions will not be easily divorced from the state after centuries of support.

Early discussions of privatization recognized that institutions of higher education—public and private—held a responsibility beyond their own interests of educating students and pursuing an institutionally focused agenda. The public college or university, in particular, held a responsibility to the local region, the state, and higher education overall. The public interest, historically, was defined more broadly to include the integration of teaching,

research, and service in ways that directly connect with the state. James Perkins, the former president of Cornell University (a public-private hybrid),
framed the issue clearly, stating that "the university's decisive role leads not
to isolation but to leadership, not to autonomy but rather to participation."[29]
Discussions of autonomy and accountability predate by several decades the
decline in state funding for public higher education and require a more in-
timate understanding of the role of the institution, its history, and mission.

By focusing the discussion of privatization first on the change and tension
in the relationship between public colleges and universities and their state
context, before autonomy and finance, we can better understand the depth
of the relationship. It is true that, historically, the states and the federal government provided significant funding for public colleges and universities,
whereas today the trend is not positive. However, we must view autonomy
and public finance from a longer perspective than just the most recent recession to understand their role in privatization. Many governors and legislators
are quick to point out that the trends of the past two decades do not erase
two centuries of deep and generous support for higher education.

Foundations of Privatization

To meaningfully discuss privatization and to bring this concept to life with
real examples, I will tell the story of three states—Virginia, North Carolina, and California—and their systems of higher education. I pay particular attention to the flagship universities, but this book also examines
the broader systems of public higher education, from community colleges
through the top research institutions. No discussion of public higher education can rest with a few states, but privatization and its impacts are best illuminated through the experiences of the broader forces of privatization in the
state. These states claim three of the finest systems of higher education in the
world, even though their history and dynamics are very different.

While this book focuses on privatization and higher education in three
states, the narrative is widely applicable across all fifty states. From Oregon to
Colorado to Wisconsin to Pennsylvania to New York to Texas, the stories of
privatization take different forms, but they are interconnected, and, increasingly, one state will attempt what has been done in another—often without
understanding the full context.

Following extensive interviews with scholars and policy makers across the
country, as well as thorough examination of financial data and a review of the

literature, I selected Virginia, North Carolina, and California as the best examples of how different states have dealt with the forces of globalization and the elements of privatization. I chose them because of their vast differences historically in how higher education was envisioned, created, funded, and managed; their individual paths of privatization therefore make clear the differences in how states and institutions can manage today's rapidly changing environment. By understanding what has happened in these three states, university leaders and public officials can make more informed decisions about how to proceed in the public-private partnership that is higher education in the twenty-first century.

Significantly, the stories are told through the experiences and insights of public officials and institutional leaders who have a vested interest in the future of public higher education in the United States. Their words help to illuminate the critical state of public higher education today and offer hope for a renewed compact between the public and public higher education.

State Context Is Vitally Important

It is critical to understand what has happened in Virginia, North Carolina, and California and why the approaches taken by different colleges and universities to meet their respective missions are so different. Several foundational elements define an institution and its propensity to privatize, and they must be understood before any serious discussion of the effects of privatization is possible. My data revealed that although autonomy and finance remain strong forces in privatization, other core elements—most significantly, the mission, history, and culture of an institution and its state—are necessary to fully understand it. By analyzing and comparing privatization among the states, I identified six distinct *foundations of privatization*—each of which could be viewed as a distinct continuum—by which to examine an institution (see figure 1.3).[30]

Similar to Maslow's hierarchy of needs, the foundations of privatization build upon one another in such a way that each additional foundation is influenced by and helps to interpret the previous foundations. The foundations are weighted more heavily toward those that are more central to an institution's identity and role within the state. Mission, history, and culture—together known as *state context*—are the core elements of any institution and therefore constitute the primary foundation of privatization. The vision and focus of the institution helps us to understand whom the institution sees as its "publics"— in other words, whom or what the institution serves.

FIGURE 1.3   Foundations of privatization: A model for public colleges and universities

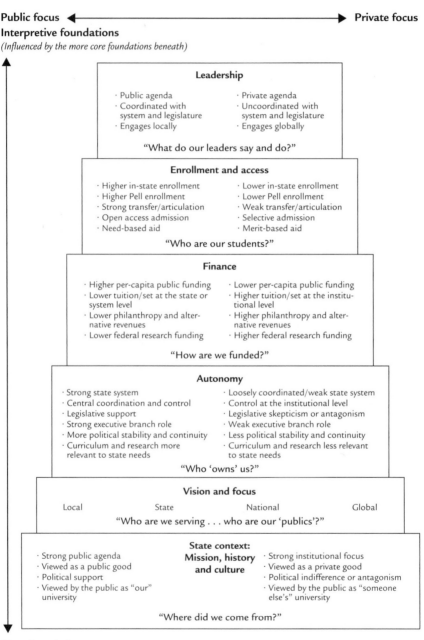

Public focus ◄─────────────────────────────────────► **Private focus**

Interpretive foundations
(Influenced by the more core foundations beneath)

Leadership

· Public agenda   · Private agenda
· Coordinated with   · Uncoordinated with
  system and legislature   system and legislature
· Engages locally   · Engages globally

"What do our leaders say and do?"

Enrollment and access

· Higher in-state enrollment   · Lower in-state enrollment
· Higher Pell enrollment   · Lower Pell enrollment
· Strong transfer/articulation   · Weak transfer/articulation
· Open access admission   · Selective admission
· Need-based aid   · Merit-based aid

"Who are our students?"

Finance

· Higher per-capita public funding   · Lower per-capita public funding
· Lower tuition/set at the state or   · Higher tuition/set at the institu-
  system level   tional level
· Lower philanthropy and alter-   · Higher philanthropy and alter-
  native revenues   native revenues
· Lower federal research funding   · Higher federal research funding

"How are we funded?"

Autonomy

· Strong state system   · Loosely coordinated/weak state system
· Central coordination and control · Control at the institutional level
· Legislative support   · Legislative skepticism or antagonism
· Strong executive branch role   · Weak executive branch role
· More political stability and continuity · Less political stability and continuity
· Curriculum and research more   · Curriculum and research less relevant
  relevant to state needs   to state needs

"Who 'owns' us?"

Vision and focus

Local   State   National   Global

"Who are we serving . . . who are our 'publics'?"

State context:
Mission, history
and culture

· Strong public agenda   · Strong institutional focus
· Viewed as a public good   · Viewed as a private good
· Political support   · Political indifference or antagonism
· Viewed by the public as "our" · Viewed by the public as "someone
  university   else's" university

"Where did we come from?"

Core foundations
(Influences the more interpretive foundations above)

The model's most significant departure from conventional thought is that autonomy and finance are seen as the third and fourth foundations—not the first and second. Presidents, chancellors, legislators, and governors, as well as alumni, faculty, and students, often focus on privatization in terms of funding (declining) and autonomy (increasing). I found that while autonomy and finance are significant factors in privatization, it is more important to first understand the state context and vision to see where the institution has been and where it is going.

My model of privatization, visually arranged as a pyramid, depicts the layered nature of privatization. At the top of the pyramid are the institutional leaders—those selected to lead the institution, interpret the issues facing it, and make sense of how best to maintain the public focus even while pursuing private means to achieve it. The foundations at the top of the pyramid are not necessarily less important than those at the bottom, but they build upon the foundations that precede them and help to interpret earlier foundations under current circumstances.

I employ this model throughout the book to illustrate the many foundations, each of which at times takes on more or less importance as privatization evolves within higher education. Though no model is perfect, these six foundations account for the complexities of a higher educational system as diverse as the fifty states. This conceptual framework allows me to highlight the similarities and differences among the three states and their universities in regard to how the public mission and public purposes are defined today; the privatization push from the state and pull from the federal government; and the insights of legislators and their perceptions of higher education as a public good or private benefit. I will discuss the model more fully in chapter 8, but it is introduced here so you can refer back to it as different examples of privatization are highlighted.

A wise scholar once told me, "If you know one state, then you know one state." In higher education public policy, she was to a large extent correct. However, my model was developed across three very different in-depth case studies and is applicable and helpful for interpreting privatization from coast to coast in states large and small, and from community colleges to comprehensive universities to the elite public research universities. After testing this model on many more states, I am more certain than ever that privatization can be understood more broadly than in just one state. That same scholar later quipped that "every state is unique, but no state is as unique as it thinks it is."

The Dichotomy of Mission

Privatization will likely continue to proliferate in the years ahead as constraints on state resources and increases in institutional ambitions lead to a further alteration of the funding and governance models for public higher education. Granted, not all of the nation's public colleges and universities are blessed with the same opportunities. Some elements of privatization may be feasible only for the most selective among these institutions, but all will face the same challenges, so privatization in some form will touch nearly all of them. As a result, some public colleges and universities are being pulled in two directions and are experiencing a dichotomy of mission as they seek to navigate the current realities.

One mission—the historic public purpose of these institutions—is to remain accessible, affordable, and focused on the needs of the community or the state. A second, sometimes unspoken mission—driven by the ambitious, competitive, and market-based nature of these institutions—is to ensure the strength of the institution by attracting the very brightest students, talented faculty, and adequate funding to support the institution's aspirations.[31] This institutional ambition was most often expressed to me by leaders of colleges and universities in words like, "I will not allow this institution to falter on my watch," or, "We aspire to be among the world's great colleges and universities." The dichotomy in mission can produce tension. Students, faculty, and funding are much more mobile across state and national borders today, which leads to this sense that state-based higher education matters less than it did a few decades ago. The national and global focus of these public institutions has challenged their historic mission and definition of public purposes.

To achieve both missions, the relationships and historic agreements between public institutions and the state are rapidly being reframed, rewritten, and reconfigured. Public colleges and universities face a perplexing challenge: they must balance the short-term and long-term needs of the state's citizens—such as economic development, teacher training, and medical treatment—against the institution's own beliefs about how to conduct its business and what mission it should pursue. In an ever-evolving funding and governance structure, this balancing act is daunting. These institutions and their leadership must, however, take seriously the tension between being what James Duderstadt described as "an enduring social institution with a duty of stewardship to generations past and a compelling obligation to take whatever actions are necessary to build and protect its capacity to serve future generations."[32]

The tension between achieving institutional priorities and serving larger public purposes reflects the complexity of the challenges that lie ahead for public colleges and universities. Institutional leaders describe their struggle to maintain the quality, prominence, and stability of the institution, and they profess to remain committed to the public ideals of higher education. Indeed, institutional leaders have long connected the elements of cost, quality, and access in an indivisible "iron triangle," where any change to one element inevitably affects another.[33] Roger Geiger suggests that before we can clearly articulate the duality of mission in public colleges and universities, we must answer fundamental questions, including "how much quality is needed?" and "who among the state's citizenry should enjoy the privilege of attendance?"[34] Such questions are not easily answered, but they are critical to understanding the varying goals universities face.

Each of the key stakeholders—institutional and legislative leaders and the public they serve—requires a deeper understanding of privatization and the balance between institutional interests and the public good. The legislative and gubernatorial perspectives are especially important because they are virtually undocumented in the scholarly literature.[35] Though I did not endeavor to conduct an anthropological study, at times I fancied myself a sort of Jane Goodall, observing these public officials in their natural habitat and trying to understand why they make the decisions they do in the context of the challenges facing them, particularly about higher education.

One legislator summed up the frame of mind for many of his colleagues when he told me, "I didn't come to [the capitol] to cut budgets, but that's all we can do today. You can't be visionary and forward-thinking when the state is bleeding, and right now [this state] is close to life-support." But, ironically, some of the most significant expansion and funding for higher education *has* come during periods of national crisis, often more severe than the recent "Great Recession." Among these are the aforementioned Morrill Act, passed one month after twenty-five thousand men died at the Battle of Shiloh during the Civil War, and the massive federal and state investments following World War II, such as the GI Bill and the National Defense Education Act. In many cases, higher education was used to expand opportunity and to strengthen areas of national interest when resources were limited.

In today's environment of hard decisions and scant options, how do public colleges and universities balance the pursuit of public purposes with the demands of a competitive marketplace? In an era when the marketplace is becoming increasingly crucial in determining the focus for higher education, is it possible to imagine a scenario whereby institutions can remain focused on their core mission with a connection to the public good while also advancing their globally competitive market position and their own institutional interests?

The two missions driving public colleges and universities need not be mutually exclusive, but in a market-based system, many of these institutions find the state to be a less reliable partner and, as a result, have begun to seek alternative revenue sources and greater autonomy and control. These trends are not new, and they are not caused solely by a decline in state revenues. But they are proliferating across public higher education, and they may be irreversible.

Public colleges and universities and their states must find an appropriate balance so that both institutional interests and the public good are served. The most significant gap that persists today between the two is the loss of the focus on the public good—meeting the needs of the state—and the autonomy and flexibility that institutions seek in order to thrive and survive in an era of limited state resources.

Rather than framing privatization as an either/or concept, where institutions gain freedom or states and the public maintain control, we need to understand how the changed relationship between universities and the states is affecting the balance between institutional interests and the public agenda.

CHAPTER TWO

The Historic Role of Universities in State and Society

[T]here is nothing which can better deserve your patronage than the promotion of science and literature. Knowledge is, in every country, the surest basis of public happiness. In one in which the measures of government receive their impression so immediately from the sense of the community as in ours, it is proportionably essential. To the security of a free constitution it contributes in various ways: by convincing those who are entrusted with the public administration, that every valuable end of government is best answered by the enlightened confidence of the people; and by teaching the people themselves to know and to value their own rights.

—George Washington[1]

FROM THE EARLIEST days of the United States, education was a crucial function for the fledgling democracy. The previous chapter set the context for a deeper exploration of the history of higher education in the United States, with a focus on public colleges and universities. As our first president noted, education and knowledge are central to a functioning democracy, particularly one where liberty and representative government are so "essential."

If the country is to retain its competitive edge in a rapidly globalizing, knowledge-based world, we must reformulate the relationship between universities and the state. Public colleges and universities have been steadily increasing tuition as sources of government funding have declined, but the story is far more complex and can be fully understood only in its historical context.

As noted in chapter 1, higher education in the United States is distinct from that of most nations in the breadth, diversity, and scale of its institutions, and the greater access they offer for citizens. Throughout the nineteenth and twentieth centuries, U.S. higher education, together with primary and secondary education, was viewed as a public good that benefited society overall. An educated population was considered critical to maintaining a democratic system, and higher education was viewed as an engine of economic growth.[2]

Even before the musket and cannon fire of the American Revolution had dwindled, it was a common hope among America's founding fathers that both knowledge and education would be the new weapons with which future generations would protect themselves against such tyranny. In the winter of 1779, Samuel Adams wrote to James Warren, a fellow Son of Liberty and Massachusetts patriot, "If Virtue & Knowledge are diffused among the People, they will never be enslav'd. This will be their great Security."[3]

In short, higher education in the United States has long served as a central and primary force for the betterment of society and, more recently, the growth of the vast middle class. There existed a social compact between the state's citizens and the public universities that supported public funding for higher education, even though only a small portion of the population directly benefited.[4] This compact was manifested in private institutions that received significant public support, both directly and through the tax laws' encouragement of philanthropy, as well as in public institutions that represented the public's desire for excellence in higher education.

After a long history of well-funded and high-quality public higher education, however, the past few decades have seen a growing debate over higher education's public and private benefits. This debate is not new, but it becomes more prominent each time a major recession forces people to focus on the financial and governance model for public higher education. The most recent recession has certainly fueled the debate fervently.

In this chapter, I highlight the history and mission of public universities and their historical roots in the states; the history of public higher education finance; the public and private benefits of higher education; issues of control related to governance and regulatory autonomy; the significant role of the federal government in higher education; and how the academy has played an important role in larger issues of national security. Additionally, I examine changes in the competition for faculty and students because they are part of the context required to understand the competitive marketplace that public research universities are facing.

Autonomy and Accountability

Direct institutional support, though it has been declining slightly, is actually one of the last sources of funding affected by privatization in higher education. State governments have historically provided most of the direct institutional support from annual appropriations. Since World War II, higher education public policy has focused largely on building, maintaining, and overseeing institutions of higher education on behalf of the state to ensure an efficient allocation of resources. However, states historically appropriated aid in the form of block funding, which was the previous year's appropriation adjusted for enrollment and inflation, with few strings attached. Beginning in the 1980s, the focus on accountability and outcomes resulted in much greater attention paid to the impact of state funding even as the state decreased appropriations.[5] States mandated accountability so that universities would remain beholden to state goals even as they gained more autonomy in raising revenue from tuition, philanthropy, and other sources.

Certainly, institutions and systems of higher education in the United States have historically been among the most autonomous and market-focused in the world by any measure. Autonomy was once critical to both society and higher education, as universities were able to pursue roles and purposes that conflicted with the state from time to time. Some have even argued that one notion of accountability is that higher education institutions must tell society what it should want from them. However, the recent corporatization of higher education, largely based on shifts in state funding and poor public policy, has made some public universities unwilling or unable to speak to public issues, including the improvement of K–12 education; racial, ethnic, and socioeconomic tensions; social and political partisanship; and broad social problems.[6]

The challenge lies not only in the vision and focus of an institution, but also in how that institution's leadership frames its relationship and responsibility to the state and to larger social issues. Even with the focus on accountability, some public universities—particularly flagship institutions—have benefited from their recently gained autonomy, as they can raise revenue from a variety of resources. However, most public universities have been ill served by such a system, given rising tuition, an achievement gap based on income, and a struggle to maintain an adequate number of programs in areas that are costly but important to public need.[7]

Full autonomy, with minimal connections to the state, might not serve universities or society well. Such a system would prove feasible for only a small number of selective research universities, because few public universities would be able to fully replace state appropriations with tuition revenue while maintaining stable levels of access. In 2011–2012, state and local governments appropriated $63 billion and $10 billion, respectively, to support public degree-granting institutions. In fact, of the $323.8 billion in total revenue that public degree-granting institutions received, state governments provided the largest share. (Tuition provided close to $60 billion, and the federal government provided $29.8 billion in grants and contracts.)[8] Even beyond the question of finances, a state that sees its universities as a state asset would not likely allow full autonomy. While it seems unfair that states are providing less support and demanding more accountability, that is the reality in a political system of public universities. This reality will be a major focus of the case studies later in this book.

Because of this reality, elements of privatization will more generally prevail when pursued with a more realistic approach to reframing universities' relationship with the state. Both autonomy and accountability are necessary to ensure institutional success and a connection to the state. Such a balance requires a clear mission and a focus on meeting public goals, so that higher education can be more "flexible, entrepreneurial, customized, accountable, and able to meet the state's needs." Even where highly selective public universities have advocated for greater autonomy, they know that "without some form of accountability to the body politic, the public purpose of the university is at risk."[9]

By strengthening the connection between higher education on the one hand and economic development and community engagement on the other, institutions and systems are better able to secure additional state appropriations. Finding the right balance between mission and market is why public institutions, in particular, must strive to reframe their relationships with both the state and the wider public that supports them. Indeed, the traditional conception of the public purposes for these institutions, from the Morrill Act onward, was tied to the agrarian, mechanical, and manufacturing economy in many of the states. Ironically, the focus on the "practical" arts did not sustain most of the land grants. Rather, it was their liberal arts programs that had the biggest draw. In some ways, the liberal arts saved the land grants. Thus, the initial agrarian and practical purpose of the land grants floundered at least in some ways. In the twenty-first century knowledge economy, many of these institutions are again reimagining their role in serving the public, becoming economic generators and talent magnets for a region and a state. As the needs of states evolve, public universities will have to use their greater autonomy to innovate while also producing clear and measurable results that will assure the public that they are meeting the state's needs.[10]

The Federal Role in U.S. Higher Education

For most of U.S. history, higher education was largely a state affair, because the states were the epicenter of higher education policy. Since the mid-twentieth century, however, the federal government has taken a larger role, particularly with financial aid and research funding.

In the nineteenth and early twentieth centuries, public higher education was predominantly open to a relatively small slice of the population, but it was fairly inexpensive and had strong state ties, in keeping with the country's colonial heritage. Each colony, and then each state—not the federal government—established charters for colleges. The U.S. Constitution makes no mention of education, and the federal government's involvement was essentially limited to establishing two service academies, as the United States never had a Ministry of Education or any other form of national oversight over its institutions of higher education. The colonies' strong sense of independence would also prevent the formation of any central, national university that could have promoted national unity and created common standards to which individual universities and colleges could aspire.[11]

In fact, so as to ensure doctrinal consistency and service to society, the colonies did not even permit the establishment of rival institutions. Accordingly, the original colleges, founded during the colonial era, sought primarily to educate leaders for both the church and province, and so they focused on producing ministers, teachers, and lawyers. However, colonial and later state governments never became directly involved in governing colleges and universities. The 1819 Dartmouth College case codified the universities' autonomy by establishing that the charter from the state government allowed an institution of higher education to act independently. A board of trustees was essentially responsible for managing these institutions and acted as a buffer against state interference. Given universities' relative autonomy, they were always responsive to the market, competing for students and resources. The later development of systems of higher education was thus a result of institutional competition rather than centralized legislation and involved a mix of public and private support, initially with more reliance on the church or wealthy benefactors, though students often did pay a minimal tuition.[12]

The Northwest Ordinance (1796) was the first significant federal legislative act related to higher education, with provisions mandating that township lands be used for schools. Significantly, however, the establishment and administration of these lands were left largely to the states' discretion. Given authority but without much revenue, state governments often supported existing private, largely church-chartered institutions with these federal land grants and authorized lotteries to benefit the institutions; the first truly public institution of higher education was in fact established only in the late eighteenth century.[13]

As the United States expanded during the early to mid-1800s, hundreds of colleges were established, though most failed. This change occurred because states no longer encouraged monopolies on higher education, granting charters more readily and directly supporting institutions of higher education through general tax revenues. With no national system, each state sought to create as many institutions and programs as its neighbors did so as to educate various professionals and be more competitive. Religious groups in particular founded many colleges and universities in the new territories to provide a structure for civilized life; however, hundreds of these institutions lacked sufficient state support or student constituency.[14]

This expansion also brought some important regional differentiation in higher education. The newer territories become the bedrock of the public sector of higher education and of small, independent liberal arts colleges. With its religious activism, denominational colleges in particular dominated the West. The South, in turn, saw a proliferation of state universities, and the Northeast took on a strong commitment to private education, given the private institutions' strong roots from the beginning.[15]

The legacy of this early trend can be seen today through the number, varying by state, of private and public institutions of higher education. In 2010–2011, 67 percent of Massachusetts institutions were private, as were 45 percent in Pennsylvania. In the southern states of North Carolina and Virginia, only 32 percent and 29 percent of institutions were private, respectively. This trend is perhaps not as clear as it once was, but the effects of higher education's regional roots have been lasting.[16]

Later federal legislation would make possible another significant expansion of the nation's system of public higher education, even though the federal government did not take direct ownership of or manage any institutions. Republican Representative Justin Smith Morrill first introduced the groundbreaking Land-Grant College Act (Morrill Act) during James Buchanan's presidency; however, Buchanan vetoed the bill because of political pressures from dominant Democratic senators and later called it "inexpedient and unconstitutional."[17] Morrill did not have enough votes to overturn the veto and so waited to reintroduce a revised version of the bill until December 1861 under President Lincoln. Under this version of the Morrill Act, the federal government gave states portions of federal land in the West to be sold for a profit that could then be used for advanced instructional programs and to establish collegiate programs in practical fields of study such as agriculture, mechanics, mining, and military instruction, without sacrificing other classical studies. With this new source of funding from the sale of lands, state governments could either create new institutions or support existing ones.[18]

Western legislators opposed such a bill because they thought speculators would claim public lands before states could reserve the lands for schools. Kansas Senator James Lane introduced an amendment limiting any state's land grant to 1 million acres, and President Lincoln signed this version of the bill into law in July 1862. This significant investment during the darkest hours of the Civil War was an example of foresight, vision, and courage. It served the betterment of all people, creating greater access to education that was crucial for a democratic society while also focusing on practical and applicable education for the citizens, which would ultimately benefit the state and the nation.[19]

As an illustration, the land-grant colleges created by the Morrill Act let women, African Americans, the working classes, immigrants, and other minorities enroll in higher education; the Act opened the door to low-income students, as states offered education at public expense and broadened the scope of education to include vocational training. The second Morrill Act of 1890 allowed for the creation of dual systems made up of institutions that served both black and white populations given that the funds were equally divided.[20]

The legacy of the Morrill Acts still lingers—according to the Association of Public and Land-Grant Universities' (APLU) 2012 Annual Report, just about one-third of its 221 member institutions are land-grant universities resulting from the 1862 and 1890 Morrill Acts. The APLU also boasts high enrollment—3.6 million undergraduate and 1.1 million graduate students enrolled across all member institutions.[21] These statistics make clear the lasting success and growth of land-grant institutions.

As higher education became more accessible and more open to qualified students, the number of postsecondary institutions increased, from 563 in 1869 to 997 in 1900, and the number of enrolled students increased from 52,286 to 237,592. Additionally, the second Morrill Act of 1890 began to provide direct federal funds in support of national educational interests and developed the concept that the states should provide matching dollars (according to some ratio) for a directed purpose. However, revenues from land grants, augmented by direct state appropriations derived from general tax revenues, still mostly funded these universities, even though some of them charged a nominal tuition.[22]

Another revolutionary development was the emergence of the research university. The Hatch Act of 1887 provided federal funds for experimental research stations in land-grant colleges and laid out requirements for granting them university status, setting the foundation for the state research university. By the beginning of the 1900s, these state universities had adopted the German research university model, though they made several changes. German universities, importantly, provided graduate and doctoral training, and Americans transformed their universities by emphasizing the concept of community service, showing the direct links to industry and agriculture, and developing degree programs for vocational fields. Americans also made departments the basic academic units, and introduced the PhD as well as the position of assistant professor, thus allowing young faculty to research independently. The Johns Hopkins University, founded in 1867, was the first new research institution in the United States, and, like other research universities to come, it provided a "locus of lofty and abstruse research and specialized graduate training."[23]

Without much government involvement or interference, these universities were able to raise substantial new revenues with the rise of large corporations and large-scale philanthropy in the late nineteenth and early twentieth century, as corporate leaders and religious groups contributed significant sums of money.[24] Additionally, with the growing focus on regional government in the states, there was increasing institutional diversity that suited a fast-changing society with different, regional needs. Unlike continental Europe, universities developed their own standard practices that helped organize these growing institutions. Presidents and faculty were not public employees and enjoyed extensive academic freedom, and faculty increasingly became specialized experts in fields and formed different departments with their own appointed deans.

These professors were able to emphasize their own research when instructing undergraduates, dictating the course of curriculum and study. Such a system allowed American universities to be innovative and entrepreneurial while still serving a wide range of social interests. However, the federalist system of government and the decentralized nature of American higher education did deny universities a significant source of funding that was available to universities in other countries. Hence, state funding was historically the largest source of revenue for all types of institutions—public and private.[25]

Though such a system of higher education made sense during the large growth periods of higher education in the past, many outside the academy see these institutional silos today as outdated, redundant, unnecessary, and detrimental to the goals of student learning, greater productivity, and reduced costs. The reluctance of some universities to evolve is one reason that legislators and governors today see higher education as out of step with the public at large.

Higher Education Gains Prominence

World War I influenced the next stage of university development, as universities allowed on-campus training programs funded by the federal government. These programs were seen as a patriotic duty, but they also provided compensation to colleges, which were lacking tuition with the loss of many men to the war effort. Further, while there was a broad militarization of the curriculum, the universities played no major role in providing either scientific or technological research, though the formation of the National Research Council and the Naval Research Laboratory in 1916 allowed industry, university, and government scientists to coordinate with one another. This coordination formed the basis for future partnerships between the universities and the government that President Franklin D. Roosevelt would exploit during the New Deal era.[26]

Given the universities' very strong regional ties, the Roosevelt administration used them to help the federal government connect with the American people. At land-grant universities in particular, programs in agricultural adjustment, student work study, and civic education all contributed to improving national opinion of the federal government.[27] As federal funding grew, there was also generous funding from state legislatures and alumni donors.

In the 1930s, a university degree still marked the entry into the upper mid-dle class, but most occupations did not require specific academic credentials. Universities would take on the role of economic engine only after World War II, when they underwent a lasting change in their structure and purpose. So-ciety would become willing to make massive investments in basic research conducted at universities, with the promise of long-term economic benefits, even while leaving universities autonomous in performing that research.[28]

Higher Education Expands in Access, Research, and Service

When the United States entered World War II, American colleges and uni-versities mobilized quickly to provide numerous specialized services for fed-eral agencies. As an example, many professors willingly applied their expertise to wartime services such as providing advanced instruction in esoteric lan-guages. Faculty in the physical sciences undertook defense-related research, including the atom and hydrogen bomb projects. The universities' success in large-scale applied research projects during World War II convinced many in the federal government to pursue future partnerships, bringing the university to the forefront of national security.[29]

Colleges and universities were now regarded as multipurpose institutions responsible for producing cutting-edge defense and medical research. The federal government also found that higher education could help create psy-chologically adjusted democratic citizens who better appreciated American society and culture. The 1944 passage of the Servicemen's Readjustment Act, more commonly referred to as the GI Bill, allowed all qualifying veterans to pursue educational benefits. These tuition and benefit payments were por-table, and 2.25 million veterans enrolled in some accredited institution of higher education, leading to massive growth in the student body on college campuses.[30] Though some university leaders doubted these men were intellec-tually or psychologically ready to succeed in college, the many veterans who took advantage of these educational benefits proved to be serious, focused stu-dents eager to secure their place in the middle class with a college education.

In 1945, Vannevar Bush published *Science, the Endless Frontier,* which sig-nificantly influenced government action in higher education. Bush argued that the federal government should fund basic and advanced research and de-velopment in the sciences, because the nation's health depended on advance-ments in this kind of knowledge. His writing led directly to the creation of the National Science Foundation and, later, the National Institutes of Health, as well as the creation of research and development initiatives funded through different departments and agencies that encouraged academic experts to apply for specific research assignments. Additionally, the government began to directly subsidize the graduate training of future engineers and scientists and provided relatively unrestricted, competitive federal grants to support on-campus research that would eventually become the basis for a small number of powerful, well-funded research universities.[31]

During this time, U.S. universities led the world in fundamental scientific knowledge. They produced well-trained personnel capable of applying scientific knowledge to achieve breakthroughs in agriculture and health care while laying the technological foundations for new industries such as biotechnology. However, this new form of federal involvement encouraged the applied projects and short-term payoffs favored by military-related federal agencies; accordingly, it would create the problem for sufficient, sustained federal funding for pure science that exists today. The form of federal involvement in higher education in the aftermath of World War II was a monumental change from the late nineteenth century, when the government built its own labs, agencies, and research infrastructure. After World War II, the United States had a growing public sector and a corresponding demand for highly trained personnel in many different occupations.[32]

In 1948, the Truman Commission on Higher Education examined the U.S. college and university system, focusing on access and enrollment, and it concluded that the nation was investing too little money in postsecondary education. The commission argued that postsecondary education should be expanded, with no discrimination in terms of race or religion in college admission. However, though the commission focused on the federal government's involvement in higher education, the state governments and private foundations still ultimately carried out the recommended initiatives in terms of financial investment, since they were still the primary sources of revenue for enrollment. The federal government was not yet actively involved in directly funding higher education enrollment, focusing instead on research initiatives and encouraging state action.[33]

From 1940 to 1960, state and local governments provided the largest source of increased revenue for all institutions of higher education, increasing aid by $1.35 billion. In comparison, over the same time period the federal government provided $998 million more, and tuition and fees provided another $956 million.[34]

Universities often preferred the lack of federal involvement and regulation, as they did not welcome federal educational policies that would threaten traditional university autonomy and self-determination.[35] Additionally, although the federal government increased higher education appropriations by $7.86 billion from 1960 to 1980, a small number of federal agencies provided all the funding, so that it was concentrated in a few fields—physical and biological sciences, health sciences, and engineering. Teaching and normal institutional operations received little grant support. Moreover, just six universities received 57 percent of the funding, and 79 percent of the funding could be traced to just twenty universities.[36]

The Federal Government Increases Its Direct Role in Higher Education

Though the first wave of federal funding stabilized in the late 1950s, Congress initiated a second wave in response to the Soviet Union's launch of *Sputnik*. Given the increased acceptance of the idea that higher education was crucial to national welfare, universities were expected to educate citizens about democracy and provide research expertise that could contribute to national security. Scientists also said that education was the best protection against radical policies and dangerous factions in the nation and would strengthen the nation's ideological center.[37]

With the growing Cold War threats around the world, the federal government passed the National Defense Education Act in 1958, further highlighting the national interest in education. This legislation established the system of federal student loans and provided more funding for advanced scientific research, vocational education, national defense doctoral fellowships, and foreign language and area studies. The focus on national strategic interests was clear in the government's effort to use universities' expertise to promote national defense.[38]

With the additional federal funding, academics had many opportunities to apply for research and development grants in the 1960s. The federal government believed that researchers' expertise would be essential to surpassing the Soviet Union and other countries that threatened U.S. interests during the Cold War. In fact, the federal government became such a predominant source of research funding for universities that some foundations withdrew from sponsored projects. This federal funding of research would stimulate approximately half of the nation's economic growth during the latter half of the twentieth century, especially given that the federal government was also the primary supporter of graduate- and professional-level advanced education.[39]

With massification efforts driven by the GI Bill as well as Lyndon Johnson's "War on Poverty" and the civil rights movement of the 1960s, more people generally had access to college after World War II. The nation was aiming for greater equality for people from all walks of life, and the federal government actively enforced civil rights after President Johnson signed the Civil Rights Act of 1964. Title VI of the Act explicitly decreed that institutions that discriminated on the basis of race, color, or national origin would receive reduced funding.[40]

The Economic Opportunity Act of 1964 was also central to President Johnson's War on Poverty. It focused on increasing adult literacy and building on basic education. The Higher Education Act (HEA) of 1965 was a product of the sustained national focus on ensuring more equal access to higher education, supplying the original Educational Opportunity grants that were given to students from low-income families. The federal government also gave limited amounts of funding to institutions, such as historically black colleges and universities (HBCUs) and women's colleges, that served groups that had suffered from discrimination.[41]

Higher education, therefore, became a major focus of public policy at both the federal and state level, with the federal government providing funds for advanced research and improved access, and state governments providing significant blocks of funding for basic operations. Clearly, the benefits of both education and research were viewed as crucial for national security and for society, and therefore worthy of significant investment by government.

All of these federal investments in higher education built on the Morrill Acts, but they also increased the size, focus, and complexity of higher education, particularly the public university system.[42] Given the influence of democracy and accelerating demands for specialized knowledge and a qualified work force, access to higher education continued to expand after 1890. By 1920, 582,000 undergraduate students and 15,600 graduate students were enrolled in higher education. From there, enrollment jumped to just under 1.5 million in 1930, and in 1970, enrollment in institutions of higher education increased to just over 7.9 million students. The baby boomer generation contributed to a sizeable expansion in higher education; from 1960 to 1970 alone, the numbers for enrollment grew from 3.58 million to 7.92 million. The huge growth in community colleges especially contributed to this vast increase in enrollment, as many Americans wanted affordable vocational training. Community college enrollment jumped from 500,000 in 1960 to more than

2 million by 1970, 4 million by 1980, nearly 5.5 million by the end of the 1990s, and over 7.1 million by 2009.[43] Figure 2.1 shows the dramatic growth in the number of institutions and enrollment over the past 150 years, while figure 2.2 shows the growth in the different degrees over that time period.

The Beginning of the Era of Privatization

Higher education's comprehensive growth over the twentieth century led to a shift in the nature of the university, which moved from a simpler institution focused on teaching toward what Clark Kerr described as the *multiversity*: a more complex collection of "communities and activities held together by a common name, a common governing board, and related purposes."[44] This organization, which grew to encompass a diverse collection of pursuits, was fed by massification due to federal legislation and demographic changes as well as significant federal and state investment. However, following decades of investment in higher education—in support of facilities, instruction, research, and financial aid—the economic stagnation and inflation of the 1970s into the early 1980s forced a national reconsideration of government subsidies and spending and served as one driver of privatization.

The stagflation of the 1970s and the declining birth rate, along with the end of the U.S. military draft, also made colleges less attractive to youth

FIGURE 2.1   Growth in U.S. higher education institutions and enrollment, 1869–2009

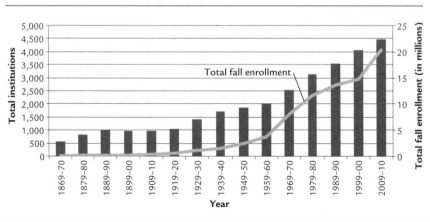

Source: National Center for Educational Statistics, "Digest of Education Statistics, 2012," table 220, http://nces.ed.gov/programs/digest/d12/tables/dt12_220.asp.

fresh out of high school. Colleges now had to cater to the part-time student, who tended to be on the older side; this led to, in part, an emphasis on pre-professional studies. The trend continued so that by 2000, when over 82 percent of students were enrolled in publicly funded institutions, 43.5 percent of the total student population was over twenty-five, with 43 percent enrolled part-time.[45]

Even as the structure of the university changed, President Ronald Reagan cut federal funding for higher education. He wanted to decrease the size of the welfare state in the face of international economic competition, a nation-wide recession, double-digit unemployment, and revenue shortfalls, all at a time when public service was in high demand. In targeting higher education to make it market efficient, he decided to reduce taxes and increase user fees for higher education while simultaneously reducing federal support for state and local government. This reduction in federal spending invigorated state governments, and governors and state legislatures introduced numerous initiatives and innovations, making education reform central to improving economic competitiveness.[46]

State governments convened numerous summits and engaged in such collaborative efforts as *Time for Results*, a set of recommendations to improve education at all levels. Additionally, whereas states previously relied on institutional

FIGURE 2.2   Degrees conferred by U.S. institutions, 1869–2009

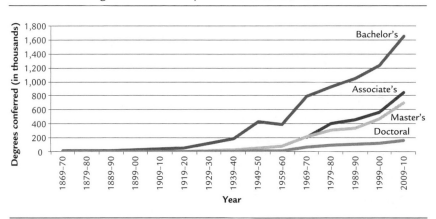

Source: National Center for Educational Statistics, "Digest of Education Statistics, 2012," table 220, http://nces.ed.gov/programs/digest/d12/tables/dt12_220.asp.

Note: Until 1959–1960, first professional degrees (e.g., law, MD, and DDS) were included with bachelor's degrees.

mechanisms for assessment and accountability, guided by presidents and provosts of universities, they now raised questions about outcomes and demanded accountability for state appropriations spent for general or specific purposes. At the national level, the Reagan administration started comparing states' K–12 test scores and other indicators of success as a way of promoting accountability after the 1983 publication of *A Nation at Risk*, which was produced by a national commission on excellence in education.[47]

Once the economy began to rebound in 1983, state political candidates increasingly supported greater cooperation among universities, industry, and government, and the federal government started to fund some social programs again. Federal programs, such as the Experimental Program to Stimulate Competitive Research (EPSCoR), distributed research funding more evenly by giving money to institutions without strong federal research records in underserved states, to HBCUs, and to programs that encouraged female scientists. Additionally, numerous universities did indeed partner with state governments to subsidize research parks and new centers for innovative technology, such as Silicon Valley in California and the Research Triangle Park in North Carolina.[48]

Overall, however, the general structure of the university became somewhat strained with the transition toward multiple functions (teaching, research, and service) and universal access at a time of stagflation, so universities began to more extensively raise funds from other sources (most significantly, tuition). As a result, Roger Geiger describes the 1980s as the beginning of an "era of privatization" that would forever shift the financial and structural models for public higher education. Public universities quickly lost their perceived role in economic development and thus saw a further decline in their relative share of government spending. Some now thought that a market-based system that focused on student demand would provide an optimal mix in higher education at market-based prices. Accordingly, the burden of cost shifted significantly from the state to the student, where it remains today.[49]

Under these conditions, larger and more selective institutions that have more diversified revenue streams will be able to secure funding from auxiliary services and other ventures in addition to philanthropy, as they can raise tuition while still getting competitive applicants and can raise funds from wealthy alumni and federal research agencies. In contrast, smaller and less selective institutions do not have as many options, and contrary to what many lawmakers assert, as state appropriations stagnate or decline, so too does philanthropy, resulting in a further stratification of public universities. However, from a broader perspective, all universities have had difficulty promoting fields of study that do not garner external support and providing advanced education to a broad range of students. Moreover, given the massification of higher education and globalization, economies are no longer limited by national or state boundaries, and neither is knowledge, causing institutions to push the limits of their mission, which had been historically tied to the state.[50]

As public universities have needed to raise more revenue and as students have come to be generally regarded as consumers, universities have necessarily become somewhat more autonomous. The federal government has supported campus autonomy by providing matching grants, but it has mostly concentrated on financing specific research programs and granting financial aid to students predominantly in the form of private loans. The federal government has only ever given direct institutional aid to the five service academies and to institutions serving groups that historically faced discrimination.[51]

In observing state appropriations, one should understand that higher education receives the second greatest share of many states' budgets; however, funding tends to be cut harshly during difficult years because higher education can replace public support with tuition. In fact, higher education likely gained more state revenue during the 1980s, as the national economic recovery and tax increases allowed higher education appropriations to increase between 1980 and 1987. However, the rate of increase in tuition was 30 percent greater than the rate of increase in state appropriations, and the taxpayers' revolt and nationwide recession in the early 1980s led to a tax system that was less progressive and less responsive to demands of education, in accordance with President Reagan's goals.[52]

More recently, the Great Recession has led to another precipitous decline in government appropriations. The decline in state appropriations is also occurring at a time when economic forces are spurring higher enrollments due to unemployment and significantly greater demands for financial aid. Overall, the "disinvestment" of state funds in higher education has most heavily impacted the instructional function. The result has been the flight of top faculty to private institutions, and larger numbers of part-time adjunct faculty teaching at public institutions.[53]

Accordingly, tuition and fees have now become the most stable, fastest-rising source of revenue for public universities. Between the 2000–2001 and 2010–2011 academic years, the average cost of undergraduate tuition, room, and board at public universities rose 42 percent after being adjusted for inflation, to $13,297, up from an average of $5,938 in constant 2009–2010 dollars.[54] Given the push of privatization, the federal and state government's relationship with universities has been affected in three fundamental areas: financial aid for students, direct institutional aid, and research.

The federal government has long provided funding to public universities in financial aid and research; state governments have long provided direct institutional aid and financial aid. As privatization has become more prevalent, the effect on national security in the era of globalization is becoming more acute. Through the nineteenth century, the public university was key to agricultural and industrial development, and it provided crucial help with national defense during both world wars. Even today, public universities make important intellectual contributions crucial to national security.[55] We turn our attention next to financial aid and its impact on access to higher education.

The Effect of Privatization on Financial Aid

Relatively inexpensive loans are central to most students' ability to fund their higher education, but the forces of privatization and larger economic forces in the past decade have put significant pressure on the financial aid model. As universities have turned to alternative sources of revenues, higher tuition has been a key component of privatization. Yet higher tuition often conflicts with the states' access goals if not paired with sufficient need-based financial aid.[56]

Partially as a result of the shifting economic, social, and political forces of the past forty years, higher education is more commonly viewed today as a private benefit to the individual—serving as the primary means for personal advancement, better job prospects, and higher income—than as a public good.[57] For this reason, there is greater emphasis today on the need for individuals to personally bear the true cost of their higher education, since they stand to gain the most. Chapter 3 will delve more deeply into understanding the value of higher education for the individual and society, but financial aid has been the main way to ensure that people from all walks can achieve a higher education.

Direct federal grants administered through universities were once the most common form of financial aid. The recent trend has been toward higher tuition coupled with financial aid that relies more on loans. The financial aid programs established by the Higher Education Act of 1965, and later amendments and reauthorizations, represent a progression from direct aid to federal loans.

As discussed earlier, the Higher Education Act showed a sustained national focus on granting more equal access to higher education, authorizing major financial aid programs to postsecondary students and creating the first grants and loans. The Higher Education Amendments of 1972 further extended the government's promise of financial aid to all low-income students, especially at the baccalaureate level, as the Title IX amendment provided legal protection for women and minorities by codifying their rights. These grants and loans were administered by colleges and universities but were given directly to students, after an effort to give direct federal aid to institutions in the form of unrestricted grants was defeated, thus reaffirming that states ultimately organize and fund systems of higher education.[58]

President Richard Nixon expanded the federal financial aid program and encouraged the high tuition–high financial aid model in which tuition was set at a high level and financial aid was used to provide access. Given the high tuition pricing during the late 1970s and early 1980s, political pressures extended financial aid eligibility to middle- and upper-middle-class students through programs such as the Middle Income Assistance Act, which broadened eligibility for Pell Grants and loans to middle-income families.[59]

During the 1980s, in part due to President Reagan's emphasis on decreasing the size and scope of the federal government, federal programs began to offer more student loans than grant aid by expanding student eligibility for loans. Between 1980 and 1988, lending under the guaranteed student loan program increased 96 percent, and loans became the predominant form of federal financial aid by 1990. As a result, the government spent less money. Between 1980 and 1988, funding for elementary and secondary education was reduced by 12 percent, and federal funding for higher education, while increasing by 7.4 percent, fell short of rising college costs. As a further illustration of the predominance of loans, in 1979, two-thirds of federal assistance to students was offered through grants and work-study jobs; in contrast, in 2003, two-thirds of federal aid was in loans, with the percentage of tuition covered by federal aid for low-income students further decreasing over time.[60]

As financial aid changed from grants to loans, there was a noticeable shift away from the idea that higher education was a social investment. Even though the expansion of loans was linked to improvements in enrollment, several analyses have shown that need-based grants were better for low-income students. The changes in financial aid have shifted the focus away from economically disadvantaged and minority groups, and although state governments have encouraged initiatives focusing on such groups, U.S. higher education has made very little progress in addressing participation gaps related to income and ethnicity.[61]

The Pell Grant program is one of the few remaining major federal need-based grant programs in the twenty-first century. Founded in 1973, the program provides need-based, voucher-like grants given directly to students by the federal government. Colleges disburse the funds, but the amount of funds each university receives depends on the number of low-income students enrolled. All other federal grant programs, such as the State Student Incentive Grants (now known as LEAP), have been limited and underfunded, and recently there has even been a large and rising gap between the maximum Pell Grant and the cost of attending a college or university.[62] Figure 2.3 shows the purchasing power of the Pell Grant has not risen over time. Sara Goldrick-Rab, one of the leading researchers on Pell Grants and affordability, notes, "Forty years ago, a needy student could use the Pell Grant to cover more than 75 percent of the costs of attending a public four-year college or university. Today, it covers barely 30 percent."[63]

Though this form of privatization was the most economical way for the United States to promote college access, the massive investment of private

FIGURE 2.3   Maximum and average Pell Grants, 1976–2012 (in constant 2012 dollars)

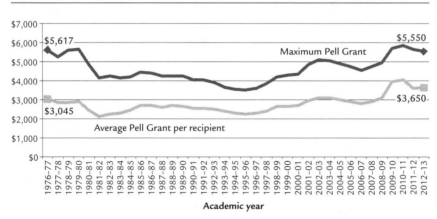

Source: College Board, "Trends in Student Aid 2013," Figure 13B (p. 24), http://trends.collegeboard.org/student-aid.

Note: The College Board uses CPI-U for its inflation adjustment.

capital in guaranteed loan programs skewed financial aid toward wealthier middle-class families, and current state and federal merit-based financial aid proved incapable of easing inequities. Federal loans for college students (known today as Stafford loans) provided about $13 billion in loan capital in 1980, rising to about $38 billion in 2001–2002.[64] In fact, in 2007–2008, federal Stafford loans averaging $5,000 apiece serviced 41.8 percent of all undergraduates, but the guaranteed student loan program experienced a high default rate, as the banks did not strictly police collection on loans given that the federal government backs them. Additionally, the average student debt grew from $9,188 in 1992–1993 to $16,928 in 2002–2003 and over $29,400 in 2013, emphasizing how the burden of cost had shifted to the student, thus affecting access to higher education.[65]

The federal government also introduced parent loans, known commonly as PLUS loans, the second biggest federal program that uses private capital to provide loans for higher education. Developed through the 1992 reauthorization of the Higher Education Act, PLUS loans provided financial aid for 3.8 percent of all undergraduates in 2012, averaging $10,800 per loan.[66] The burden of repayment has limited the potential for students from low-income families to attend institutions of higher education.[67]

Another noticeable shift away from the concept of financial aid as a social equalizer was an emphasis on tax credits that primarily benefit the middle and upper classes. In 1997, the federal government developed the Lifetime Learning tax credits. These supported higher education through the tax code and showed that the government was moving away from direct investment in students. These programs amounted to a massive middle-class entitlement program, though legislators portrayed them as a $40 billion national investment in higher education.[68]

By 1990, corresponding cuts in state support caused tuition rates to further increase, and higher tuition and higher loans became an international pattern. In this manner, institutions of higher education gained student dollars while governments simultaneously reduced spending. The loan programs as a whole became another major stimulus for this form of privatization, given that they were developed using private capital. However, in 2010, the Obama administration engineered the Health Care and Education Reconciliation Act, which extensively reformed the mechanism by which the federal government awarded financial aid. The Act codified the discontinuation of the Stafford or federally guaranteed Student Loan Program, with all new loans originating from the Direct Loan Program since July 1, 2010. Students receive the same benefits, but the federal government now provides loans through federal capital rather than private lenders.[69]

The Obama administration is also attempting to improve access to higher education by reforming Pell Grants and restructuring student loans so that interest rates are more market-based. The Act included the provision of $36 billion over ten years to increase the maximum Pell Grant to $5,550 in 2010 and to $5,975 by 2017, while indexing the Pell Grant to the Consumer Price Index starting in 2013. The Act also provided $2 billion over four years for community colleges and $2.55 billion in mandatory funding for minority-serving institutions and HBCUs, including programs to help low-income students obtain degrees in STEM majors. Additionally, the government has created a $1 billion "Race to the Top" fund to support competitive grants for states that reform higher education while decreasing tuition and increasing graduation rates.[70]

The perception of high tuition cost tends to discourage lower-income students, even with generous financial aid. Some states have further aggravated the problem by granting merit awards that divert resources away from low-income students, as merit awards overwhelmingly go to students in the middle and upper classes because of their access to quality preK–12 education. However, when universities charge tuition that is too low, they sacrifice revenue that could be used to fund expansive financial aid programs. The general public and the legislature tend to favor low tuition and prefer financial aid based on merit. In contrast, most university leaders and policy analysts favor the high tuition–high aid model with public subsidies for low-income students. The system of financial aid in the United States today is far more complex and expensive while at the same time, some might argue, less expansive than at any time in our history.[71]

Privatization and Research

Together with financial aid, research funding has been the federal government's other major contribution over the past century. Basic research is expensive and is not generally prompted by a specific goal or product but instead by a desire to seek the truth and to expand the borders of humanity's knowledge. Lofty as that may sound, basic research has led to some of the most significant breakthroughs in technology, medicine, and our understanding of our world. Some of that research brings significant economic payoffs for the researcher, the university, and the nation, but much of it may not be valued as highly for decades—or ever. While many outside of academia think of the "useless" research that occasionally makes headlines, such as mating patterns of ants or the psychology of rock 'n' roll, research is one of the essential functions of higher education.

The American public research university has provided highly trained specialists, expert knowledge, and scientific advances that can be used for national defense, life-saving treatments, and greater efficiency in production. Some examples of discoveries in which university research has played an essential role are radar, synthetic insulin, computers, magnetic resonance imaging, and lasers. More generally, federally sponsored research has been responsible for countless advances in chemistry, agriculture, and medical science, and laid the groundwork for the integrated circuit, the computer industry, and Internet. Advances in the life sciences from federally sponsored research have drastically decreased mortality and morbidity rates, and federal investments in military technology directly underpin the modern military. Public universities enroll over 75 percent of college students, providing 75 percent of doctoral degrees and 70 percent of engineering and technical degrees while conducting most of the nation's campus-based research.[72]

The U.S. higher education infrastructure has historically combined financial autonomy with public funding so as to ensure local economic and social benefits while also focusing on problems of agriculture, public health, and industry as well as providing advanced research and education. The federal government has also recognized that universities' partnerships with the private sector allow technology to be effectively transferred from universities to the commercial marketplace. The government has used this relationship to establish markets for key technologies such as the integrated circuit memory chip, and it has also given subsidies for various university-business partnerships to help apply the discoveries of academic science to practical ventures more quickly.[73]

The federal Bayh-Dole Act of 1983 allowed universities to own and license patents on discoveries made through research supported by public funds. This step provided strong incentives for further partnerships between universities and industries. Previously, in the 1970s, the federal government retained its title of ownership, but made the inventions available through a nonexclusive license; since industries did not have exclusive rights to manufacture and sell such goods, companies were less willing to invest. After Bayh-Dole, many university-linked companies were created, reaching their peak of activity in the late 1990s; the Act was instrumental in transferring basic science and technology from the university to the private sector and creating a significant number of jobs. In fact, by 2000, universities were earning more than $1 billion per year in license fees and royalties, while corporations further increased research support.[74]

Expanding basic research with the support of public funds while partnering with the business sector has also been necessary so that universities can conduct research at a sufficiently large scale. And when universities conduct research, undergraduate and graduate students who are assisting faculty are effectively trained to become part of the country's science and engineering work force and to continue to assist private firms in developing and applying new technologies.[75]

In the United States, the university partnership with government and industry was directly responsible for the creation of hubs in which start-up companies, research labs, financiers, and corporations created an environment that combined knowledge, finance, and opportunity to bring about advances essential to economic progress. Universities use public funding to conduct cutting-edge research activities and train highly skilled workers, providing the infrastructure that forms the basis of research clusters; firms can then use the new technology in the commercial marketplace and hire talented personnel from these universities. Additionally, the universities help to highlight the reputation of clusters so that foreign firms may invest in the region. The development of the transistor by Bell Labs in 1950s, as well as the growth of the semiconductor industry and birth of Silicon Valley, exemplifies this sort of partnership well.[76]

As corporations have funded more basic research, the federal government has decreased its share of funding for such research from 70.3 percent in 1980 to 57 percent today.[77] However, corporations are often disinclined to focus on basic research that may not be immediately ready for commercial use, preferring to invest in applied research and development.[78]

Without federal funding, university-based research could shift away from basic research and focus on training and applied research, as the social benefits of basic research usually exceed private returns and cannot not be quantified by corporations. Additionally, due to competitive pressure to introduce new products quickly, most large firms simply cannot afford to support basic research and the indirect costs that come with deteriorating science facilities and equipment and concerns about hazardous waste.[79]

Perhaps most importantly, the government has stopped partnering with universities by funding basic research and has instead become a procurer of research. Government staffers make sure that research universities meet every detail of their agreements with government, imposing restrictions on such research. Currently, university research essentially tracks federal priorities; at a time when fields are becoming increasingly interdependent, many are calling for more balanced funding to achieve the best results for economic productivity.[80] Without sustained federal involvement, public universities will potentially shift toward applied commercially funded research rather than basic inquiry, and may sacrifice educational quality by trying to extract as much profit as possible from extension divisions and distance learning.

Overall, universities' commercialization of technologies has slowed since 2000, a slowdown that persisted even after the economic recession of the early 2000s. According to the World Economic Forum, given other countries' rapid innovations, the United States is now ranked seventh in the world in terms of innovative capacity. This suggests that the federal government, even as it accepts and encourages forms of privatization, must fundamentally invest in basic research, aid the transfer of research to the marketplace, and make sure that the university and private sectors are given enough incentives to invest in basic research and development.[81]

Success at the scientific frontier does not guarantee national economic rewards. Technology breakthroughs are expensive, difficult to achieve, and not always applicable for practical purposes such as the distribution of goods. However, higher education serves the instrumental role of bringing technological innovations to companies of all sizes and in all sectors.[82]

Global Shift to Privatization

Around the world, nations have been embracing an ideology of privatization contained within a broader set of reforms, as government funding has been far outstripped by rising unit costs and increasing demand for higher education. Thus, governments all over the world have pushed for universities to better respond to external market pressures and the broader global economy while also relying more on private sources of revenue to meet their commitments. In fact, national leaders from around the world seem to think that global contracts, innovation, and the construction of international research networks would be more likely to occur if there is more competition between the private and public sectors.[83]

Even countries with national education strategies and ministries of education are unable to accommodate all secondary school graduates who are eligible for and want to pursue further study. As a result, one solution is greater managerial autonomy over central planning and export competitiveness, as well as efforts to diversify the financial base of universities and allow free-market principles to drive higher education, especially in terms of directing research for national needs. The governments of developing countries, especially, hope that privatization will prevent academics from going to work at universities in the West, given that private enterprises and competition tend to encourage flexibility and financial rewards.[84]

Higher education in countries such as the United States, Japan, and South Korea has long depended on private funding; in fact, the ratio of private investment to public investment is three to one in both Japan and South Korea. However, China and countries in Central and Eastern Europe have just begun to look to private sources to relieve the strain on the public government. For example, in the 1990s, China was actively drawing multinational corporations to the country and investing about $30 billion per year in research and development to further increase its role in the global economy. By 2000, China was supposed to quadruple its agricultural and industrial output; however, given the country's extensive government control, its leaders realized that the system could be much more cost efficient and effective and decreased the government's share of funding from 96 percent in 1978 to 45 percent in 2005.[85]

The Chinese government has also recently encouraged university-based research and university-industry linkages, as the Chinese Ministry of Education has acknowledged that commercialization of research and technological inventions is necessary if the economy is to benefit from such advances. The Chinese government directly assists the commercialization of research by supplementing the shortage of capital from private and local investors, and the country has done better than the West in terms of commercializing advanced technologies.[86]

The Indian government, too, has extensive control of its higher education sector. It invests $4 billion in higher education to develop and maintain a system of national education that could train the masses and ultimately produce a skilled work force as well as a research and development infrastructure that would allow the country to generate, access, and share knowledge. Even now, the Indian government is still investing money to build more than one thousand new universities and fifty thousand new colleges in an attempt to double its higher education enrollment over the next ten years. However, India's public research universities are still overpoliticized, undermanaged, and undermodernized, with overall relative underinvestment by the Indian government. In this environment, private investment is necessary. When the government does not respond fast enough, private initiative establishes institutions to meet the demand for higher education; in India today, a majority of students are educated in private universities.[87]

Great Britain in the 1980s is another example of the forces of privatization. The government dramatically altered its relationship with its universities and polytechnics, allowing them greater autonomy and freedom to pursue entrepreneurial activity at the expense of ministry and local control; it also reallocated resources and increased students' tuition, so that taxpayers were no longer bearing a significant portion of the cost.[88] This is part of a worldwide trend that has effectively shifted the burden of cost to the student.

Is a National Strategy Possible? Is It a Good Idea?

Even as the forces of privatization grow stronger, the Four Asian Tigers (Hong Kong, Singapore, South Korea, and Taiwan) and other countries with flourishing systems of higher education still have a national strategy that depends on significant government investment, and these countries have reached such great heights only through an aggressive development strategy. The successful East Asian governments all implemented higher education plans through legislation and played a key role in building the infrastructure and helping students pay for entry into higher education in the early stages of development. These governments also set targets for real improvement and adapted specific measures to increase capacity in the sciences and technologies; as a result, research institutions in these countries have gained incredible prestige.[89]

South Korea has one of the highest proportions of students in private universities. In fact, the Pohang Iron and Steel Company funded the establishment of a private research university—Pohang Institute of Science and Technology—so as to increase revenue. However, the South Korean government still allocated approximately $4.1 billion for higher education in 2009 alone while also launching the Education Capacity Enhancement Project, which provides grants to campuses to meet industrial demands for a qualified work force.[90]

South Korea has extensive coordinated control of its higher education system. The government controls the expansion and direction of higher education through legislative directives and provides large subsidies that make up about 95 percent of institutions' development and recurrent costs. Singapore, another successful country, has also closely coordinated the development of higher education institutions so as to produce the correct quantity and type of labor for the economy, with access to institutions determined by objective criteria tied to a ten-year enrollment plan. Taiwan's Ministry of Education approves the appointment of university presidents, tuition, student enrollment, and faculty salary, among others. All these countries have developed their higher education systems in tandem with industrialization policies that have fixed growth targets and manpower forecasting, even as they target areas of research to maximize investment of resources.[91]

These countries can invest so extensively in research because they force students to compete for places in elite schools that automatically offer superior life chances, and this competition ensures that families pay tuition fees, given Confucian societies' intrinsic commitment to education. Because public resources that might have gone to tuition can then be applied to research and development, as well as financial aid for high-quality students and researchers, East Asian research funding and investment has grown faster than anywhere else. However, these countries have a more utilitarian emphasis on research, where close state supervision may stifle creativity and cause civil disillusionment.[92]

India, Singapore, and China have also clearly shown that developed countries cannot maintain their competitive advantage merely by adopting some elements of privatization, such as allowing patents in universities, running entrepreneurship classes, and spinning off new companies; these developing countries have used such methods even while the government actively invests in education. They have invested in training students through graduate school, especially in science- and technology-related majors, at a time when fewer students are pursuing such majors in the West. Overall, Britain, China, France, Germany, India, Japan, Singapore, and South Korea have all established national grant programs for students. At the regional level, the Bologna Process and the Lisbon Declaration of the European University Association have also provided student grant programs. Most of these countries have better tertiary participation rates than the United States, and grants have proven to be viable so as to increase equality in participation.[93]

In comparison, the U.S. government also first invested heavily in universities by funding research and subsidizing the attendance at the university. As a result, enrollment increased dramatically, which spurred a rise in real income and a rise in economic productivity and innovation. However, though the

U.S. system has always been decentralized so that universities have had significant autonomy, the public funds available for higher education have not kept pace with demands for increasing enrollment, despite increasing federal aid. Even though the federal government increased its revenue by 29 percent per full-time equivalent (FTE) student between the 2005–2006 and 2010–2011 academic years, state revenues decreased by 12 percent in the same period.[94] Because other sectors of the nation's economy have competed for the government's scarce resources, and demand for education has risen even as it has become increasingly regarded as a private good, the government hasn't been able to provide sufficient funding to maintain the competitiveness of the higher education system.

The United States reached academic superiority through significant investment in research, access, and a more diverse system of higher education than is found in most countries. However, following several major recessions and facing increasing global competition for students, faculty, and funding, the nation needs a fundamental remodeling of the higher education funding and management structure. After looking at sixteen key indicators—such as the number of scientists and engineers, corporate and government research and development, venture capital, productivity, and trade performances—the July 2011 *Atlantic Century* reported that the United States has not improved its international competitiveness since 1999; as of 2011, the country ranked fourth in innovation-based competitiveness. A national report published in 2005 showed that foreign students made up 40 percent or more of graduate enrollments in physical sciences, mathematics, computer science, and engineering, and about two-thirds of graduate and undergraduate students in engineering were white males.[95]

The federal government needs to ensure that more U.S. citizens, particularly women and minorities, have access to higher education in the vital STEM fields so as to protect national security and economic competitiveness at a time when other countries are fast advancing their education systems. However, in comparison to the other national systems of higher education, the U.S. system is still seen as superior because of its great diversity of offerings. From Harvard and Stanford to the local community college, there is an option for everyone in the country. But the question remains, how long can they remain competitive as individual institutions facing global competition? A national system of higher education that is centrally controlled will likely not be the answer in the United States, but a more coordinated emphasis on reaching national goals in areas of greatest need may well be required.

Is Higher Education Too Valuable Not to Privatize?

The nation's system of higher education was born locally, grew, and has been sustained within the states, and today many universities are national institutions with wide-ranging impact. What many fear about privatization (again, often without a proper understanding of its definition, broadly speaking) is that it will unduly loosen state and federal control of the system of higher education. Instead, we may be at a point where these institutions are too valuable to be left to the whims of federal and state funding, which fluctuates wildly depending upon the economy, the politicians in power, and the priorities of the day.

For institutions with broad national appeal, including many of the flagship public universities, letting them remain state institutions may impact our national security in significant ways, since these institutions are responsible for the lion's share of defense- and security-related research. If a state decides it no longer has the ability or interest to support that university and federal research funding declines, there could be significant ripple effects for decades to come. The question, therefore, centers on understanding what the true value of higher education is, to whom, and for what. Economic analysis can help shape our understanding of that perennial conundrum of who pays, who benefits, and who should pay? Our discussion moves next to some of the answers to these questions.

CHAPTER THREE

The Value of Higher Education

There is no education that is just for earning a living; it is also for living a life.

—W. E. B. Du Bois[1]

It is not the individual, but the society, that creates wealth.

—Andrew Carnegie[2]

IN ALMOST EVERY MEETING I had with state legislators, governors, or members of Congress, they made clear to me that they value colleges and universities and see them as engines of prosperity and ladders to the middle class. In other words, across the country, those charged with deciding where to allocate public dollars and influencing public policy see higher education as very valuable. Why, then, when universities are recognized as creators of value, is there so much chatter publicly and privately about outrageous increases in tuition and the need to constrain costs? If the return on an investment in higher education is so high, not only for the individual but also for the society, why is the burden of cost shifting from the state to the student?

One ranking state legislator in California summed up an important reason for such a gap between perceived value and public investment: "I think people understand that [higher education] is important, but when you talk about a shrinking pie, we're choosing between seniors and single mothers without child care or the university system, which is perceived as being able to take care of [itself]. So we tend to focus on those who are the most at need, which are those who cannot take care of themselves." Higher education doesn't stand a chance if policy makers are drawing stark lines narrowly focused on the most immediate and pressing social needs or on the voting bloc with the most consistent turnout and historically lowest support for education—senior citizens.

Whether higher education is a public good, a private good, or both, it is imperative to understand more deeply its value. If states and the federal government are to decide whether or not (or how much) to invest in higher education, policy makers need a full understanding of its costs and benefits—and just who stands to gain. Tax dollars are spread among many competing priorities, and with competing interests comes the need to explain value and return on investment.

Governments and individuals invest hundreds of billions of dollars each year in higher education. In the United States, a large proportion of the country's national wealth is spent on education. Combining private and public sources, the United States spends around 7.3 percent of its GDP on all levels of education. This is significantly higher than most advanced economies and is one of the reasons why we are one of the most educated societies in the world. Higher education contributes substantially to that total sum—around 2.6 percent of total GDP, accounting for both public and private spending. In the Organisation for Economic Co-operation and Development (OECD), a group of highly industrialized countries, the average is around 1.6 percent of GDP.[3]

Remarkably, a higher than average proportion of U.S. spending on education comes from private sources. In the United States, only 38 percent of higher education expenditures comes from public sources, and the other 62 percent comes from private sources. Comparatively, across all OECD countries, 70 percent of higher education expenditures comes from public sources and only 30 percent from private.[4]

The merits, value, and perceived returns on those investments inform much of the debate surrounding higher education policy today. The forces of privatization have been gathering steam since the 1970s, gradually at first, then more rapidly in the past two decades. According to the College Board, since 1996 tuition at public institutions has risen 28 percent in real terms. However, net increases of tuition, including financial aid and other sources of aid, rose only 7 percent. Meanwhile, public funding to higher education

institutions per FTE student has declined, but there is considerable variation in tuition among the states. The lowest average tuition stands at $4,125
dollars in Wyoming, while the highest average tuition is in New Hampshire
and stands at $13,705. In 1996–1997, the average published tuition and fees
for four-year public schools was $4,280, while the amount of net tuition and
fees was $1,910. In the 2011–2012 school year, the average published tuition
and fees was $8,240, while the amount of net tuition was $2,490. In 2010
constant dollars, state appropriations per full-time student stood at $8,300 in
the 1980–1981 academic year. By contrast, in the 2010–2011 academic year,
state appropriations fell to $7,200.[5] Federal and state financial aid has not
matched the rising costs of higher education. In reaction, universities have
begun to explore different sources of revenue, resulting in the current general
trend of privatization.

Stuck in the middle of this policy shift are families and students who find
it increasingly difficult to pay for college. According to a 2012 College Board
Report, for those who do not receive financial aid, the cost to attend an in-
state public college for the 2012–2013 academic year rose 3.8 percent, to a
record $22,261. This figure includes tuition, housing, food, books, and other
fees. Averaging for all students in calculating the net price, total costs minus
scholarships, grants, and federal tax benefits, in-state public colleges rose 4.6
percent. This figure is more than twice as high as the rate of inflation, which
was just 2 percent in the same period.[6]

The forces driving the privatization and rising costs of higher education
are numerous, and this book expands on the legislative and historic reasons,
with a heavy emphasis on qualitative data from hundreds of interviews with
state and federal policy makers. Though I am by no means an economist, I
have found economics most useful in providing an essential perspective to
help understand what's going on. At the heart of my discussion is the need to
understand the value of higher education, both public and private.

Historically, institutions of higher education in the United States were
founded with roles conceived for the public good. In 1803, Bowdoin College
President Joseph McKeen said, "institutions are founded and endowed for
the common good and not for the private advantage of those who resort to
them for education."[7] As the culture of individualization grew in American
society, the discourse about the benefits of higher education has gradually
shifted to the individual. Moreover, public support for investing in higher
education began to focus on individual monetary gains and higher earnings
over the student's lifetime, and other market-based benefits.

Throughout most of the twentieth century at the macroeconomic level, higher education was increasingly seen through the perspective of human capital theory, where the drivers of economic growth were skilled labor, innovation, productivity, and individuals' ability to harness technology. For many students, the decision to invest in higher education began to be based on rate of return. Whether they were actually calculating an institution's rate of return or not, they believed that a college degree would mean greater earnings. For the government, higher education began to be seen as an engine for productivity and economic development, with public investments leading to economic growth for all. Governments increasingly began to understand that there was something about higher education that appeared to improve the society. Countries soon discovered that societies with higher levels of education had reduced levels of crime, greater civic participation, and improved health.[8] Governments, just like individuals, began to calculate a social rate of return for investments in higher education. The movement to reform the classical curriculum to make higher education more relevant to modern society in the nineteenth century was in many ways an economic argument rooted in social goals, and it was also a motivation of the Morrill Act of 1862.

Today, the trends of privatization in higher education result from multiple variables that include a fundamental shift toward thinking about the benefits of higher education as increasingly private—individual—benefits. Rising costs of higher education and the public's perceived lack of both private and social returns on an investment in higher education have created market inefficiencies, where the optimum private or social good is never fully realized. This chapter highlights the fact that higher education has several nonmarket benefits that are often omitted when individuals think about its value, distorting their decisions about whether to invest in it. This chapter will show how misinformation about the potential benefits of higher education results in its devaluation, and therefore, market failure in providing the best outcome to the most people.

The fact that 62 percent of higher education expenditures in the United States comes from private sources raises some interesting questions. Why is the proportion of private sources in higher education expenditures greater in the United States than elsewhere, and has this always been the case? Given such large expenditures on higher education, what is the return on investment in higher education to individuals and societies? Finally, what is the government's responsibility in providing access to higher education for its citizens? All these questions lead to a central question of this book: is higher education a public good or a private benefit?

To answer these questions, a modest understanding of critical economic theories on higher education is required. For readers who prefer fingernails on a chalkboard to reading about economic theories, my goal here is to make clear foundational work that even I (not an economist) can understand readily. The first part of this chapter outlines the fundamentals of human capital theory and introduces private investment calculations of rate of return for higher education. Next, I introduce, in monetary terms, the private value of higher education, the principles of market failure in higher education, and the notion of economic efficiency. Third, I shift to a discussion of the social, or public, value of higher education; the monetary value of the social benefits of higher education; and the role of government and the concept of higher education as a public good.

The Evolution from Public Good to Private Benefit

In an idealistic description of the university as "a basic commitment to the life of the mind" with a focus on "the advancement of knowledge, the increase of understanding among men, and the unending search for truth," higher education maintains its role as society's central laboratory for the creation and dissemination of knowledge.[9] Public universities, in particular, have long fulfilled this mission but also fill another role by serving the people and the needs of the state and the nation more broadly.

Over time, however, the shifting focus and financing of public higher education led to a change in perception about its benefits. The nature of "public" in public higher education—accessible, accountable, and affordable—is coming into question even as the nation realizes the importance of greater attainment for more citizens in order to meet the needs of a changing global economy. The challenges ahead are significant when we consider that over three-quarters of all students enrolled in higher education are at a public college or university in an era of flat or declining funding for such institutions.

Partially as a result of the shifting economic, social, and political forces of the last twenty years, it has become increasingly apparent that higher education is viewed more commonly today as a personal benefit to the individual—serving as the primary means for personal advancement, better job prospects, and higher income—than as a public good.[10]

One recent report examined both the benefits and costs to society and taxpayers for public, private, and for-profit institutions of higher education. At "highly competitive" and "most competitive" public universities, a college graduate gained, on average, an additional $525,000 in lifetime earnings as compared to a high school graduate. Taxpayers also gained with an average of $98,000 in additional lifetime federal and state taxes from the graduates of these public institutions. The costs to the taxpayers per bachelor's degree are significant, however, and averaged between $75,000 and $108,000 for degrees from these most competitive public universities.[11]

Even a rigorous economic evaluation of the costs and benefits to the individual and society lacks any discussion of the public good that the institutions serve or the wider economic benefits to the state, which may balance out the additional costs to the taxpayers via forgone taxes and state appropriations to the public universities. Governors and state legislators should rightly focus on the direct costs and benefits of public higher education, but this and other reports highlight the gap in the understanding of these institutions' connection to the public good and the need for dialogue between institutional and state leaders.

Just as privatization occurs along a series of continua, the line between public goods and private benefits in higher education is murky; the discussion is framed most often as a benefit either to the individual or to the society. Milton Friedman argued that higher education had no broad benefits for society beyond those created for the individual, but there is research to suggest that the benefits to the individual resulting from greater access also have broad "spillover" benefits for society.[12]

What has been lost in the debate, however, is the public consensus that both society *and* the individual benefit from higher education. Higher education is not a perfect public good or a truly competitive market because it has some elements of both public good and private benefit and cannot be clearly differentiated.[13] Indeed, there are significant public and private benefits, viewed through the framework of social and economic benefits as seen in table 3.1. These benefits may only be correlated with investment in higher education, rather than causally related, but it is still worthwhile to see the significant benefits to society *and* the individual.

Many institutions are seeking to balance their core public mission with the realities of the competitive marketplace. The lack of differentiation between public and private benefits is one contributing factor in the pursuit of dichotomous missions. Finding the right balance between mission and

TABLE 3.1   A classification of higher education benefits

	Public (societal)	Private (individual)
Social	· Reduced crime rates · Increased charitable giving/ community service · Increased quality of civic life · Social cohesion/appreciation of diversity · Improved ability to adapt to and use technology	· Improved health/life expectancy · Improved quality of life for offspring · Better consumer decision making · Increased personal status · More hobbies and leisure activities
Economic	· Increased tax revenues · Greater productivity · Increased consumption · Increased work force flexibility · Decreased reliance on government financial support	· Higher salaries and benefits · More stable employment · Higher savings levels · Improved working conditions · Personal/professional mobility

Source: Institute for Higher Education Policy, *The Investment Payoff: A 50-State Analysis of the Public and Private Benefits of Higher Education* (Washington, DC: Institute for Higher Education Policy, 2005).

market is why public institutions, in particular, must strive to reframe their relationships with both the state and the wider public that support them. Zemsky, Wegner, and Massy astutely noted, "Administrators and politicians must publicly reaffirm the principle that the American university, an educational asset, can powerfully serve both public and private purposes."[14] There remains a need to reconnect higher education to the public good and to develop a new model of what has been called a "public-purpose institution" that can survive and thrive in the twenty-first century.[15] As the needs of the nation and individual states evolve, these institutions are seeking greater autonomy to allow them to innovate. Public purposes have shifted rapidly, and that has been an important driver of the evolution of these public universities—both socially and economically.

Human Capital Theory

Several key concepts are central in understanding the economics of higher education. Perhaps none is more applicable or crucial than the theory of human capital. The theory originates from the work of Gary S. Becker, who defined *human capital* as the "knowledge, skills, and attributes accumulated through the investment in education and health, work experience, and learning that occurs throughout the duration of an individual's life." Human capital can be accumulated at home, through social interaction, and through on-the-job training.[16]

Before we get into too much detail regarding economic theories, it may be beneficial to outline certain sources of human capital. To do so, we must first accept that harsh yet undeniable reality that not all people are created equal and not all people have an equal chance with the circumstances into which they are born. For example, a child born into wealth is not only much more likely to attend college, but will probably go to one of the best universities.[17]

The first source of human capital lies in the innate abilities or skills an individual possesses. Although this is highly debated, some research in biology attests that individuals can have different levels of skills (human capital) because of inborn differences.[18] The second source, schooling, is one of the most observable components of human capital development, and the primary focus of this chapter. Third is the murky role of school quality and nonschooling investments, which affect the quality of education an individual receives (not all schools are equal) and the student's decision to study certain subjects that may improve human capital, such as developing communication, public speaking, or study skills. The fourth source is training, which improves human capital for specific industries; it includes on-the-job training and workshops.

At the heart of human capital theory is the principle of improved productivity—that an educated population is, in fact, a productive population.[19] For example, an office with employees who have similar levels of higher education will likely work more effectively and productively than an office with a mixture of educational and experiential backgrounds. There is firm-specific human capital, which has little value if the worker moves between firms. There is industry-specific human capital, which is mobile between firms in the same industry. Finally, there is fully mobile human capital, which tends to be the most general education (quantitative skills, writing ability, communication, and critical thinking). The more specific information and knowledge you have, the better you can perform tasks. This is one of several reasons why many jobs have a tiered wage structure—increased levels of experience result in increased knowledge, which, in turn, warrants higher wages. This concept views human capital as directly useful in the production process, represented by a "stock" of knowledge or skills that is directly part of the production function. In classic economic growth models, the output of an economy is a function of two primary factors of production: capital and labor. Human capital, through the improved productivity of labor, greatly increases the possibility for economic growth.

Modern human capital theory expands to include the improved productivity of the household and society as a result of skills and knowledge accumulated by an individual. Inherently, human capital belongs solely to the individual. Until death, human capital is used only at one place at a time. However, an extension of the theory is that human capital skills are not just used on the job or in the labor market. Human capital skills are carried home with the individual, and that has an effect on the productivity of the household.

Although human capital belongs solely to the individual, skills and productivity may be transferred through *externalities*—the spillovers from human capital that affect others, and one reason why higher education has been viewed historically as a public good. These characteristics have huge implications for the development of the society through social nonmarket benefits, which will be discussed in the second part of this chapter. Therefore, it is important to emphasize that modern human capital theory has incorporated advances in measuring these crucial nonmarket benefits that lead to improved productivity outside the working environment.

Now that we have discussed the theory of human capital in general, our focus can return to higher education. To understand the potential value of education, we must first understand how individuals decide whether to invest in it. Formally or informally, many students and parents will calculate a net present value of their education that will assure that the dollar investment put forth today will be returned and yield higher benefits in the future. If the investment in higher education does not satisfy this criterion, it likely will not occur. Quantifying this cost-benefit analysis for an individual can yield a concrete value of higher education. Until recently, it was often assumed that completing college would guarantee entry into the middle or upper class. However, with rising tuition and uncertain job prospects, students and families are beginning to question that assumption. Some researchers argue vigorously that we are educating too many people and that the jobs they are performing don't require higher education.[20] There is hope, though, in Val Burris's 1983 study of the various effects of overeducation on the American public. Burris evaluated overeducation's impact on job satisfaction, political leftism, and alienation. The study concluded that the effects of overeducation on these worker attitudes were minor.[21]

Apart from the individual, state and federal governments also have a strong interest in the returns on education. According to Joseph Ayo Babalola, the case for investment in human capital is based on three arguments. The first is that every new generation must be given the appropriate parts of the knowledge that have already been accumulated by previous generations. Second, new generations should be taught how existing knowledge should be used to develop new products and to introduce new processes, production methods, and social services. And third, people must be encouraged to develop entirely new ideas, products, processes, and methods through creative approaches.[22]

Measuring the social benefits of higher education is crucial for the federal and state governments. Policy makers and elected officials need to calculate whether the social costs of investments in higher education—such as taxpayer money to fund public universities, financial aid, and research—are higher or lower than the social benefits. Even if decisions are made based on the political winds of the day, as many legislators and policy makers made apparent to me, the facts about the costs and benefits must be understood.

Rates of Return on Investments in Higher Education

While education can be considered a consumption good, human capital theory treats it, particularly higher education, as an investment, because it is an action that incurs costs in the present but raises productivity in the future. There is considerable evidence that a college graduate will be able to obtain higher paying jobs than an individual with only a high school diploma.[23] Even though the recent recession made finding a job harder for many college graduates, the long-term employment and income prospects for those with a college degree are still much higher than those with only some college or a high school diploma. Using data to evaluate the likelihood that a person of working age with a college degree would earn less than the median worker with a high school degree, figure 3.1 makes clear that the evidence points to greater returns for the college graduate a majority of the time.

The decision to invest in education can be explained through a cost-benefit analysis and calculation of the rate of return of the net present value, where the costs of human capital accumulation can be divided into direct and indirect costs. The direct costs are payments for tuition, books, and other instant payments. The indirect costs are the opportunity costs of forgone

FIGURE 3.1   Percentage of college graduates earning less income than the median high school graduate, 1964–2010

Source: R. Archibald and D. Feldman, 2013; used with permission.

Note: Calculated using Current Population Survey (CPS) data from the Bureau of Labor Statistics.

earnings and increased job experience. The estimated costs and benefits of a college education are illustrated in figure 3.2, a graph that is frequently used in economic literature on educational gains. The y-axis displays the monetary costs and earnings of a high school graduate and a college graduate. The x-axis shows the age of individuals, beginning at eighteen, the typical entry age for higher education, and ending at sixty-five, the average age of retirement.

Figure 3.2 shows that when an individual decides to attend college, there are opportunity and monetary costs, represented by forgone earnings and direct costs. Think of the job you could have had right out of high school versus the tuition and living expenses of college. Taking these costs into account, most people will invest in human capital (higher education) only if the future returns outweigh the costs. That implies that future earnings of a college graduate should be able to cover the lost wages forgone by his or her not working immediately after high school and the institutional costs of attending college. The area labeled "Monetary benefits" in figure 3.2 represents the monetary gains from a college education. For an investment to be profitable, the "Monetary benefits" area must be larger than or equal to the area of "Forgone earnings" and "Direct costs" in present-value terms.

FIGURE 3.2   Costs and benefits of four years in college

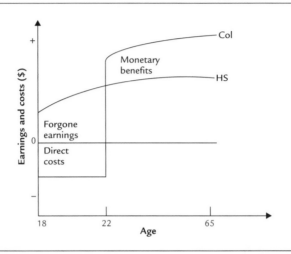

Source: Campbell McConnell, Stanley Brue, and David MacPherson, *Contemporary Labor Economics*, 10th ed. (New York: Irwin Professional Publications, 2014), 301.

Economists quantify the costs and benefits using the present-value (PV) formula. The formula takes into consideration the present and future costs and benefits of attending college, such as increased earnings and tuition fees. Present-value calculations discount the value of future earnings to present-day value simply because of the lengthy time needed to realize those investments. Discounting is important because it acknowledges that a future value may be lower than a present one. Consider, for example, whether you'd rather receive $20 today versus $20 in five years. Receiving $20 today is more valuable than receiving $20 in the future (even if just five years into the future). The present-value formula calculates future income to current value, given the number of years and the market rate of interest.

To calculate the present value of an individual's lifetime stream of income along with its costs and benefits, the net present value takes the sum of each present value for each working year of an individual, to calculate the combined present value for each year in the future. We can calculate the decision to invest in higher education by comparing the net present value of the two income streams and choosing the highest present value. Intuitively, what the net present value calculates is the total future earnings as a result of higher education, discounted to a present value using a market interest rate and reduced by total direct costs and forgone earnings from the investment. This compares the value of future income depending on two scenarios, which are often the choices of investing in higher education or not.

The results of the present-value calculation can be illustrated again through figure 3.2. The present value for college graduates is characterized by the area under the college (Col) curve subtracted by the "Forgone earnings" and "Direct costs" boxes. Similarly, the present value for high school graduates is characterized by the area under the high school (HS) curve. The decision to invest in human capital depends on whether the Col area minus the "Forgone earnings" and "Direct costs" boxes is greater than the area under the HS curve, or whether the college graduate present value is higher than the high school present value. Therefore, if your return on investment and calculated future earnings from investing in higher education are greater than the total calculated earnings without a higher education degree, then investing in higher education is the more profitable option.

Expected Wages from Higher Education

While economists may calculate the expected value of higher education, it is understandable that, for many reasons, this calculation may not be straightforward or understandable to individuals or families trying to decide whether it makes sense to go to college and what the value of a degree will be. The premise of human capital theory and the benefits from higher education are based on higher wages for skilled workers. In economics, skilled workers, or individuals in the labor force with higher education, have increased productivity. The rate translates directly to wages. Higher education creates a larger stock of productive human capital skills, which are in demand in the labor market. Employers continue to pay more for skilled workers if increased productivity improves the efficiency of the firm and brings lower cost per unit.

Two immediate challenges arise when individuals and families are considering higher education. First, the need for immediate income may hinder investments in higher education—particularly in some low-income and minority populations, where children are working to support parents and grandparents. Second, and more common, is the lack of information on the benefits of higher education. As mentioned earlier, there is substantial evidence that education raises earnings. Individuals with a bachelor's degree earn more and are less likely to be unemployed than those with only a high school diploma.[24] In 2011, the median weekly earnings for individuals with a bachelor's degree were 65 percent higher than those with a high school diploma—$1,053 compared to $638, as shown in figure 3.3. More students

FIGURE 3.3   Median weekly earnings in 2011

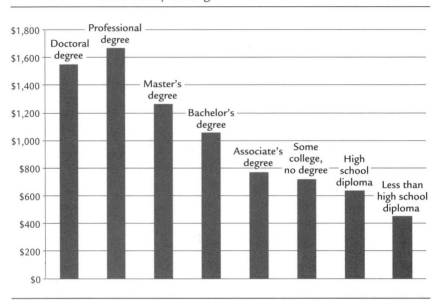

Source: Bureau of Labor Statistics (2012).

Note: Data is for individuals age twenty-five and over. Earnings are for full-time wage and salary workers.

and parents are using information of this kind, although some remain skeptical. However, this type of information, even using these calculations, grossly excludes the nonmarket benefits. If private nonmarket benefits of education were more commonly included in present-value or rate-of-return calculations, the evidence of the benefits of higher education might greatly increase.[25]

From the perspective of both governments and individuals, to determine an accurate cost-benefit calculation in the public and private returns from higher education, there must be accurate information—information that is not always easy to obtain. Traditional human capital theory measures only the monetary benefits of the job market and its returns to individuals. Modern human capital theory greatly expands its perspective on higher education beyond the traditional focus on market benefits. Again, it is important to note that the use of accumulated human capital does not stop at the end of a nine-to-five work day. Expanding the concept of externalities and indirect effects, modern human capital theory incorporates using learned skills and knowledge at home and in the community. It measures an individual's productivity during leisure time and other nonworking hours. Time spent at home or at a community event produces nonmarket private satisfactions that may improve health, longevity, and happiness.[26] Time spent in the community generates social outcomes that may improve democratic society and civic order broadly, as well as in individual institutions.

It is often the case, however, that individuals and policy makers measure only market returns when making an investment decision or grossly underestimate the nonmarket benefits. This is certainly the case with education overall and higher education specifically in most states. Modern human capital theory, through the advancement of measuring the value of time, has significant implications for public policy. Nonmarket benefits in addition to market benefits can reveal accurate values for human capital outcomes in relation to their costs. This link will help governments create policies that decide the optimum level of investment required for economic growth or development in a state.

Private Nonmarket Returns on Education

To measure market and nonmarket benefits, we need clear definitions of the two terms. *Market benefits* are additional earnings from the productive use of higher education or increased human capital on the job. They are extremely important because they accurately measure income, not simple wages. Traditional labor market economics relates human capital with increased productivity as measured by wages. For example, 70 percent of national income is directly related to wages that reflect human capital and productivity (more recently, this percentage has declined and is one reason for the dramatic change in the distribution of income that has created most of the college affordability problem.[27] The remaining 30 percent of earnings—such as interest, rent, or other forms of income—is also affected by human capital but is usually not included in standard rates of return. Walter McMahon's work on private nonmarket benefits is an important focus in this chapter, as it diverges from the traditional understanding of the value of higher education.[28]

Nonmarket benefits of human capital are accumulated when an individual carries human capital from the job to the home or community and uses it to improve the productivity of time there. Some private nonmarket benefits of higher education include improved health for the individual and his or her family, greater longevity, and greater happiness. Human capital influences these nonmarket variables by altering an individual's behavior and lifestyle choices. People with more human capital modify behavior to eat healthier, exercise, reduce smoking, take better care of children, avoid risky behavior, and so on.

To many people, measuring these nonmarket benefits may appear unrealistic and almost impossible. However, certain statistical techniques that can be used to estimate these kinds of variables have gained recognition by the academic community. Economists measure nonmarket benefits by placing a monetary value on them. Using regression techniques, economists can, for example, measure the nonmarket benefits of improved health as a result of increased human capital. In a regression measuring the impact of income on health, the income coefficient demonstrates on average how much additional health will be produced when income increases.[29] Depending on the data set, this statistical method uses thousands of data points to gather an estimate of the correlation between two variables that is based on average trends.

Using another regression that models the relationship between levels of education and health, an education coefficient indicates how much more health is produced when education increases by one unit. To measure the nonmarket benefit of education on health, the ratio of the education to the income coefficients will indicate the income-equivalent value of the improvement of health due to an increase in education. Though it has its critics, this regression technique is broadly accepted as an accurate way to measure nonmarket benefits.

These advances in measuring nonmarket benefits and the economic value of time have considerable implications for policy. If human capital accumulation is improved by higher education, which results not only in increased earnings but also better health and other nonmarket benefits, then why aren't more people investing in education? One reason is that a lack of understanding, or a lack of accurate measurement of private nonmarket benefits, distorts the perceived value of higher education. This often leads to poor public policy and poor household decisions in which inaccurate calculations are made about value. It also leads to some of the combative public posturing we've seen from governors, legislators, and members of Congress criticizing higher education in recent years.

In the previous section, the present-value calculation for private returns on higher education was computed entirely from direct earnings. The wage was the direct measurement of productivity. Modern human capital theory includes the important private nonmarket benefits in the calculation to provide a more accurate cost-benefit analysis. With tuition in the United States increasing rapidly in the past few decades, it is crucial that students and families confidently understand what they should expect in return from the high cost of investing in higher education.

In the search for more accurate rates of return from investments in higher education, we need to clearly separate the various channels that feed human capital. Earlier in this chapter, human capital was introduced as the knowledge and skills accumulated through education, on-the-job training, and lifelong learning. To measure the value of private market and nonmarket benefits of education, we must separate the outcomes of higher education from those of basic education. Taking these caveats into consideration, economists have been able to place value on the nonmarket benefits of higher education.

McMahon's extensive 2008 study found that there has historically been a remarkable underestimation of the private nonmarket benefits. Most standard private rates of return, which often inform legislators and other policy makers, do not accurately highlight nonmarket benefits. Using regression techniques, McMahon measured ten private nonmarket benefits: 1) personal health benefits, 2) smoking cessation, 3) longevity/mortality, 4) child health, education, and cognitive development, 5) spouse's health, 6) fertility and family size, 7) happiness or well-being, 8) consumption and saving efficiency, 9) job and location amenities, and 10) lifelong learning.

The study standardized the outcomes of previous studies to make the various estimates comparable (by converting variables into the same units of measurement). For example, income is often measured through either monthly or weekly wage. Education is measured as years of schooling or through an index of education levels.[30] Placing a monetary value on these private nonmarket benefits further highlights higher education's positive impact on a person's standard of living.

Value of Personal Health Benefits

There is significant evidence that additional years of schooling improve overall personal health.[31] This can be attributed, in part, to the fact that individuals with higher education have a greater capacity to choose healthier lifestyles and value the future more highly. These studies are important because they explicitly control for potential determining variables such as income or occupation, and they have found that each additional year spent in college contributes to increasingly better health, and in due course, greater longevity.[32]

McMahon found that higher education's mean value for personal health is around $16,800 per year through one's lifetime. This figure relates to an individual who has finished college, using an assumption of 4.5 years as the average time required to complete a bachelor's degree. Over the sixty years of the typical graduate's lifetime after college, this nonmarket benefit totals almost $1,008,000 in future dollars. Partly as a result of good health, research has shown that, on average, higher education leads to almost five added years of life.[33]

Children's Health and Education

There is substantial evidence that children's health benefits substantially from the higher education of their parents, especially their mothers. Children with parents who have completed college are less likely to get pregnant or suffer from domestic violence, and are less likely to be sick as infants. The private nonmarket benefit of improved child health to a parent with a college degree is around $4,340 per year. The benefit to the child's education from the mother's level of education is even greater. The average value for a child's cognitive development when the mother has a bachelor's degree is around $10,178 per year.[34]

Household Efficiency

The rationale for measuring the productivity of education in producing nonmarket outcomes in the household is based on Gary Becker's Nobel Prize–winning work on the theory of the allocation of time in 1965 and 1976. The theory expresses the logic of individuals' utilizing their human capital in the home or the community. Moreover, benefits from higher education mean greater efficiency in consumption and improved management of savings. McMahon demonstrated that a bachelor's degree would improve household efficiency by almost $3,401 per year in monetary terms.

Adding up the values of other calculated nonmarket benefits, the total annual private nonmarket benefits of higher education reach around $8,462 for each additional year in college. Assuming an average college completion rate of 4.5 years for a bachelor's degree, the nonmarket value per year after graduation equates to approximately $38,080 in 2007 dollars.[35] This astounding figure indicates that standard rates of returns for higher education are grossly misleading, a fact that is often unknown to most families and students, contributing to market failure in higher education and external inefficiency. The average wage of males with a college degree in 2007 (using 2007 dollars) was around $66,400. Take into account these private nonmarket benefits, and the total expected value of higher education is considerably higher. If it were incorporated into an individual's decision about whether to invest in higher education, a more comprehensive estimate of the potential benefits of higher education might positively influence the decision to apply and enroll. Table 3.2 highlights the substantial private nonmarket benefits of higher education per graduate per year.

Market Failure in Higher Education

The valuation of private nonmarket benefits indicates that total benefits from higher education—commonly measured as income after graduation—are grossly underestimated or inappropriately communicated to the public. The result usually leads to market failure, which distorts the ability of markets to function efficiently.

Within economic theory, *market failure* describes a situation where the allocation of goods and services is not efficient, as there is a potential outcome that could make individuals better off without harming or making other people worse off as a result.[36] In the market for higher education, market failure occurs when education markets fail to produce an economically efficient result that would lead to optimal investment levels in higher education.[37] Among the classical sources of market failure are three primary ones particular to higher education:

TABLE 3.2   Private nonmarket benefits of higher education

Private, nonmarket benefits beyond income	Value of private benefit per year as a result of a bachelor's degree
Own health benefits	$16,800
Longevity	$ 2,179
Children's health	$ 4,340
Children's education	$ 7,892
Spouse's health	$ 1,917
Fertility and reduced family size	$ 1,551
Consumption and saving	$ 3,401
Total private benefits	$38,080

Source: Adapted from Walter McMahon, *Higher Learning, Greater Good: The Private and Social Benefits of Higher Education* (Baltimore: Johns Hopkins University Press, 2009).

- The lack of accurate information for individuals seeking to invest in higher education
- The presence of social externalities that benefit others and future generations
- A monopoly that distorts markets (particularly financial market failures wherein students and families are unable to borrow because of lack of collateral)

In standard economic theory, market failure calls for government intervention to correct inefficiencies and make the market work better. If any of these sources distort higher education markets, full privatization will not produce an economically efficient solution.[38] Though the debate on whether higher education markets actually possess such characteristics is not settled, the implications of market failure remain important nevertheless. As I've demonstrated, underestimating private nonmarket benefits can lead to poor information that produces an inefficient allocation of higher education, because only those who understand or are exposed to accurate information about the benefits of higher education will invest in it.

Market failure occurs when markets are unable to coordinate actors, usually through supply and demand, to reach a point where the maximum number of individuals benefits from the market. It is often the case that markets, higher education markets included, serve only the few (those who value or understand the benefits of higher education).[39] This situation may be efficient if any other allocation of supply and demand would make another worse off. In higher education, because too few individuals understand the value of higher education, not everyone is benefitting from it, which leads to an inefficient market. If more individuals invested in higher education (the argument goes), then through social returns and certain nonmarket benefits more individuals would enjoy the benefits of higher education without making anyone else worse off as a result. Because of poor information, this optimal market equilibrium never materializes; instead, market failure continues.[40]

The second source of market failure in higher education is in the theory that higher education leads to positive social externalities. Already, the evidence of improved child health and cognitive ability indicates that education has a permeating quality. In the second part of this chapter, I discuss the numerous social benefits of education. More than any other, this discussion has a strong bearing on legislators and higher education policy makers. The trend toward privatization may be fraught with the risk of market failure. State and federal governments, which have historically been the primary source of funding for higher education, need to accurately understand some of these shortcomings as well.

The Social Value of Higher Education—a Public Good?

As I've said, the Morrill Act of 1862 fundamentally altered the involvement of the federal government in higher education and provided new sources of revenue for states to create or fund existing institutions. The Act led to what some historians consider the start of the social compact between public universities and society.[41] Through the Morrill Act, research became a mission of public universities and their role was defined in public service. The returns of higher education were understood to benefit society and be shared among individuals. Fundamentally, this "contract" between society and public higher education was based on the understanding of the implicit value of higher education as a public good—both the education of the students and the research and extension activities.

Today, society's valuation of this contract appears to be rapidly eroding, and the status of higher education as a public good is being constantly questioned. This can be seen most clearly in the increasing cost for students of higher education, which is occurring in part because state and federal support to finance higher education institutions has diminished. The fact that government support to help students finance the rising costs is no longer sufficient highlights the ideological shift toward privatization.

Privatization, as defined in this book, therefore, is both a result of and a solution to the challenges that colleges and universities face across the country. The private returns on education, as this chapter shows thus far, appear to far outweigh the social benefits. So it appears, objectively at least, that one explanation is that higher education in the United States is increasingly viewed as a private good.

Many academics have pointed to financial and economic crises as the reason for this change in perception. Historically, states have limited subsidies and appropriations to public higher education during financial downturns only to support them again when economic conditions improve. The present situation, however, does not appear to follow such a trend. In fact, there seems to be a fundamental shift in the valuation of public higher education from public partnership to private perk. If there is to be any chance to alter this trend, higher education must first be proven to be a public good. In the eyes of some economists, if this happened, then government intervention would be justified to address any imperfections in market efficiency (although others would argue there are plenty of government failures, too). Regardless of which political ideologies policy makers maintain, we need an impartial understanding of the social benefits that higher education provides in the form of externalities and spillovers from private investments.

Tracing the philosophical debates surrounding the public good discourse sheds light on why education can be regarded as a public good. Early in the Middle Ages, philosophers began to focus on the duality and conflict between the common good and private gain. The concept of public good was not yet defined as an aggregate of individual goods, or of individual actions. It was Adam Smith, through his seminal piece, *The Wealth of Nations*, who argued that private action could enhance the public good. Political philosophers soon embraced this idea, although the channels of practice often took the form of individual devotion to civic duty. Thomas Jefferson, for example, referred to the process of individual gain through devotion to the common good as a "co-incidence of interests," although he greatly valued the benefits of public good over private interest.[42] It was in this spirit that the early American universities were founded and further developed through the creation of land-grant institutions as defined by the Morrill Act of 1862. In exchange for resources, universities would produce research for the common good and train workers for the local, state, and national economy.

Although it was committed to the public good, higher education in the United States at the beginning of the twentieth century was still largely limited to the affluent. Though few people at the time spoke about the right to higher education, President Franklin D. Roosevelt first began to articulate a rights-based approach to his education policy. Some scholars believe that Roosevelt articulated a right to education on three grounds: "education as indispensable to a decent prospect to life, education as a basic safeguard of security, and education as a necessity for citizenship."[43] Moreover, there was growing international acceptance that the right to education was an integral human right. The 1948 Universal Declaration of Human Rights boldly includes the right to education at all levels. To some, then, higher education is considered a public good because it is fundamentally a human right (and they don't care who gets the benefits).

Although it is not well known, there is evidence related to civic participation to reinforce the idea that higher education is, in fact, a public good. The

National Center for Educational Statistics conducted a study of young adults over three decades, from 1974 to 2006. According to this study, within all four of the cohorts examined, students who planned to obtain a bachelor's degree or higher were, on average, more likely to have voted in elections than their high school–educated counterparts. The first cohort, examined in 1974, reported that 77 percent of students expecting to complete graduate or professional degrees had voted, as had 72 percent of students expecting a bachelor's degree. But the percentage for high school graduates rested at 50 percent. The final cohort in 2006 reported slightly less voting overall, but showed an even greater gap between those planning to pursue a college education and those concluding their education with high school: 66 percent of students expecting to pursue a graduate or professional degree had voted, as had 61 percent of those expecting a bachelor's degree, but only 35 percent of those with a high school education had done so.[44]

The notion of public goods today has two main qualities. First, the benefits of public goods are *nonrivalrous* in consumption and, second, public goods are *nonexcludable*. One individual's consumption of a nonrivalrous good does not in any way affect another individual's opportunity to consume that good. A private good, in contrast, does not have this characteristic. Once someone eats a burger, no one else can eat that same burger. Furthermore, a private good is excludable. A restaurant can simply refuse to sell you a burger. Examples of classic pure public goods are national defense and lighthouses—things that can't be excluded from someone's use.

In reality, pure public goods are very rare. Most public goods are either nonrivalrous or nonexcludable, but not both. Goods that only partly meet either or both of the defining criteria are called *impure public goods*, which often fall into two categories. Goods that are nonrivalrous in consumption but excludable are *club goods*, and goods that are mostly nonexcludable but are rivalrous in consumption are called *common pool resources*.[45]

The case of education is particularly interesting—education is often considered an impure public good, yet it bears all the characteristics of both a rival and an excludable good. For example, having more students in a classroom may lower the quality of instruction and diminish the amount of time a teacher or professor can spend with an individual student, making education a rival good. Education is also excludable because not all individuals can receive an education at the school or university of their choice—some schools decide which students to accept, and although primary and secondary education are free and compulsory, higher education is not.

Despite these limitations, education is still considered to be a public good, which governments have historically provided to their citizens. Whether the justification is philosophical or embedded in the Universal Declaration of Human Rights, economists have considered higher education to have some properties of a public good due to the number of public benefits (positive externalities) that are derived from it, and that justify a government role in its provision.

As mentioned earlier, the idea that private returns spill over to the benefit of society began to gain traction in the early nineteenth century. The usual understanding, pioneered by the work of Adam Smith, was that aggregate benefits of individuals would lead to combined social value. This concept evolved to include externalities, which are crucial for understanding the impact of higher education, since it is argued that private investments contribute significantly to society. For example, private returns on education can spill over to future generations, for example, through improved care for the environment. This permeating quality of education is often the main rationale behind considering education to be a public good.

If education is an impure public good, and if several important spillover qualities of higher education can benefit society, then what is the optimal level of social investment required for efficiency? To answer this question, we must calculate a monetary valuation of the social benefits. Several studies have attempted to measure the positive externalities of higher education. One of the externalities most often cited is increased social productivity.[46] If a higher level of education makes a person more productive, then society can benefit from education in terms of the higher standard of living that comes with increased productivity. Social benefits from higher productivity generally occur through two channels. The first is spillovers to other workers. A productive worker can raise the productivity of coworkers by improving the overall production of the group. Second, social benefits can occur through taxes. Higher productivity often results in higher pay, which results in greater tax revenue for the government to use on public purposes.[47]

Measuring productivity and social benefits is not straightforward. Yet the economic explanations of this point hold great value for our understanding of who should pay for and who benefits from higher education. Economists have typically quantified social benefits through taxed benefits, and they formally define social returns as the total benefits of higher education, private plus social, including the externalities minus the total costs. The social benefits of higher education can be measured in three primary ways: the social rate of return, the contribution of education to national income growth, and the economic impact of universities.[48] Recent advances in measurement methodology have provided a more accurate and representative accounting of higher education's social value. The following section identifies, measures, and quantifies the value of social benefit externalities.

The Social Rate of Return

The social rate of return is theoretically based on the idea that there are certain returns from investing in higher education that benefit society. For many centuries, scholars have tried to grasp exactly what those benefits are. Economists, who always lean toward quantifiable variables, have sought to measure social benefits in terms of revenue gained by the greater community, and, in macro terms, the government. As a result, the traditional method of measuring the social benefits of higher education is based solely on monetary earnings, including taxes paid.

In measuring the social rate of return, all costs and benefits of investing in higher education—both public and private—are calculated. The social rate of return is calculated as an aggregate component of private returns and involves finding the pure internal rate of return that discounts the future stream of earnings of high school graduates into present value.[49] This is not, in fact, a new concept. Remember that this calculation is similar to the one introduced earlier explaining net present values. Again, future returns are often discounted when calculated in the present because they are valued less in the future. What is different from private rates of return is that social rates calculate combined total private and public costs and benefits of investing in higher education. These include public investments such as state subsidies, appropriations, or any financial aid the state provides. Specifically, the social return reflects the facts that people pay taxes on their income, which benefits society as a whole, but not the individual directly, and society pays some portion of education costs through the state and federal subsidies.[50]

The social rate of return, then, calculates the additional tax levied by the increased average income generated by individuals minus the subsidies provided for the investment in higher education. Naturally, the social rate of return is lower than the private rate of return. For the United States, this conventional measure of the social rate of return for higher education is around 16 percent for females and 14 percent for males.[51] Compared to other OECD countries, the social rate of return in the United States is relatively higher.

In one study, the social rates of return were found to be 6.5 percent in the United Kingdom, 7.8 percent in Denmark, 5.5 percent in the Netherlands, 13.4 percent in Japan, and 13.5 percent in Spain.[52]

Though the standard calculation of the social rates of return is used extensively, there are considerable shortfalls in its measurement. The most crucial shortfall is the underestimation of nonmarket benefits and of the spillover effects of human capital into society. These nonmarket benefits, similar to those in the previous section discussing the private rates of return, have been underrepresented in traditional calculations. In fact, given the immense benefits to society of such things as civic participation, productivity, and increased standard of living offered to future generations, the social rate of return should be considerably higher. Just as with calculations of private rates of return for higher education, poor information may lead to an under- or overvaluation in levels of investments, which, in turn, distorts the market and creates inefficiencies. Once again, most people involved in the investments surrounding higher education (students, families, university leaders, legislators, and policy makers) may not know the actual value of higher education.

Education in Economic Growth

The impact of education on economic growth has both intuitive appeal and a theoretical foundation. The classic Solow economic growth model of two factors of production—labor and capital—emphasizes that long-run economic growth can be achieved through the accumulation of technology, either through innovation or importation.[53] In both cases, education plays a role in spurring entrepreneurship and using new technology. Intuitively, higher education improves the productivity of labor, an important factor of production in economic growth theory.

Measuring the impact of higher education on economic growth is crucial to understanding its social value. Growth accounting, the classic method of measurement, indicates that basic education contributes around 17 percent to economic growth, and higher education around 5 percent.[54] However, this simple method does not consider the lag effects of education (the impact of education is not immediate) or the all-important positive externalities. Growth accounting methods, therefore, lead to a high-unexplained residual of 20 to 40 percent.

The endogenous growth model, which currently dominates, considers indirect effects and externalities of education within the growth process, a fundamental advance in understanding education's value in long-term economic growth. It was first believed that only a direct increase in capital or labor would result in greater economic growth. The extension of the Solow model included the important roles that technology and innovation play. Now education and human capital have become additional key features for understanding improved growth and productivity, in acknowledgment that education permeates and improves other variables that have an impact on growth.

Through econometric models, researchers are now able to quantify the indirect effects of education on other important variables that factor into economic growth. For example, the strength of civic institutions may account for economic growth, and a more educated population is able to demand improved governance. Economists measure the impact of education on civic institutions by first using standard regression techniques, then filtering back to measure the impact of civic institutions on growth, but only when the strength of civic institutions is the result of education. Such indirect effects are ultimately externalities of education, since all other effects are filtered out.[55]

What is most important to take away from endogenous growth theory is that education is considered to be very valuable because it indirectly affects variables that directly increase growth. The fact that modern endogenous growth theory is the dominant model suggests that there is already considerable consensus on certain social benefits of higher education. The most notable social benefits of higher education are considered to be: 1) the development of political institutions, 2) human rights, 3) political stability, 4) life expectancy, 5) reduced economic inequality, 6) reduced crime rates, 7) reduced welfare, medical, and prison costs, 8) better care for the environment, 9) social capital and happiness, and 10) the use of technology and knowledge.[56]

The Economic Impact of Universities

The third way to estimate the spillover benefits from higher education is through economic impact studies. Today, nearly every college and university in America can point to the economic impact it creates and has produced a study to share with legislators; some are good, but many are not. Such impact studies estimate the total economic activity generated by colleges or universities. One thing no legislator will debate is that an improved economic environment is a social benefit. According to one estimate, every dollar spent by a two-year college generates $1.50 to $1.60 in the local economy. For four-year institutions, the impact is around $2.20 per dollar spent.[57]

Despite such evidence, economic impact studies are not accurate measures of social benefits because they, again, omit nonmarket social benefits and spillover costs. Most economic impact studies are very difficult to administer at an aggregate level and so are only estimates of the local economy. For these reasons, economic impact studies are probably the least insightful approach for measuring the social value of higher education, though they are the one that universities rely on most heavily.

The Value of the Social Benefits

Identifying possible social benefits is possible only through accurate calculation of the social value of each benefit. There are several methods for estimating the social value of higher education; all have pros and cons, and they vary in their accuracy. Yet they do provide an opportunity to quantify the social value of higher education in monetary terms. McMahon was the first to comprehensively identify and value the social benefits that do not overlap with earnings benefits and other benefits of education, and his estimates demonstrate how the social value of higher education is misunderstood.

According to McMahon's study, the value of direct nonmarket social benefits of higher education is $27,726 per graduate per year, in 2007 dollars. This valuation breaks down the value of each social benefit from higher education, such as improved political institutions, human rights, political stability, social health, improved environment, and reduced crime.

One of the presumed social benefits of higher education is that it increases effectiveness of government (although the idea is controversial—many legislators wanted to debate this very notion with me!). In addition to improved governance, higher education is argued to improve people's ability to organize political parties, limit the domination of certain groups, and increase the likelihood of fair elections, political equality, and opportunity.[58] Improving these political institutions involves two primary groups, the citizenry and the public officials who hold government posts. Historically, higher education institutions in the United Kingdom and the United States were established to train individuals for religious or civil service. Political institutions, especially democratic ones, require a large and politically active population to hold elected officials accountable. The extensive scholarly literature on what produces improved political institutions indicates that education, and to a certain extent, higher education, is a critical variable.[59] McMahon's study values the social nonmarket direct effect of higher education on improved political institutions and improved governance—resulting from both public and private investments—at $1,830 per college graduate per year.

Improved human rights, which are related to political institutions, are a considerable benefit to society. There is micro-evidence that higher education contributes to attitudes that support human rights, and college graduates are more likely to question authority and be more tolerant of diversity. Individuals with higher education are also more likely to support and be active in civic institutions that support human rights. Measuring human rights through the definition of the Freedom House Index, McMahon values the human rights benefit of an individual's investment in higher education at $2,865 per college graduate per year.[60]

Political stability, as measured by the International Country Risk Guide, includes political and economic risks. Since political stability contributes to earnings and growth, its enhancement is an indirect effect of education and an education externality.[61] The value of higher education's contribution to political stability is estimated at $5,813 per college graduate per year.

The health, environmental, and community benefits of higher education are also high. The value of increased life expectancy essentially reflects the improvements in health as a result of higher education. Although most of the benefits in health are private, there are also nonmarket social benefits as a result of higher education. Wheeler analyzed data on U.S. metropolitan areas and found that higher education was associated with lower mortality rates.[62] McMahon estimates that the nonmarket social benefits of higher education in improved life expectancy is around $2,308 per college graduate per year. He also estimates that the nonmarket social benefit of higher education in reduced crime is around $5,647 per college graduate per year. These social benefits include improved security and lower incidences of rape, murder, theft, and property crime.

There is some evidence to suggest that individuals with higher education are more environmentally conscious and aware of the detriments of overconsumption. McMahon measures environmental benefits through three primary variables: water pollution, air pollution, and deforestation. Intuitively, increased awareness of the environment might produce many other results, such as lower population growth rates and reduced carbon emissions. Therefore, it may be the case that this valuation is slightly underestimated. Nevertheless, McMahon estimates that the social nonmarket value of an improved environment as a result of higher education is $5,609 per college graduate per year.

Finally, higher education is connected to social capital through improved trust and social cohesion.[63] Improved community relations, participation in clubs, and networking, some argue, have positive social benefits that are not market based. However, it is still unclear how to accurately measure these nonmarket social benefits, and a monetary value of social capital as a result of higher education has not yet been estimated.

Table 3.3 summarizes all the social benefits calculated from higher education. These estimates of the nonmarket social benefits of higher education highlight the common undervaluation of standard social rates of return. To set the value properly, we need a new social rate of return that combines both higher education's market benefits and the nonmarket social benefits just described. By combining the two calculations, we can develop a comprehensive and more representative social rate of return. The results are impressive: the standard market-based social rate of return for a bachelor's degree is around 15 percent. When we add the missing nonmarket social benefits, the new social rate of return for a bachelor's degree is 41 percent—a tremendous increase in value. Moreover, the total externalities come out to around 52 percent of the total benefits of higher education. This figure has huge implications; it

TABLE 3.3   Direct social benefit externalities of education

Social benefits	Value of social benefits as a result of bachelor's degree
Political institutions	$ 1,830
Human rights	$ 2,865
Political stability	$ 5,813
Life expectancy	$ 2,308
Reduce inequality	$ 3,110
Lower crime	$ 5,647
Lower public costs	$ 544
Environment (indirect)	$ 5,609
Total social benefits	$27,726

Source: Walter McMahon, *Higher Learning, Greater Good: The Private and Social Benefits of Higher Education* (Baltimore: Johns Hopkins University Press, 2009).

can be interpreted to mean that for every investment in higher education, public and private, 52 percent of all returns spill over to society as externalities, while 48 percent of the benefits accrue to the individual achieving the degree. Thus we have the beginning of an answer to our question about who benefits from higher education—a slight majority of the benefit goes to society and the public at large, but the individual also gains.

The Role of Government in Higher Education

Though the social value of higher education has been implicitly understood, these empirical results place a monetary value on the social impact of investments in higher education. If individuals are primarily concerned about the private returns on higher education in the form of higher wages and improved private nonmarket benefits, then the government should have a significant interest in higher education's social benefits. In the United States following World War II, the public discourse over access to higher education was driven by social and political concerns over equity. Governments, particularly at the state level, have continued to play a major role in financing higher education, based primarily on two arguments: 1) access to higher education is a human right and the government should support individuals who are not financially able to invest in higher education; and 2) there is high social value in investing in higher education.

In economic terms, arguments for using public resources to support investments in higher education also touch on rights and social value, but they are ultimately based on the concept of efficiency. The first reason for government involvement is to address credit market failures, which are linked to the right to access higher education. In a world without government involvement, individuals would have to independently provide the finances required to cover tuition and other expenses of higher education. In practice, private credit markets might not be willing to provide loans because of the perceived risks and the lack of a clear collateral for education loans, potentially leading to underinvestment as a result. Economists define this problem as *educational credit market failure*, where the credit market's failure to provide loans means that total social surplus is not raised through productive education.[64] To address this market failure and the potential reduced social surplus, the U.S. government provides grants and loans to individuals. State governments more commonly directly provide a fixed level of publicly funded education, through public universities and state appropriations.

Another form of government involvement would be redistribution, a concept hotly contested by politicians today. In a privately financed education model, as long as education is a normal good (demand rises with income), higher-income families would provide more education to their children than would lower-income families.[65] Because higher education leads to higher wages and earnings, the absence of government intervention might increase inequality and reduce income mobility.

Finally, governments today have an intrinsic interest in higher education due to the high correlation with economic growth. As briefly mentioned earlier, the endogenous growth model is considered to be the most advanced and accurate model for economic growth and development. At the heart of this model is the emphasis on education and, in industrialized countries, higher education. As we have seen, there is immense economic value in higher education's tremendous impact on innovation, the creation of new technology that improves productivity and spurs business, and the dissemination of and ability to use technology for productivity.

Lack of investment in higher education is a result of many factors, such as market failure and misinformation, as well as a shift in priorities for spending tax dollars away from higher education and toward other areas, such as prisons, health care, and transportation. The considerable undervaluation of the social and private benefits of higher education can result in severe inefficiencies, where the optimal allocation and investment in higher education is not reached because of market failures. As a result, governments and individuals may never realize the tremendous benefits that result from increased higher education.

The economic case for higher education is becoming clearer, but public universities exist in political environments where politicians' interests are not always aligned with the economic analysis of market and nonmarket goods for the individual and society. Privatization in higher education, therefore, would be simple if it were based on economic analysis alone. However, the policy makers responsible for higher education face many other forces competing for dollars and attention. One major reason for market failures in higher education public policy is that legislators and the public are ill informed about the value of higher education to both the individual and society. My own belief is that higher education is a public good worthy of significant public and private investment, and this research has led me to the conclusion that it is tremendously undervalued by most legislators.

Higher Education as a Public Good

The rising costs of higher education are all too apparent for the many hopeful high school graduates thinking about pursuing a college degree. The rise in higher education prices has largely been the result of state subsidies and appropriations not keeping pace with inflation *and* a proliferation of the curriculum (a topic discussed later in the book). The cost of higher education to the end user has increased substantially relative to state subsidies, and students and universities themselves must bear the expense.

In an attempt to understand the rapidly rising cost of higher education, some policy makers have blamed mismanagement by higher education institutions or claimed that universities are already well funded ("Just look at all those shiny new buildings and rock climbing walls"—two examples quoted often in my interviews). Lost in this logic is the reduced recognition for higher education's contribution to the common good. Higher education has been steadily redefined in the public mind as yielding mainly private benefits, and this redefinition has been central to the erosion of support from state legislatures across the nation. As the quantitative work cited in this chapter shows, the benefits of higher education are largely social. A majority of the benefit—52 percent—of returns on higher education accrues to society; thus, higher education has clear social value.

Several somber university presidents told me after I cited this data: "That's all well and good, but that's not what a legislator wants to hear. They want to hear about low tuition and employability for graduates. It's not easy to talk about social benefits when you are testifying before a hostile legislature." Politics outweighs economics in many cases, a reminder that no matter how good and true the story is, it sometimes doesn't change the reality of politics.

Access to higher education, whether we approach it from the perspective of human rights, equity, markets, or economic growth, improves the overall standard of living for the public. The positive externalities that spill over to society confirm that higher education is a public good. The social benefits of higher education can be seen, therefore, as nonexcludable and nonrivalrous. The benefits of improved political institutions, reduced crime, and social cohesion include all individuals, and one person's use of these benefits does not interfere with another's. Defining higher education as a public good deepens our understanding of the social value of higher education, which may stimulate a more objective discussion in this rapidly privatizing sector.

CHAPTER FOUR

The Business of the Business

Administration is not the business of the business.
—Robert Zemsky and William F. Massy[1]

The obvious attraction of most commercial ventures to their university sponsors is the prospect of bringing substantial new revenues to the university. In the hands of academic officials, such funds have the ennobling quality of being used, not to line the pockets of private investors, but to help fund scholarships, purchase library books, pay for new laboratory equipment, or support any one of a number of worthy educational purposes.

—Derek Bok[2]

IN THE EARLIEST DAYS of the academy, the "masters," or faculty, took responsibility for all aspects of the institutions they oversaw, from teaching to discipline to maintenance of facilities to religious instruction. As these colleges grew and became more complex, administrators were added to the ranks of faculty to take on some of the functions less directly relevant to the core function of teaching (today, the core functions are considered to be teaching, research, and service). My grandfather, for instance, graduated from college in 1927, then received his graduate degree in psychology in 1929 and began teaching that same year. As the years progressed, he took on additional roles, and at one point he was at the same time professor of psychology, dean of students, and university registrar. Today, each of those roles is quite specialized and often supported by a large staff.

To understand the role of privatization in public—and private—higher education, we must step back and ask: what exactly is the "core" function of higher education, and what is ancillary to that core mission? Privatization as a word and as a concept strikes fear into the hearts of many people because they loathe the idea of the private sector encroaching upon the "purity" of the academic mission. However, when privatization touches the business of higher education in areas such as parking, housing, dining, and bookstores, should we really be afraid? Do we really think that universities or the administrators and faculty who oversee them are better at managing a dining hall than Aramark or Marriott? Do faculty trained in the classics know more about information technology than Google or Cisco? How many courses in graduate school do physics faculty take in the economics of parking services?

In the management of business-related services, there is tremendous potential to improve when the private sector is involved. Where we can and should ask hard questions about privatization is when it touches functions central to the university—teaching, research, service, and the student experience. In other words, let's step back and think about the "business of the business" differently from the auxiliary functions less key to the actual educational experience.

This chapter examines the meaning and examples of outsourcing and privatization in the wider society and then in the academy. I focus on several case studies of public entities and institutions and examples of different forms of privatization to better understand the various ways an institution's core "business" may or may not be affected by the outsourcing or insourcing of certain functions. Before we delve into privatization in higher education, it is helpful to understand the broader context of the evolution of privatization in government and public agencies more broadly.

Privatization in Wider Society

The many forms of privatization in the university coincided with a larger movement that swept U.S. policy beginning in the late 1970s and early 1980s. The election of Ronald Reagan marked the beginning of the drive to privatization (although its antecedents stretched much further back). Reagan and others argued that the public sector had become bloated, backward, and inefficient. Privatization was seen as the key to success; Reagan and others argued that we must starve the "beast" (the public sector, namely government) of funds, which would prompt it to seek revenue from the private sector and, more importantly, to compete.[3]

One of Reagan's first actions was to commission what became known as the Private Sector Survey on Cost Control. The commission claimed that the federal government could accrue over $1 trillion in savings through multiple forms of public-private partnerships. The Reagan administration urged state and local governments to privatize public functions as a way to reduce the size of the public sector, and, during the 1980s and the 1990s, many local governments obliged.[4] Competition was viewed as the best method to encourage efficiency, and public control was seen to inhibit efficiency because of the absence of competition. Without competition, it was argued, there is no incentive for units to produce because they are not sufficiently challenged.

While the federal government dabbled in privatization, local and state governments were the undisputed leaders. Nearly 40 percent of the cities surveyed in the 1996 Congressional Quarterly report noted some type of privatization and contracting service. One notable example came from Indianapolis, where, in 1992, Stephen Goldsmith was elected mayor and led a massive privatization effort, most notably by forcing city departments to bid for jobs and compete with private-sector companies. The result was considered a tremendous success: it was estimated that by 1996, the city had saved over $26 million. Goldsmith and others argued that competition was at the heart of the Indianapolis success story.[5]

Roads

In 1991, President George H. W. Bush signed the Intermodal Surface Transportation Efficiency Act (ISTEA) into law, allowing states to sell noninterstate highways, bridges, and tunnels to private enterprises. In 1992, the president also signed an executive order that aimed to further help state and local governments sell or lease infrastructure to private companies. In 1995, a fourteen-mile toll road between Dulles International Airport and Leesburg, Virginia, became the first road in the United States to be privatized in a century. Three months later, another private toll highway opened in Los Angeles, and in the two decades since, several cities and states have sold ninety-nine-year leases to private companies to operate stretches of highway.

When President Bush signed ISTEA in 1991, he remarked how the Act would usher in a new era in transportation history. Transportation would no longer be solely the domain of government entities, but also of the private sector, whose involvement would bring new opportunities and partnerships to the beleaguered public sector.[6] ISTEA's supporters argued that it would aid states in dealing with their crumbling infrastructure because they would not have to scramble for tax dollars; instead, they could call on the private sector. Presidents of both parties have subsequently embraced the privatization of transportation, particularly roads.

Further road privatization and the involvement of the private sector may increasingly become an attractive option for cash-strapped public entities, as well as for political candidates who find generating tax revenue more difficult in the current environment. One related example is the deal that the City of Chicago struck when it sold its parking meter system to private investors. The City is now locked into a decades-long agreement that some regard as detrimental and exorbitant because of hidden costs and user fees as well as lost oversight and regulation, but it is a long-term contract. This is, of course, an extreme example, but transportation privatization is still in its infancy, and there is much to be learned in the years ahead.[7]

Military

Perhaps no other public institution has seen privatization on a scale quite like the U.S. military. After the terrorist attacks of September 11, 2001, security and national defense became public priorities and funding was massively increased for several war efforts. Defense contractors such as Lockheed Martin and Northrup Grumman secured billion-dollar contracts to produce military and surveillance technology for the government, and then private security companies began taking on greater responsibility, a phenomenon referred to as the "McMilitary" effect.[8] Private companies were given contracts to build military installations, complete with fast food chains and spas, all privately owned and operated. Although the actual defense of the country was left to the military, many private mercenaries were employed from companies such as Blackwater (now known as Academi). By 2008, there was a one-to-one ratio of military personnel and mercenaries hired by the U.S. government, mostly from Blackwater.[9]

The U.S. government's funding of such services with tax dollars raises important questions. For example, if national defense is a public good, how does the profit motive affect national security? In other words, if a private company is hired to carry out the will of the public and maintain the public good, what are the rules of engagement? National defense is a quintessential public good, but the introduction of market-based privatization has the potential to skew this notion. When a public entity, such as the military, is no longer directly accountable to the public, does it change the focus on the public's best interest and the notion of the public good?

Prisons

Another area that has undergone privatization over the past few decades is the prison industry. In 1980, there were no private prisons in the United States. During the mid-1980s, a group of Tennessee investors saw a business opportunity. The number of inmates in the United States was on the rise, due mainly to the expansion of law enforcement powers under the Nixon administration. The United States turned increasingly to incarceration as the method of choice to deal with its criminal and mental health problems. The investors' argument to policy makers was the same as in education and other sectors of government: privatization will save the state money. And so the Criminal Correctional Agency (CCA), the first for-profit prison company, was born. By 1990, almost eight thousand prisoners were incarcerated in private prisons, and by 2009 almost one hundred thirty thousand prisoners were behind bars in these for-profit prisons.[10] The United States, which makes up only 5 percent of the world's population, imprisons 25 percent of the world's incarcerated population, so there is significant growth potential for the privatization advocates as prisons become more overpopulated.[11]

The United States Postal Service

The United Stated Postal Service (USPS) occupies a curious position on the public-private spectrum. Its appropriations have not come from Congress since the 1970 Postal Reorganization Act. However, as many critics on both the right and left will argue, Congress often prevents the USPS from operating like a true business because it imposes certain mandates, such as not allowing it to reduce service or change prices without strict regulation from Congress. It should be noted that (unlike with education), the U.S. Constitution does call for the government to create, establish, and maintain a post office. Furthermore, the mandates placed on the USPS by Congress, such as the requirement to deliver mail to all Americans and to establish a uniform price for first-class mail, are seen as an intrinsic part of the USPS mission. It must be a universal mail system, which serves all Americans, no matter where they live.

These examples of privatization in transportation, the military, prisons, and the postal service offer some insight into how privatization of other public entities has—or has not—affected the focus on the public good, but most of these are very early into new territory. As a public entity, higher education may be the most crucial instrument for maintaining and furthering the public good in the twenty-first-century knowledge society.

Layers of Privatization: Outsourcing, Contracting, Partnering, and Hybridization

With some context of privatization in broader society and in other public agencies, we will now explore the many forms of this phenomenon in the academy. To understand outsourcing in higher education, it is helpful to trace its history, especially how the meaning and use of the term has evolved over time; determine the extent to which the practice is being embraced (or not) in higher education; evaluate the benefits and limitations of its usefulness as a strategy; and explore how it relates to the missions of colleges and universities.

The term *outsourcing* stems from the corporate sector, which employs the term to describe a strategy that a company uses to manage its supply chain, and often refers to international partnerships in which a company looks outside the perimeter of its own national borders to acquire lower-cost labor.[12] In higher education, however, the term is more specific and refers to how higher education institutions enter into contractual agreements to help manage designated services. It is often used interchangeably with terms such as *privatizing, partnering*, or *contracting out*. Broadly speaking, each of these concepts aligns with one definition of outsourcing as "the process of a campus contracting with an outside vendor to provide a service rather than providing the service itself."[13]

Although the scholarly literature often treats *contracting, privatizing*, and *outsourcing* synonymously, there are several distinctions among the terms, especially in the higher education context. For example, *contracting* can be thought of as a fairly straightforward process by which a buyer obtains goods or services from a provider; *privatization* commonly refers to a public agency, especially one that enters into an arrangement with a private entity to fulfill one or more services; and *outsourcing* is a relatively newer term connoting a contractual arrangement that is intended to be "a means to promote efficiency, enhance technology, and provide better services."[14]

Perhaps even more crucial to a meaningful understanding of outsourcing as a concept is the fact that the relationships between corporations and campuses take a variety of forms. In that sense, the terms *outsourcing, privatizing*, and *contracting* are worthy of closer scrutiny to understand the different manifestations. One framework suggests three groupings that characterize outsourcing relationships: outsourcing, collaboration, and co-branding.[15]

In a complete outsourcing relationship, the institution ostensibly delegates full management responsibility to an outside firm. In collaboration, the institution and the private partner share jointly in an undertaking that will be of some benefit to the institution, such as real estate development or a preferred-provider relationship where institutional constituents receive some advantage as a result of the exclusive contract. And in co-branding, the institution may license or otherwise give permission for the use of its name and trademarks in conjunction with a product, service, or activity marketed or performed by an outside provider.[16]

Trending Phenomenon

In a 2012 study, Christopher Bradie found that outsourcing is already quite widespread in higher education and represents a growing trend. The majority of the nation's academic institutions outsource at least one nonacademic service, and the number of private contracts continues to rise.[17]

With state funding reduced, tuition constrained, and a call to offer additional programs and services, the 1990s forced colleges and universities to seek ways to manage their finances differently. But they faced several challenges. Robert Zemsky and William Massy postulated that higher education institutions had intrinsic disincentives to make noticeable improvements. For public colleges and universities, cost savings reverted to the state rather than the institutions, resulting in a zero-sum gain; for publics and privates alike, any savings they achieved only called attention to their previous inefficiencies. Even as universities argued the need for efficiency in order to gain a competitive advantage, they acknowledged that some critics would cite the adverse political impacts surrounding any institution that took a hard stance in questioning faculty productivity or cut staff too broadly. In fact, Zemsky and Massy warned against any widespread actions of cost reduction lest the institution inadvertently "demoralize the administration, eventually sapping the energy of the institution as a whole."[18]

These paradoxes pointed to the fact that new and innovative solutions were needed. During the heart of the crisis, institutions employed a number of traditional strategies to respond to the economic pressures. Freezing salaries, deferring maintenance expenses, and postponing capital investments were among the most commonly implemented. But such measures were not sufficient and proved only to be short-term tactics rather than sustainable long-range strategies.[19]

With traditional methods failing to alleviate the financial pressure, institutions looked for strategies that increased revenue, reduced administrative costs, enhanced services, and improved efficiencies while avoiding any number of pitfalls that would result in political backlash. Collectively, these needs eventually led colleges and universities to enter into more contracts with private firms to manage nonacademic campus services—a strategy that they believed had the potential to achieve one or more of the desired goals without impacting the core missions of teaching, research, and service.

This strategy seemed to be the panacea that institutions were seeking, and the practice of outsourcing accelerated greatly during the 1990s. As an example, in 1994 private contractors were responsible for managing 915 campus bookstores; only five years later, the number had grown to 1,250—a 36.6 percent increase of private control in an industry that had approximately $5.8 billion in the annual sales of course materials.[20]

The growing financial challenges that the academy faced in the 1990s persisted into the twenty-first century. In 2001, a survey of more than one thousand campuses found that 94 percent of the institutions outsourced at least one service and 34 percent outsourced five or more services.[21] In the first decade of the twenty-first century, 75 percent of campus dining services contracted their food services to companies such as Aramark and PepsiCo; 48 percent of college bookstores were outsourced to companies such as Follett and Barnes & Noble; and, toward the latter part of the decade, institutions increasingly outsourced information and Internet technology services such as e-mail to external firms, including Google and Microsoft.[22]

Further testament to the pervasiveness of outsourcing is the variety of services that colleges and universities tend to privatize. The extensive list includes traditional auxiliary services such as bookstores, dining, vending, printing, parking, transportation, mail, and facilities maintenance. But examples of privatized services also include campus security, daycare, travel services, ID card services, payroll preparation, conference services, fundraising, and alumni relations. Of these services, some of the most frequently outsourced are those that typically fall under campus-life operations, such as vending, dining, college bookstores, and custodial services.[23]

Perceived Benefits

Cost savings from outsourcing may come in the form of reducing expenses that the institution would have otherwise incurred from providing the service itself. When a college or university operates a service itself, it faces expenses associated with day-to-day management. These might include labor, supplies, equipment, and investments in new technologies necessary to continue providing quality services. A contract with an outside provider might reduce the expense or even avoid a deficit. Such losses divert financial resources from the institution that might otherwise have been directed to the academic core. Secondly, programs and services managed by the institution often require capital investments in facilities, technology, equipment, or other infrastructure. Outside partners may offer economies of scale that partnering institutions can leverage. Lastly, one of the most commonly referenced examples of cost savings results from direct and indirect labor expenses, which represent another area where institutions incur considerable expenses that could be reduced or eliminated in an outsourcing arrangement, especially given the fact that employee benefits at institutions tend to be quite high.

Consider two examples that illustrate the dynamics of cost savings through outsourcing. As an example of cost avoidance, the University of Arizona, an institution with over seventy thousand students, relied on copy machines that were between fifteen and twenty years old. The institution entered into a leasing contract with Canon Business Services, which provided the campus with between two thousand and three thousand new, upgraded machines as well as provided repair services—all without any capital outlay from the university. Such an example is consistent with the earlier definition of a collaborative partnership, where the institution offers long-term exclusivity to a provider in exchange for favorable rates on future services so long as the designated provider exclusively serves the account.

As an example of savings on labor, Sodexo employs five hundred staff members who provide food services support at George Mason University, Virginia's largest university at thirty-five thousand students. According to a representative from the university, without that contract, the institution's work force would increase by 10 percent, and the institution would bear the associated costs. This example represents a contrast to some institutional contracts in which the terms stipulate that the employees remain on the payroll of the institution. However, in the case of George Mason, the labor savings that the school achieves is substantial, and, in turn, Sodexo receives more freedom in managing staff performance, scheduling, and wages.[24]

The opportunity for increased revenue is another reason that institutions turn toward outsourcing. A common practice in privatizing services is the sharing of profits between the company and the college or university. DePaul University entered into a contractual relationship with Brailsford &

Dunlavey to manage a recreational facility—a project that entailed a $45 million investment in its first phase. In addition to providing expertise for the development and construction, DePaul partnered with the firm to create a new entity, Centers LLC, to provide the dedicated management needed to ensure the success of a very large and specialized operation. This partnership was identified as "one of the few outsourcing arrangements identified across the country that actually generates, from previously untapped user-fee resources, a positive cash flow of new money into the university budget." Also, vendors may sometimes provide direct infusions of cash to the university, especially as an investment in infrastructure. Another example is a university that entered into a fifteen-year food service agreement with a private company in exchange for $35 million of investment over the life of the contract.[25]

Enhanced service and improved efficiencies are a third category of benefits often cited as goals that institutions hope to achieve through contracts with private providers. Particularly in the case of public colleges and universities, an outside provider may be able to circumvent the bureaucracy and politics associated with managing the operations. External providers may have access to technologies and economies of scale beyond those of the institution, allowing the operation to be more profitable. Wesley College identified a preferred provider to which it outsourced its long-distance telephone services. Before outsourced models became prevalent, many universities provided telephone services by serving as actively involved intermediaries that brokered services between the telephone companies and the students—in effect, schools were "retailers" of phone services. As a result of the corporate partnership at Wesley, students' installation fees and damage deposits were eliminated, resulting in as much as a $150 out-of-pocket reduction for the students. Additional digital features were added, and students' monthly service charges decreased by 40 percent. Further, the institution enjoyed reduced costs for its own local and long-distance phone services. Jean Marie Angelo encapsulates the benefits of service enhancements, efficiencies, and economies of scale: "The basic rationale for a college or university to outsource to a vendor could be summed this way: I can't do this, others can, I think I'll let them."[26]

The pressures of the past several decades have caused more than one public institution to rethink its government-buoyed, seldom-checked operations model. In many more than the following cases, states and universities have looked into restructuring their relationship to match the demands of a slowing economy, rising enrollment, decreasing quality, and so forth. No single process can be generalized and labeled privatization, and each of these examples is different in its proposed and actual transformation, but they all exhibit a significant divergence from the standard framework that public colleges and universities used to follow. Any such alterations carry trade-offs, but the following institutions have, to some degree, succeeded with their new strategies while occasionally encountering new challenges. In many cases, the outcome of privatization remains to be seen, but, as I emphasize throughout this book, privatization is best considered as a continuum, rather than in black-and-white terms of public *or* private.

Examples of Outsourcing, Partnering, and Privatization in Higher Education

University of Pennsylvania

It is possible for each of the aforementioned types of partnerships to exist within a single institution.[27] The University of Pennsylvania (Penn) illustrates this point and illuminates the differences in outsourcing implementations. As an example of complete outsourcing, in 1996 Penn entered into a contract with Barnes & Noble College Bookstores (BNCB). This agreement transferred all financial and operational management of the campus bookstore from Penn to BNCB. Before the agreement, all of the staff members of the campus store were employees of Penn, and all revenue, liability, and execution of services belonged to the institution. After the agreement was signed, while Penn still owned the facility, all other aspects of the operation were transferred to BNCB. Of note, the bookstore terminated its employment relationship with the staff, and workers were left to seek positions with BNCB or find jobs elsewhere. In exchange for a portion of the proceeds from product sales, Penn achieved financial savings from the transfer of labor and operating expenses to BNCB. Penn's executive vice president, who was responsible for the decision, succinctly stated the rationale for the decision: "The partnership with Barnes & Noble College Bookstores will enable [Penn] to focus our resources on our academic mission, and let the business professionals do what they do best."[28]

As an example of a co-branding partnership, in 1997 Penn negotiated a contract with MBNA Corporation to offer a credit card and other financial products to Penn's faculty, staff, and alumni. In exchange for the opportunity to promote its services to the Penn community, MBNA created a credit card uniquely branded for Penn constituents, prominently featuring the university's logo, colors, and campus images. The endeavor allowed Penn to offer a service that was perceived to be of value to its community, and it earned royalty income from the endeavor as well. The program was well received and, at its height, approximately twenty thousand faculty, staff, and students carried the card. As Penn itself was not a bank and therefore could not legally create such a product, the credit card offering could only have been achieved with the help of an outside private partner.

Lastly, as an example of collaborative outsourcing, in 2008 Penn entered into an agreement with United Parcel Services (UPS). The contract designated UPS as Penn's official provider for outbound package shipments. As a result of this venture, Penn departments received favorable rates on shipping services; easy-to-use online tools that facilitated their shipping needs and the associated billing; and enhanced services, processes, and technologies related to packaged mail. However, despite this relationship, Penn continued to manage certain campus mail services and maintained in-house department and staff to perform those tasks.

The Ohio State University

In 2012, the Buckeye state's flagship university—The Ohio State University (OSU)—accepted a $483 million bid from CampusParc, a parking services company, to run the campus parking system for fifty years. While it is too early to tell the effects of the privatization of the parking system at OSU, the $483 million was invested in the endowment and has already earned significant returns, with about $20 million directly invested in core university functions such as staff grants, student scholarships, and new faculty positions. OSU still retains oversight of the parking system through a parking advisory committee. The deal has been estimated as yielding the university $3.1 billion over the course of the fifty-year contract—dollars that will be invested back into the core university functions.

The OSU case may be indicative of the future for many public universities as they consider new revenue streams for the business side of the academy. As state appropriations continue to dwindle, universities will be looking for new and more efficient ways to generate revenue, and the OSU model appears to be a successful example of privatization that doesn't threaten in any way the core "business" of teaching, research, and service.[29]

UVA's Darden School of Business

Virginia as a state and the University of Virginia as an institution will be examined in depth in chapter 5, but the Darden School is a case study of privatization in itself. In the 1990s, under the plan devised to rescue it from declining state funding, the Darden School became financially independent of the parent organization whose name it would still bear. State funding was cut, as was government control, and tuition subsidization became essentially unmanageable; interestingly, while state legislators were intensely focused on undergraduate enrollment and tuition, they paid very little attention to Darden and other graduate programs. On the other hand, Darden gained the ability to embark on independent revenue-seeking ventures, to set tuition and faculty salaries as it saw fit, to recruit professors freely, and even to build its own campus. In everything but name, Darden became a private, specialized spinoff of UVA.

The outcome of the Darden School's steps toward autonomy has been mixed. On the one hand, Darden's new capabilities have allowed it to compete more successfully for top-notch students, faculty, and resources. The state government need not brood over the quality of its education, and students are no longer confined by state capabilities. However, Darden represents, to some, the loss of the public good that is so central to public higher education, and raises serious questions about the consequences of commodifying education.[30]

UCLA's Anderson School of Management

The implementation of the new model at UVA's Darden School had ripple effects all the way across the nation. In 2010, the dean of UCLA's Anderson School, Judy Olian, announced her intention to follow the same sort of plan. UCLA is also a world-class institution and a leader in the University of California system, which also has a history, until recently, of providing its exceptional education at an insignificant tuition rate; this will be explored in greater depth in chapter 7. Therefore, maintaining a public agenda focused on access and affordability would be crucial for legislators in approving such a change in the Anderson School.

In forming her plan, Dean Olian guaranteed no alteration in governance, public mission, or percentage of in-state students. In making the case for change, she cited the fact that halfway through the 2010 fall semester, the state's budgets, upon which UCLA greatly depends, had not been set. Under the new agreement, the Anderson School would gain significant flexibility in setting tuition and making financial decisions, and would sacrifice a chunk of state funding in return. In Olian's own words: "To our students and faculty, in evaluating excellence, I don't think it matters one iota to them if we are public or private. They want to go to the best place."[31]

In July 2013, the proposal was partially enacted, and the MBA program at the Anderson School, which received 6 percent of its funding from the state of California, officially severed ties with the state and began to receive 100 percent of its funding through student tuition. Though the MBA is only one program, it is nonetheless the largest professional program in regard to both enrollment and funding at UCLA.[32]

Then University of California President Mark Yudof, in approving the plan, stipulated that the MBA program must continue to offer financial aid to students at a rate commensurate with what full-time students get at other UC-supported MBA programs. In addition, Yudof demanded that the now self-sufficient MBA program still operate like a public institution. Yet critics point to the fact that although the business school was built with state money, the public no longer has a stake in the MBA program. Such a move might have damaged the performance of UCLA as a whole, but privatization did little harm to Anderson. The desire for greater flexibility and autonomy are the new driving calls for change, even if it means forgoing state revenue.

St. Mary's College of Maryland

While St. Mary's College of Maryland, a small public liberal arts honors college, did not diverge quite so far from the public model, it did make an influential bargain in its governance. In return for a significant reduction in appropriations from the state of Maryland, St. Mary's was afforded greater autonomy in finances and operations that would help the university achieve its own ends more efficiently. The decision, which passed the state senate in 1992, gradually reduced government subsidies as a percentage of St. Mary's budget from 49 percent to 41.3 percent over five years. At the small liberal arts school, this loss in revenue would be compensated by tuition.[33]

The drawback to the plan for legislators was, predictably, the tuition hike. St. Mary's made up for the loss in state oversight by founding a powerful board of trustees that could be exclusively responsible for the well-being of the college. The state would also continue to monitor the college's public mission, which ended up giving St. Mary's two observers of its accountability. In the end, it was possible for the state to loosen its institutional controls without St. Mary's College or the state losing their "rigorous evaluation of the public ends."[34] While most privatization cases are so new there is a paucity of research about them, the case of St. Mary's illustrates how privatization efforts might play out over the decades ahead.

The University of Wisconsin

The flagship University of Wisconsin–Madison attempted a solution to perceived restrictive governance in seeking to separate the campus from the state system. Unlike some other states, Wisconsin formed its system long after the flagship had been an independent campus. The plan was spearheaded by former Chancellor Carolyn "Biddy" Martin in 2011 with similar goals as in other case studies—setting tuition, recruiting faculty, and setting budgets independent from state mandates. Martin suggested separating the Madison campus from the system and its board of regents, which directs all affairs in the University of Wisconsin system.[35] The plan was eventually dubbed the "New Badger Partnership" and while the plan itself was controversial, the method in which the plan was crafted was a main reason it drew the ire of critics in the state. Martin met with Governor Scott Walker behind closed doors without consulting the system president, board, or her faculty. While Martin had some support from inside the university, lawmakers struck down the plan.

As in any attempt to break the union between higher education and the state, there were concerns about the responsibility and accountability each had to the other. Beyond that, the other University of Wisconsin campuses were worried the Madison campus's departure would leave them without a leader in their own autonomy and budget battles. In Martin's own words, such a drastic change "would be unprecedented, obviously," and would hardly be accepted by the public. Serious questions arose about the impact on the public good and the state's agenda when the flagship university sought to separate itself through a form of privatization.[36]

University of Oregon and Oregon Health & Science University

Throughout this book I have argued that you must situate privatization in its historical context. The case of Oregon Health & Science University (OHSU) is illustrative. The privatization movement in Oregon started in the 1980s. By the 1990s, as was the case with public colleges across the United States, OHSU saw its funding declining. A recession in 1991 prompted voters in Oregon to approve a measure that limited property taxes; this was a severe blow to public funding because of Oregon's reliance on the income and property tax, as well as the fact that Oregon did not have a rainy day fund. The time was ripe for exploring alternatives to public funding in Oregon.

In 1995, OHSU became one of the nation's first hybrid public-private universities. That year, autonomy legislation passed by the Oregon legislature reconfigured OHSU to be a public corporation, under the supervision of a board of directors appointed by the governor and confirmed by the state senate. OHSU would now be funded entirely by patient fees and tuition. OHSU had been one of eight public universities in Oregon, but when these changes were enacted, it became the first academic health center in the nation to become privatized. The legislation gave OHSU a new governing structure and more procedural autonomy that administrators at the university hoped would allow the university to seize business opportunities, finance future growth, and become more competitive in the health care marketplace.[37]

Many people associated with the university supported privatization. State Senator Gene Timms argued that there was no real alternative, because OHSU had "reached its limit" as an institution of public higher education and privatization was the next logical step.[38] This actually points to a wider issue—the notion of the public good is not a static one. Rather, it is continually redefined by the polity and is configured by policy. One of the biggest boons of institutional autonomy for OHSU was the ability to independently negotiate contracts. The shedding of constraints and regulations made OHSU more able to compete with other health-care providers.[39] The legislation was also crafted so that OHSU could continue to serve its public mission. The policy secured the support of the governor and legislators. What this case makes clear is that privatization of OHSU was driven by market-based pressures, accelerated by the continuing reduction in state funding, but that attention to the public mission is still paramount.

Two hours south of OHSU on Interstate 5, the University of Oregon was looking not only for greater latitude to manage its own affairs, but also for a state bond issue to serve as an independent endowment toward its budget in 2010. Oregon's solution, which would allow the university to free itself from the state's annual budget cycles, encountered too much opposition in the legislature and from the state board to be well received at the time, and President Richard Lariviere was fired by the board in 2011. Here, as was the case at the University of Wisconsin-Madison, the campus leader found himself in a difficult position between his campus's interests for autonomy and the university system and legislative leaders' interests for the larger state's needs. Several months after his firing, a campus president in another state told me this is one glaring reason why it's prudent not to speak out too vociferously for campus autonomy.

Though the flagship university's earlier attempt at separating from the state system was unsuccessful, later efforts have moved toward a new model with the state. The University of Oregon, Portland State University, and Oregon State University are in the process of altering their relationship with the state to gain some autonomy and governance at the institutional level, which will give them greater control over the hiring of presidents, issuing revenue bonds, and, of course, setting tuition.[40]

In August 2012, Michael Gottfredson was named the new president of the University of Oregon; by April 2013, he had advanced a proposal to create an institutional board for UO, citing the institutional board of OHSU as a precedent. Gottfredson emphatically stated that the board composition of OHSU "is justifiably one of the state's great educational points of pride." Since students bear a proportionate amount of the cost of their education, Gottfredson maintained that they should have more of a say in its direction. The ultimate hope is that members of the board would develop a sense of familiarity with the university and allow it to connect with local civic and business leaders in the state. Gottfredson argued that this arrangement would give the university more autonomy and flexibility to deal with changing conditions in the future.[41] The bill was signed into law by the governor in 2013, which should serve as another example that elements of privatization as discussed in this book sometimes require the right timing *and* the right messenger, as well as the right way of involving all parties in the process.[42] You will also notice the great similarities between the states (such as Oregon and Maryland, with twenty years between the proposals).

The $10,000 Degree

In 2011, Governor Rick Perry of Texas introduced a bold plan to decrease costs at the state's public institutions. In an initiative he called the "$10,000 Degree Challenge," he asked each of the state's universities to create a bachelor's degree track that would cost the student only $10,000 (he failed to clarify that it might actually cost more than $10,000 to provide the degree, but that was the total intended cost for the student). His plan brought forth a multitude of proposals on how to reduce the cost, ranging from technological innovations to a mixed community college/university program to increasing scholarships. The plan would also involve monitoring professors' efficiency, focusing on job creation and STEM fields, and reworking funding to be based on degree completion instead of enrollment—in other words, focusing on outputs instead of inputs. This predictably rubbed more than one university official the wrong way, but Perry's initiative in seeking a solution to a longstanding problem did not go unnoticed. In 2012, governors Rick Scott of Florida and Scott Walker of Wisconsin announced intentions to introduce $10,000 degree challenges of their own similar to Perry's model.[43]

The $10,000 degree has come in the context of caps on state education spending and is economic in nature, but Governor Perry did not dictate a specific method for reducing expenditures at Texas institutions. Rather, he gave them the authority to solve the problem for themselves, making it clear that the state is no longer able to fund universities at ever-increasing levels and needs to grant some autonomy in order to allow for evolution. In this way, Perry and his colleagues retain the public image and consumer focus of the public institutions, while rebranding a reduction in appropriations as a citizen-defending crusade over tuition and autonomy that is included as part of the universities' public obligation. When stripped to its core, the $10,000 degree is indeed an implementation of privatization, with the familiar elements of seeking to sustain public higher education but with lower cost to the state.

Despite the criticism these governors received, the $10,000 degree came to fruition and the initiative led to much more effective and stronger collaboration between Texas's four-year institutions and its community colleges. The University of Texas of the Permian Basin offered one of the first $10,000 degree programs in 2012 in various science fields. In 2013, Texas A&M University at San Antonio began offering a bachelor's of science degree in information technology with an emphasis on cybersecurity. The degree will cost the student an estimated $9,700. Students will begin their coursework in their junior year of high school, then take a mandatory year of community college after high school before finishing at the university. Tarleton University is planning a $9,800 degree in business administration, and Texas A&M–Commerce is planning a degree in organizational leadership.

More low-cost degrees are likely on the way, and will target more nontraditional students—particularly older and working adults. The $10,000 degree, however, may not be the panacea that many want it to be. In Texas and Florida, the degree is offered only in specialized niche areas and only for a limited number of students. As many critics note, it will be hard to replicate this pathway to a degree across a variety of disciplines. Further, while the degree may cost the student $10,000, the cost to the university will most likely be higher. Various forms of subsidies can lower the price of the degree for students, but that is different from the actual cost to produce the degree. Thus, the $10,000 degree is certainly an innovative approach and is forcing institutions to be creative and efficient (and it makes for very good politics), but it remains to be seen how widespread its success will be.

Previous research has illuminated the importance of managerial flexibility together with accountability measures in the search for autonomy, but there remains a gap in understanding how such a combination can be balanced in pursuit of both institutional success and a focus on the public good. The effects of autonomy policies on institutions and their states in regard to the balancing of interests remain largely unknown. Many of these case studies exemplify promise and potential for the institution—but at times without a balancing focus on the state's goals for access as part of the larger public mission. Little research so far examines how institutions balance both mission and market—that is, the dichotomy of mission that public universities are facing.

Vouchers: Another Form of the Public-Private Partnership

The study of public finance is essentially a study of the rationale for and different methods used to implement government intervention. While free markets have tremendous potential for economic growth, when they go unregulated, they can promote market failures. Governments all over the world are involved in public interventions and public financing of private or semiprivate ventures.

In the case of higher education, the form of state intervention is not so easy to prescribe. There are those who argue that the state should set minimum standards and give financial support to poorer families but otherwise allow education to be privately provided. Others argue that the benefits of a less regulated system of education will be more than offset by the loss of some important externalities.

In public finance, there are four general ways in which a state can intervene: finance, regulation, public production, and income transfers. While vouchers are usually viewed as instruments to finance higher education, they can also be seen as a form of income transfer. Government interventions are usually a mix of all four methods: subsidies to the universities (finance), quality (regulation), state schools (public production), and financial aid (income transfers).[44] The first three involve direct interference in the market mechanism, while income transfers work indirectly.

Moreover, these forms of intervention target either the supply or the demand side of the market for higher education. State appropriations, for example, are direct supply-side interventions. The state directly finances the supply of higher education by providing monetary support to institutions of higher education. Other interventions have traditionally targeted demand-side financing, and vouchers are a very powerful means to do so.[45] Vouchers have largely been used in the realm of K–12 education, and there is much debate surrounding their implementation and impact on education broadly, but there are applicable lessons for higher education and some examples of their use. The federal Pell Grant, for example, is one form of a widespread voucher used in higher education. The idea of vouchers is relatively simple: students or prospective students receive vouchers from the government to buy educational services from educational institutions; these vouchers, which are valued at a particular price, can be redeemed by the educational institution for payment. The government is supplying the vouchers, and the educational institution no longer receives direct government funding, because the funding is redirected to the students.

While vouchers are still considered subsidies to producers (colleges and universities), they are channeled through the individual. Unlike with other direct cash transfers made to individuals, voucher recipients do not experience an increase in their disposable income. In other words, they can use the voucher only for education, and it cannot be converted to cash. In a voucher system, the family or student receives a voucher representing a certain amount of money to be spent on education. The value of the voucher is supposed to be related to the average per capita cost of a specific amount of education (although the purchasing power often does not keep pace with rising costs of higher education). The economic theory behind vouchers is that universities are forced to attract students in order to be subsidized and are therefore forced to compete, and students are encouraged to seek the provider that best satisfies their demands.

The crucial aspect of the voucher idea is the freedom for the individual to choose, and this would require that education be provided not just by public institutions but also by private and for-profit institutions. It would also probably require a borderless system where monies could cross state boundaries, but that is not likely in our system of state-funded education today, where local and regional interests dominate the discussion.

Advantages and Disadvantages of Vouchers

Three main arguments in favor of vouchers are commonly put forward. The first is that vouchers will increase freedom of choice for parents and students.

There is a general belief among education economists that the education system is dominated by the producer, not the consumer. Curricula, for example, are largely (if not exclusively) created by faculty; students and parents have little say in the composition of the curriculum and are largely reactive to the producers.

Remember that a free-market economy is largely driven by both supply and demand for goods and services. It is argued that just as in a free-market system, providers of higher education would respond to market demand—in this case, that of students and their parents. In theory, this is expected to create more variety, flexibility, and cost containment in the provision of education. In return, universities would have to provide more information to parents and students on the quality of their services, strengthening the selection process for an institution and increasing the effectiveness of the education. As a result, universities would provide the kind of education that students want and would attract relatively more students, leading to greater financial security. Institutions that manage to attract students would in turn be able to raise the quality of their services or charge more for the educational experience. Such market forces would lead to competition, which would improve efficiency, as only the most cost-effective providers would be able to survive.

Second, voucher advocates argue that such a system would allow more money to be spent on the most visible forms of education. Because vouchers cannot be converted into cash, there is no income substitution effect to investment in education. Even in times of financial belt-tightening, parents would be able to use vouchers without harming private income.

Finally, at least at the K–12 level, advocates also claim that vouchers would actually encourage greater equality of opportunity. Proponents argue that in the current market for education, the reason for inequality is that families with lower incomes do not have the means to attend another school. Simply speaking, they cannot afford to leave a bad school to attend a good school. Vouchers, supporters argue, would be more responsive to the educational needs of minority and low-income students.

Critics cite four main disadvantages of vouchers, including that students and parents will continue to suffer from lack of information or misinformation about the value of education (explained in chapter 3). In particular, parents and students would not be able to properly assess the quality of the education provided, and schools that have the most persuasive advertising campaigns might sway them.

A second argument against vouchers is that choice in education is still limited by geography. This argument may be less pronounced in higher education than in K–12, but it still has some merit. Families in rural areas, where colleges and universities are not as numerous, would not have much choice in the kind of school their children attend. Third, vouchers and the use of parental and student choice might lead to overly specialized schools. Some universities might drop less popular subjects and courses—such as some of the foundational liberal arts disciplines—and focus instead on those most in demand by students (who would be viewed more as consumers).

Finally, many have argued that a voucher system would be massively disruptive to the current system, and administrative costs would increase. One estimate is that a voucher system in a representative U.S. context could raise public educational costs by 25 percent or more, so it would be more cost effective to strengthen the existing educational system.[46]

Pell Grant: A Federal Form of Vouchers

The federal Pell Grant was established in 1972 during the reauthorization of the Higher Education Act. It was named after Senator Claiborne Pell of Rhode Island, who championed the bill through Congress. Since 1972, the Pell Grant has been the major federal source of financial aid for low-income students and was one of the earliest forms of vouchers in higher education. The Pell Grant (first named the Basic Educational Opportunity Grant) marked the first time federal money went directly to students. The impetus for the Pell Grant grew out of the social concerns of the 1960s around access and equity, so the three main tenets of the Pell Grant were:

- *Portability.* It was not restricted to one institution but could be used almost anywhere.
- *Need-based.* It targeted low-income students.
- *Non-entitlement status.* One had to continually apply for it.

The Pell Grant has grown tremendously and today funds the higher education of over 10 million students. However, the purchasing power of the Pell Grant has not kept pace with the price of tuition and inflation (as shown in figure 2.3 in chapter 2).[47]

The transition from institutional to individual aid coincided with a larger political, economic, and social movement known as *neoliberalism*, which Henry Giroux describes as the "defining political economic paradigm of our time."[48] Neoliberalism describes the corporatization of public interests that rose to prominence initially with Ronald Reagan and Margaret Thatcher, but has been prevalent in the decades following their time in office. Giroux and some of his contemporaries described neoliberalism as devastating to the academy because citizenship is portrayed as something less important than individual interests. Others saw it as a necessary evolution of higher education whereby it is more in tune with the larger economic forces, instead of the ivory tower on a hill isolated from societal forces.

From the mid-1930s until roughly the early 1960s, some American bankers and businessmen had reluctantly supported New Deal policies and the larger role of the government in the economy. However, by the end of the Johnson administration and the Great Society, many critics began to look for a voice to rebut these policies. By the 1970s, the battle between left and right had reached a fever pitch due to the government's stringent environmental and labor regulations, such as the creation of the Occupational Safety and Health Administration.[49]

The Pell Grant fell in line with larger conservative and neoliberal theories because it promoted funding the individual directly. By 1972, a fundamental shift had taken place in regard to higher education funding. Since the last quarter of the nineteenth century, the federal government had supported higher education institutions mainly by direct funding. By the 1940s, however, a coalition of lobbyists representing various private colleges started to push for direct student aid, because private college enrollment was dropping in the face of stiff competition from much cheaper public universities. In addition, the GI Bill, coupled with the civil rights and women's movements, began to open up opportunities for traditionally underserved populations to attend college. With the switch from institutional to individual aid, private colleges could once again be competitive. Thus, the Pell Grant helped to revitalize the private college sector with government funds. This is yet another example of how both public and private institutions have, over time, come to depend on various forms of federal and state funding; there are very few solely public *or* private institutions, as most have both sources of funding.[50]

Milton Friedman: Advocate for Market Forces

The Pell Grant, though it aided individuals, also made higher education a competitive market, which was more in line with neoliberal theories. Neoliberals equated social harmony with the market and saw the market as a rationally functioning system. Government interference, in the form of subsidies and redistribution of wealth, only impedes the functioning of the market. Thus, neoliberals argued for a hands-off system, where government allows market agents to function without interference. Giving aid directly to students allows them to vote with their feet and choose an institution for themselves. Giving money to the institution directly only further enlarges the role of government and further impedes the functioning of the market. Vouchers and other aid given directly to students theoretically allow an educational market to develop and flourish.[51]

Milton Friedman, a staunch neoliberal, perhaps best encapsulated the disdain neoliberals felt for public higher education institutions and the desirability of an educational marketplace. Friedman put forth one of the most extreme arguments, calling for cutting off all public subsidies to higher education. In his work *Free to Choose*, Friedman argued that private higher education institutions were vastly superior to public institutions. This was due mainly to the fact that tuition at public institutions was kept artificially low due to government subsidies. The low tuition allowed many to attend college who would otherwise not have, and Friedman argued that many of these public university students, since they knew the tuition was cheap, did not take their studies as seriously and essentially wasted public money. Conversely, students at private institutions, where tuition is high, take their education much more seriously and outperform their counterparts at the public universities. Friedman boiled this down to the effect of the market; since students were paying top dollar for their education at private institutions, they would not squander the opportunity (he failed to note that many students at private universities have their education subsidized by parents, so there is still plenty of squandering by students at private universities).

Friedman's ideas epitomize the desire to turn education from a state-subsidized institution into a marketplace. However, he realized this was not politically feasible, so he advocated for a voucher system for both K–12 and higher education. Freidman's ideas are emblematic of the theory that underpins vouchers: that of personal choice and the creation of market mechanisms, because the market offers the best model for educational institutions to follow.

Higher Education Vouchers: The Colorado Experiment

Colorado offers one of the most comprehensive illustrations of a statewide voucher program for higher education. In 2004, an unlikely coalition of higher education leaders and conservative policy makers completely restructured Colorado's higher education funding system. Instead of direct state subsidies, Colorado employed a system of vouchers to fund higher education. The system became known as the College Opportunity Fund (COF). The driving force behind the COF was the goal of increasing college access, especially for low-income and minority youth. Many of the policy makers were influenced by neoliberalism and its explicit market focus.

In 1992, the Colorado legislature enacted a cap on taxes and state expenditures—the Taxpayer's Bill of Rights (TABOR). As a result, state appropriations for higher education dropped from 20 percent of the operating budget in 1990 to 13 percent in 2000. In 2001, the governor set up a panel to devise new ways to fund higher education in light of declining appropriations. Under TABOR regulations, if appropriations to a state-funded entity dropped below 10 percent of the operating budget, the entity could declare itself an "enterprise" and thus not be restricted by TABOR. Doing so allowed universities to raise tuition and issue revenue bonds, and then Colorado legislators redirected the funding away from institutions to vouchers (called *stipends*).[52]

More than a convenient method to drop appropriations below the 10 percent mark, James Jacobs argues that the move to vouchers aligned well with the belief of Colorado policy makers that market mechanisms are the best way to deliver goods. Along with vouchers, the state also enacted a fee-for-service contracts stipulation. This allowed universities to purchase services to meet state needs not funded through the stipend. The major fear was that with no cap on tuition, many lower-income students would be priced out, leading to further income stratification in higher education.[53]

How has Colorado's voucher system fared? By 2009, a state working committee found that after the enactment of vouchers in 2004, enrollment in public institutions in Colorado actually decreased by 2.9 percent, while the state's population increased and enrollment in public institutions across the nation increased. Black and Hispanic enrollments continued to drop (although the decrease had started before 2004) and white enrollments held steady. However, enrollment in two-year institutions dropped by 5 percent one year after vouchers were enacted, and by 9 percent after two years. Many higher education officials claimed that the vouchers were not marketed well and there was confusion over their use and the low value. The more troubling issue, however, was the rising cost for students. Even though the state called for a cap on tuition, many institutions were allowed flexibility in setting tuition. The voucher was set at $2,400 instead of the originally proposed $4,400, and many students were also charged user fees by the universities.

Though many in higher education heap scorn on vouchers and look at them with cynicism, there has been one overwhelmingly positive aspect to the voucher system, recognized by almost everyone in the Colorado higher education community. The voucher system has allowed colleges and universities in Colorado to escape the reach of the TABOR legislation. Most higher education officials, no matter how unhappy they were with the voucher policy, were unwilling to go back to the old policy and their vulnerable position under TABOR.

No other state has followed Colorado's lead and established a voucher system, although other states are considering similar options.[54] It is important to note again the political context that created the conditions for this program in Colorado. The TABOR regulations and the caps placed on public spending severely limited the universities' ability to raise revenue, leading to the search for a solution to the problem. Without the extreme pressure imposed by the TABOR legislation, the higher education community might not have agreed to the voucher system.

In addition, no institution of higher education noted any drastic changes in behavior, such as increased competition for in-state students. Since the funding formula for vouchers is based on projected enrollments, not entitlement, the state would make up the difference if enrollment fell below the previous year. Ultimately, there was no real incentive for institutions to alter their behavior. The vouchers did not create an effective market mechanism, because institutions were not rewarded or penalized for bringing in or graduating more students, so they had no incentive to become leaner or more responsive to the state or the student. Therefore, this was probably not a fair test for a voucher system in higher education.

There are several lessons from the Colorado experiment. For vouchers to work, there must be a well-established market mechanism. In Colorado, the tuition increases, coupled with low value of the voucher, eroded the market mechanism. Since many policy makers were eager to implement a market solution and many higher education officials acquiesced, the details and implementation of the policy were vague. This led to confusion and did not allow policy makers to accurately establish the conditions needed for true change. In addition, the state made concessions during the negotiations, which hurt the establishment of a true market mechanism.

Similarly, the performance contracts never had much power to influence the behavior of colleges and universities. A policy with well-defined incentives to motivate institutions to achieve certain goals and targets might have altered their behavior; instead, the policy was based on a vague philosophy of market-based behavior. Despite a focus on increasing access as an impetus for the policy change, access actually declined.[55]

Other Forms of Privatization

The insatiable demand for higher education today in the United States and around the world, coupled with declining tax revenues, has led to a variety of cost-sharing techniques. All of these techniques are moving public (and private) institutions further down the continuum from public to private. This transition from public to private has been driven by the change in public finance, but there are also policy makers across the country who believe it is time to "discipline" higher education and force it to move toward market-based privatization. This disciplining of higher education can be described as "starving" institutions of funds and forcing them to be more accountable, efficient, and productive. For this to work, some institutions would have to fail and close their doors, and more for-profit institutions would have to enter the marketplace and be given equal treatment.[56]

The deliberate attempt to restructure higher education as a market is not explicitly stated in policy texts, however. Rather, it has been carried out under the pervasive banner of accountability. When an institution is funded by tax dollars, when it is part of a democratic government, it must be accountable to the people that fund it. A democratic society has in its power the ability to continuously create and re-create the notion of the public good, and the push for accountability over the past thirty years or so may be the new iteration of the public-private divide produced by our republic.

Accountability

Accountability, by its nature, evolves with the polity, but it is a multifarious term and means different things to different people at any given time. Yet the notions of accountability touted by many (but by no means all) policy makers are now largely market-based. Many accountability measures attempt to hold higher education institutions to producing market outputs, such as STEM degrees, work force training, patents, and other revenue-enhancing mechanisms. Though these things are not bad in themselves, without a democratic component, higher education becomes solely a market-based good. If the university is a market good, how does that affect its public and civic roles? This is the crucial point.

Current accountability measures promoted and enforced by policy makers and outside accrediting agencies are implicitly framing how higher education will be perceived by the general public. As Joseph Burke argues, "the conflict over accountability is that it is eroding what was once a national consensus regarding higher education, that higher education is a public good, not a private benefit." Policy does not necessarily constrict or prohibit behavior, but prescribes a set of norms that people internalize. In some ways, current accountability measures present the notion of the public good as equivalent to private interests.[57]

Performance-based funding (PBF) is one increasingly common mechanism to hold higher education institutions accountable. PBF involves policy makers setting certain targets for a higher education institution and then rewarding it only if it reaches those targets. For example, the state legislature may set a goal that an institution will produce a certain number of STEM graduates by the end of a certain time period. If the university reaches this target, it gains a performance bonus.

From the 1970s until the 1990s, many states implemented PBF policies, which produced mixed results for a number of reasons. First, many policy makers applied a rigid one-size-fits-all model that did not account for institutional differences in demographics and mission. Second, the targets were largely set without input from the higher education community. And perhaps most importantly, failing to meet performance targets did not affect the institutions' bottom line.[58]

Privatization of Athletics

Collegiate athletics are a multibillion-dollar industry where corporate sponsorships provide millions of dollars to individual university athletic departments. The NCAA has partnered with Nike, Reebok, and other athletic equipment companies to promote teams and merchandise. On some college campuses, Nike aids sports programs in recruiting efforts, and Nike employees get offices on campus and additional perks in exchange for their support for the athletic programs. In some cases, Nike employees are there to police the sports program and ensure that their product placement is intact. In one extreme example, Nike scolded a university because a football player, when taping up his ankle, covered the Nike emblem on his cleats. Though there are extreme examples such as this, these contracts with private companies have the potential to bring in millions of dollars to universities desperately seeking funding (public dollars cannot be used to support athletics in many states, so it requires student fees or private dollars).[59]

In 1983, the Knight Commission on Intercollegiate Athletics was formed to deal with some of the ethical issues associated with the large influx of corporate money into collegiate athletics. Each year since them, the commission has released an annual report on the state of college athletics, drawn from the available data under the rules associated with Title IX funding. As one of the members of the commission recently noted: "We already see levels of spending at some universities that require them to divert substantial resources from their core academic responsibilities."[60] From 2005 to 2011, in each Division I subdivision, spending per athlete grew at a faster rate than academic spending per student. At those institutions, academic spending rose by 3 percent after adjusting for inflation, while athletic spending per athlete grew by 31 percent and spending on football players grew by 52 percent, mainly for scholarships.

Privatization of Knowledge

University-based research is one of the primary missions research universities pursue, together with teaching and service. Many place as much or more emphasis on creating knowledge as they do on disseminating it (teaching). As university-based research has grown in importance, faculty teaching loads at many universities have declined. The creation of knowledge adds to the quality of the professor who is disseminating the knowledge, but the research model is far more expensive than a teaching-only model. The focus on research is one of the forces driving the increasing use of adjunct and contingent labor.[61]

Just as universities contract out food services and bookstores to private companies, since the mid-1970s universities have delegated an increasing percentage of their teaching to adjunct and contingent faculty. One reason for this is that research, which has become highly prized as a potential revenue generator in the academy, is valued at some institutions and by some individuals more than teaching, which does not yield the same direct rewards. Thus, many universities concentrate their resources on research while contracting their teaching out to contingent labor. The wage for many adjunct faculty is $2,000–$3,000 per course, far cheaper than the average tenured professor, who may teach two to three courses per semester.[62]

Another form of the privatization of knowledge in universities is public-private partnerships with industry. Sometimes, faculty use their discoveries to create startup companies separate from the university. Again, the public-private partnership form of privatization has the potential to bring in resources to universities, but there are also potential challenges. When for-profit companies become involved in university research, the research may no longer be the objective pursuit of truth. Instead, if a company is shelling out millions of dollars for research, it wants to see results and may force faculty to alter, exaggerate, or suppress their findings.[63]

This chapter began by differentiating the core business of higher education from support functions. In this case, knowledge—both its creation and distribution—does center squarely in the core business of higher education. Of all the various forms and models of privatization, including contracting, outsourcing, and vouchers, the "adjunctification" of higher education is one area where we ought to think seriously about the changing nature of higher education and how that change impacts the core.

Focusing on the Core, Not the Perimeter

Many forms of privatization and outsourcing have not been discussed in this chapter—primarily because the forms discussed here focus more on what Robert Zemsky used to describe to me as the "perimeter" of higher education, rather than the "core." Many students won't know or care if their dinner is being served by a university employee or a Marriott employee. Am I buying my books and T-shirts from Barnes & Noble or the university? Students and faculty are unlikely to care whether trash, transit, parking, and many other areas are outsourced or privatized. They are more likely to be interested in ensuring that those employees are paid a fair wage (whether employed by the university or a for-profit corporation).

On the other hand, whether a student is being taught by a senior, tenured member of the faculty or an adjunct professor who is teaching at several other institutions at the same time may be a question of interest to the student, the parent, and the university community overall (faculty, alumni, donors, etc.).

At the core of the university is the creation and distribution of knowledge—teaching and learning, in particular. One could argue, however, that housing is a core function, because on a residential campus it is so central to the overall learning environment (even the most fastidious student may be in the classroom for only 15 hours per week, but spends another 153 hours per week out of the classroom); facilities once known as dorms are now often referred to as *living-learning communities*. Information technology, too, extends far beyond turning on a classroom projector and operating a campus e-mail system. Teaching and learning today involve information technology in whole new ways, particularly in the era of technology-enhanced learning, where faculty are attempting to "flip" the classroom—putting lectures online and using class time for in-depth discussion.

Why is the distinction between core and perimeter functions, or the "business of the business," so important? It is critical because it relates back to affordability and the cost of education. The more an institution can save or maximize revenues on the perimeter functions (bookstores, dining, trash, transit, parking, etc.), the more funding there is available to be placed back into the core—teaching, research, and service.

Let's revisit the campus bookstore as one example of the complexities. In recent years, the rising cost of course materials has garnered the attention of legislators. A 2008 study by the Government Accountability Office focused on the textbook pricing and its impact on college affordability. Two years later, provisions within the Higher Education Opportunity Act of 2010 stipulated numerous mechanisms aimed at reducing students' out-of-pocket expenditures for required texts. Coupled with the onset of online retailers and peer-to-peer book exchanges, even the privatized campus bookstores are hard-pressed to be price competitive while also generating revenue for the institution. But perhaps even more transformational is the increasing movement toward digital content and online learning systems. These trends may result in colleges and universities pursuing new forms of outsourcing partnerships beyond traditional retail operators and instead seeking to identify partners who can help transition to digital forms of learning or institutional licensing of content.[64]

That dynamic represents a paradigm shift that reflects a very different way of thinking about the bookstore than as the place where students buy individual books, a T-shirt, or a hat. It represents a tremendous cultural migration that is based on finance, to be certain, but also creates a more mission-centered focus for the perimeter operations. And yet, partnerships with corporations that have the expertise, infrastructure, and experience in facilitating transformational solutions may still be an option for institutions to consider as an alternative to devoting their own resources in pursuit of their goals.

Though researchers have acknowledged that any service has the potential to be privatized, most of the growth in outsourcing has been in nonacademic areas. One scholar aptly noted, "When colleges and universities begin to face the reality of their need to control costs, their attention first turns almost invariably to the noninstructional areas. This is as it should be."[65] Both the observation and the principle represent a belief that provides insight into a consistent theme in the scholarly literature on outsourcing in higher education—namely, that the primary mission of the academy is teaching, research, and service, and that no other efforts should divert resources from those activities. In light of that philosophy, outsourcing becomes more than just a means of cost containment; it becomes a means of making financial resources available for the academic core.[66]

Ironically, using a practice such as outsourcing or other forms of privatization to garner resources for the core mission means the institution is embracing methods that were traditionally more common in the private sector. In other words, the shift is seen as part of a larger movement toward a business model in higher education. This is a cause for distress among many higher education stakeholders. As outsourcing means that institutions rely on external corporate entities to provide services, the engagement represents a specific type of privatization.[67]

If privatization can channel funds back into the university's core mission, why do many in academia oppose it? David Kirp asserts, "If outsourcing is carried too far, there's a real danger of turning the university itself into a business and in the process outsourcing the soul of an old institution."[68] In an essay focusing on the implications of a corporate presence in an academic environment, Henry Giroux argues strongly against the direction that privatization is taking higher education: "Corporations are increasingly joining up with universities to privatize a seemingly endless array of services that universities used to handle by themselves . . . One consequence is that space once marked as public and noncommodified now has the appearance of shopping malls . . . if colleges and universities are going to define themselves as centers of teaching and learning vital to the democratic life of the nation, they are going to have to acknowledge the danger of becoming corporate or simply adjuncts to big business."[69]

Such opinions are rooted in deep-seated ideologies that consider higher education to be something sacred that should remain untainted by any endeavors to commercialize, regardless of how noble the cause. But other scholars, policy makers, and, increasingly, the general public—equally concerned about the core mission of the institution—argue the opposite. These individuals regard nonacademic services and their related costs as ancillary to the core mission and a drain on institutional resources.

For example, the 1973 Carnegie Commission on Higher Education Report recommended that "academic institutions divest themselves of their peripheral activities and take fundamental responsibility for teaching, learning, and research," foreshadowing the trends in outsourcing that we see today. As indicated by the quote at the introduction to this chapter, Zemsky and

Massy further support that philosophy as they exhort universities to recognize that "administration is not the business of the business."[70]

When we conceive of privatization as an effective public-private partnership that has many opportunities for efficiency, privatization becomes a part of the university's solution to affordability, retention, success, and possibly, innovation in teaching. Any institution of higher education would be hard-pressed to develop such infrastructure on its own. So is privatization inherently good or bad? There are so many nuances and forms that we need a fuller understanding of how privatization has affected individual institutions and states. I turn my attention next to three states and institutions that have seen drastic change over the past few decades and how these changes have (or have not) altered the focus on the public good.

CHAPTER FIVE

Autonomy Is the System's Greatest Strength

We wish to establish in the upper country [of Virginia] and more centrally for the State, a University on a plan so broad and liberal and modern, as to be worth patronizing with the public support, and be a temptation to the youth of other States to come and drink of the cup of knowledge and fraternize with us.

—Thomas Jefferson[1]

THE UNIVERSITY OF VIRGINIA (UVA) is one of only two universities in the country founded by an author of the Declaration of Independence, along with Benjamin Franklin's University of Pennsylvania. The Declaration, whose core maintains the deepest conviction in the power of the unrestrained individual and in a human purpose greater than merely living, easily underpins the principles of a temple of knowledge. Thomas Jefferson founded his university using a combination of public and private funds, and during the past thirty years, Virginia has been rekindling its appreciation for the benefits of autonomy. Autonomy has become a symbol of the state's public universities and their success, and yet it has been a hard-won identity. Because of the legacy of exceptional public colleges and universities—including the flagship UVA—higher education policy in the state reveals promise *and* some peril for other states and institutions. Today, both the flagship university and the state still grapple with how to balance a system of higher education on which, every year, thousands wager their lives, their fortunes, and, so to speak, their sacred honor.

In the past thirty years, Virginia higher education has been influenced and altered by massive changes—politically, economically, and operationally—in the way its universities are conceived as partners with the state. The state provides an extraordinary case study for the effects of wide-ranging autonomy coupled with greater accountability. The close examination of UVA within Virginia helps us to understand the impact on the public good when privatization gives greater control to the institution.

In 2005, the Commonwealth enacted the Restructured Higher Education Financial and Administrative Operations Act (commonly known as the Restructuring Act), legislation that effectively changed the relationship between the state and its public universities. The legislation created greater managerial autonomy for the institutions while also clarifying the expectations for a public university's service to the state. Legislators and university leaders in Virginia remain cautiously optimistic, though warily skeptical, of the restructuring legislation and its effects. Meanwhile, legislators and university leaders in other states are now examining or emulating aspects of Virginia's new model as they contemplate how best to react to the challenges of state funding for public higher education. The Restructuring Act was just one of many important steps in a thirty-year trajectory of change in the state and at the university following years of philosophical conversations and debates about the government's role and function in public higher education.

But while the Restructuring Act is an important milestone in the history of privatization in Virginia, there have been many gubernatorial and legislative actions over the decades that contributed to the changes in the state. There is sufficient evidence that privatization can produce positive results, increased efficiency, and greater accountability while continuing to serve the needs and people of the state. At the same time, however, fears and doubts linger among some legislators—even without any concrete evidence to support those doubts—about the state's public universities pursuing national ambitions at the expense of service to the state.

Autonomous *and* Public

Virginia relies heavily on and is quite proud of its public colleges and universities. No Duke, Johns Hopkins, or Stanford exists as an alternative for its aspiring young scholars in the state. Virginia is home to UVA, the College of William & Mary, and Virginia Polytechnic Institute and State University (Virginia Tech), among others—all public institutions, quite highly ranked and among the best public universities in the country. Indeed, James Alessio, former director of Higher Education Restructuring at the State Council of Higher Education in Virginia "can't think of another state [Virginia's] size or larger that does not have a major research institution that's private. That whole segment of higher education is the public sector." The state is therefore presented with a blessing and a curse, with a larger selection of qualified students to enroll accompanied by a larger responsibility to provide a top-notch program for more people. That isn't easy, and the public-private structure, legacy, funding, and vision of Virginia's colleges and universities reflect this situation.

Autonomy Is the System's Greatest Strength

Virginia is served by a number of different public options in higher education. It includes fifteen "senior" public colleges and universities, one two-year college, and twenty-three community colleges, which are part of a unified system, the Virginia Community College System (VCCS). Colleges and universities have many of the trappings of private institutions, and several were founded as such. William & Mary was created by royal charter in 1693 and was private for more than two centuries, but joined as an agency of the state in 1906. UVA was founded as a public institution but has retained a mixed funding model for the two centuries it has existed. Each of the colleges and universities maintains a somewhat independent status, with an autonomous board of visitors appointed by the governor and approved by the Virginia General Assembly. So, unlike many other states with a system of tertiary institutions under a central joint board, Virginia's institutions have much more control over their affairs.

A system of higher education usually describes a hierarchical organization with a president overseeing all campus chancellors and ensuring mission differentiation, proportionate funding, and strong articulation among campuses. In comparison to the "California Master Plan," often considered one of the best conceived, organized, funded, and managed systems of public higher education in the world, Virginia's system of higher education was cobbled together over time without any central authority or funding but nonetheless is a patchwork tapestry essential to the state.

In 1956, the general assembly modified the Code of Virginia to create the State Council for Higher Education in Virginia (SCHEV) to serve as a co-ordinating agency for higher education in the Commonwealth. The agency does not have authority for individual institutions but instead serves the general assembly and the governor on issues of policy, administers several programs, monitors institutional progress toward legislated mandates, and seeks to coordinate efforts of the broader system of higher education in the state. Since its founding, the agency's effectiveness has been perceived as strong or weak depending on its leadership and independence from politics. Because the members of the Council are appointed by the governor and approved by the general assembly, the political nature of its composition can be a factor in the selection and management of staff leadership and, ultimately, the perceived independence of the agency.

Arguably, the most significant period for SCHEV was the two decades during which Gordon Davies served as its director, from the 1970s through the 1990s. Davies was described by legislators and university leaders who worked with him as a singular statesman of higher education and as someone who understood that the autonomous nature of Virginia's system of higher education was one of its greatest strengths. Davies partnered with the institutions to advance the state's goals, rather than attempting to control them. The past fifteen years have seen a much reduced role and stature for SCHEV, and many university leaders and policy makers remember its decline beginning during Governor George Allen's term in the 1990s—when highly combative individuals were appointed to the Council, and Davies was forced out of SCHEV. Since Davies's departure, many university and legislative leaders described the leadership of SCHEV as "lackluster," "weak," or "irrelevant," but there is hope for a revival in the years ahead.

As a result of SCHEV's diminished role and lack of a unified board, higher education in Virginia has no strong central leadership. But legislators and university members alike do not necessarily see this as a bad thing, as one state report makes clear: "The autonomy of Virginia's state-supported colleges and universities is one of the hallmarks of the state's higher education. Other state systems do not provide for separate governing boards to oversee each institution, and we recognize that several of these systems are very good. But diversity among the states is as important as diversity within them, and we are convinced that Virginia higher education has become what it is because institutional autonomy has been preserved."[2]

Such semiautonomous policy has led, many believe, to the public universi-ties' high prestige, selectivity, faculty and research strength, and tremendous fundraising results. Former governor and current U.S. Senator Mark Warner sees it as "each Virginia institution [having] therefore evolved and matured over time to meet its own mission."

Despite the public structure's apparent advantages, however, the status quo does not go unchallenged. Statewide systems of public higher education—especially systems as loosely coordinated as Virginia's—have the potential for mission creep, where lesser institutions begin to strive for greater selectivity, compete against institutions with similar programs, and lobby for individ-ual institutional needs, often at the expense of sister institutions in the state. Warner himself qualified his optimistic position: "The principal drawback has been that, at times, institutional plans and actions have been defined more by institutional aspiration and mission than by the needs of the Com-monwealth as a whole." The public colleges and universities in Virginia essen-tially offer a mixed bag—a system whose tenets have both helped it flourish and contributed to its weaknesses.

Politics, Finance, and Leadership

Historically, at least beyond legislators who represent the Washington sub-urbs, the Virginia General Assembly has been permeated by a philosophy of low taxes and limited government, a reflection of the state's politically con-servative populace. The general assembly is a truly part-time legislature, with its 140 members convening in session for 60 days in even-numbered years and 30 days in odd-numbered years for a total of 90 days per biennium when thousands of pieces of legislation are considered. In between, members con-vene in occasional committee meetings and other general assembly work. The nature of the "citizen legislator," as Thomas Jefferson described the role and as legislators proudly characterize themselves today, generally results in government taking a more muted approach to autonomous entities such as higher education since the limited time that the legislature spends together is often determined by areas that demand more direct involvement in order to function.

Because so much of the development of financial policy, including changes in appropriations and tuition, is tied to leadership and structural changes that occurred in the past two decades, it is most helpful to discuss them together. On the whole, Virginia's public institutions have relied more on tuition and less on appropriations. But the monumental legislation passed to spur that change, and the structural decentralization aiding it, is key. The rising cost of tuition is a fundamental challenge in the current education debate, and its rise is seen as one of the few but crucial negative consequences of the structural reorientation.

Figures 5.1 and 5.2 show how the state's two- and four-year public colleges and universities have changed over a decade in terms of appropriations per FTE student and in-state tuition and fees. Virginia has moved meaningfully toward greater tuition and lesser appropriations, and the movement on the charts is visible (movement from the lower-right quadrant to the upper-left quadrant shows the changes toward more private financing of public higher education). As I have argued throughout this book, privatization is not solely defined by changes in revenues, but it is notable to see how rapidly Virginia's public institutions have moved on this foundation of the privatization continuum.

Because Virginia's higher education system is so decentralized, it is hard to pinpoint a dominant source of leadership in developing the system's identity and policy. The governor in Virginia has a powerful role in state government, as he drafts the biennial budget. With a ban on serving consecutive terms, the governor is often in a rush to move through priorities, but, fortunately, higher education has been on the priority list in the past twenty years.

Governor Robert McDonnell signed the Higher Education Opportunity Act in 2011 with a goal of attaining one hundred thousand new degrees by 2025. He also had an eye toward shifting the funding of public higher education in a more incentivized fashion where institutions receive greater funding as a reward for meeting the state's needs (*performance-based funding*, as described in chapter 4). Legislators describe a reduced appetite for block funding and greater interest in the more targeted funding that this legislation achieved. In addition to Governors Baliles, Warner, and McDonnell, and SCHEV director Gordon Davies, Virginia has had several other influential figures in higher education policy, including state Senator John Chichester, who spearheaded many education commissions in his role as Senate Finance Committee chairman, and Glenn Dubois, the chancellor of the Virginia Community College System. Commissions have been the preferred form for evaluation and change in higher education in Virginia, not just throughout the past three decades but for more than a century.

FIGURE 5.1A   Virginia public, two-year institutions, 2001 (in constant 2011 dollars)

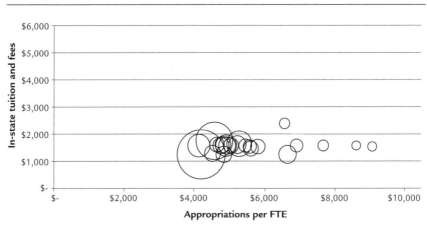

FIGURE 5.1B   Virginia public, two-year institutions, 2011 (in constant 2011 dollars)

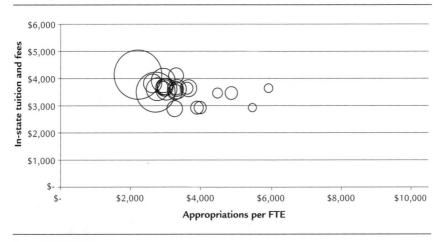

Source: IPEDS, 2012

Note: Appropriations per FTE were calculated using state appropriations divided by fall FTE enrollment. Inflation-adjusted totals were calculated using 2011 HECA. Bubble size reflects fall FTE enrollment.

FIGURE 5.2A Virginia public, four-year institutions, 2001 (in constant 2011 dollars)

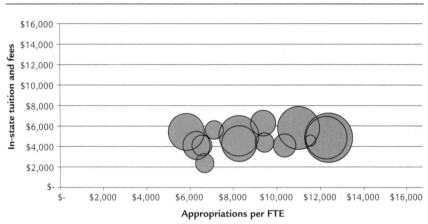

FIGURE 5.2B Virginia public, four-year institutions, 2011 (in constant 2011 dollars)

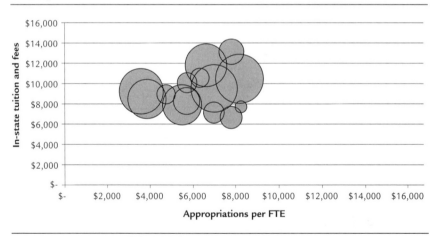

Source: IPEDS, 2012

Note: Appropriations per FTE were calculated using state appropriations divided by fall FTE enrollment. Inflation-adjusted totals were calculated using 2011 HECA. Bubble size reflects fall FTE enrollment.

Jefferson himself had a very progressive model for instituting academic change in the state, considering that the same strategy is now an invaluable, oft-exploited asset for policy leaders in Virginia. That tool is the higher education commission, used by Jefferson in 1818 to iron out the roles and responsibilities for UVA, which was founded the next year. The Rockfish Gap Commission also set another precedent for the state: it led to the formation of the university using a $180,000 government loan, with $15,000 in annual appropriations from then on, a $50,000 appropriation for the university's iconic rotunda (one of the first appropriations in the country), and, most strikingly, $40,000 in *private* support. Jefferson affirmed that his institution "would remain, be respected and preserved through the ages," and even insisted that his role in its foundation be inscribed on his tombstone, along with his great legislative compositions (the Declaration of Independence and Virginia Statute of Religious Freedom) and at the expense of including his U.S. presidency, "as testimonials that I have lived, [and for which] I wish most to be remembered."[3]

Governor Baliles's Commission on the University of the 21st Century in 1989 was the first notable modern commission to challenge the mission and direction of higher education in Virginia. One of its most important findings was that universities needed greater institutional flexibility, and it called for organizational leaders to "demonstrate creativity and willingness to take risks" to move higher education forward in the state. In its final report, the commission also pushed for university leaders to focus more on the big picture, for their mutual benefit: "The present arrangement does not encourage or reward cooperation, risk-taking, or innovation. It tends to equate effective leadership of colleges and universities with acquisition of resources: staff, buildings, and money. The institutions seldom act together because they jockey for competitive advantage among themselves . . . as if what is good for each college and university is necessarily good for the people of Virginia."[4]

Jeffersonian Vision Updated

Thomas Jefferson's vision for UVA extended further than educating Virginia's sons, and he saw UVA as a national university as much as an institution for Virginians. The recent progression of Virginia's higher education vision follows the progression of commissions. The 1989 commission that first suggested greater university flexibility came at a time of unprecedented public support. Gordon Davies described it as the "renaissance" of Virginia higher education. The report itself was issued by Governor Baliles under quite Jeffersonian principles. Baliles saw education as "a pragmatic way of achieving those ambitions" by which people "could enlighten themselves to the point that representative government would lead to progress." He linked it to something he called "the American narrative," in which "by the power of our own minds we could make our society improve and advance into the future."

The commission itself, besides stressing the need for intercollegiate solidarity, recommended a new understanding of the responsibility universities had to the state and the nation. It lamented their selfish outlook, and Governor Baliles declared that "no educational institution [is] an island unto itself . . . A university is not ministerial to society but neither is it divorced from the society in which it exists." In other words, to reach Jefferson's ideals for Virginia education, universities needed a greater focus on the public good.

Seven years later, Senator Chichester's 1996 commission focused on another service to public welfare where the universities were underperforming—providing additional seats for Virginia students, made urgent by the growing societal focus on college education as a critical driver of economic development and job creation. Chichester was also mindful of the need for funding and university solidarity to achieve these goals: "When it comes to higher education, we need to make sure that the academic community and the policy makers share the same goals and the same ideas about how to go about achieving them."[5]

These pressures are what prompted the commission to suggest structural reform for the first time. Cost was an issue that seemed unsolvable under the current system. Another cost-centered commission, empaneled by Governor Gilmore, concluded in 2000 that "the Commonwealth can no longer afford to provide funding to higher education without performance expectations to measure educational results."[6]

Written around this same time, Gordon Davies's 1997 book *Twenty Years* is an important marker in understanding the political and economic changes in Virginia public higher education because it highlights the shift in value placed on high-quality, low-cost public higher education from a public good to a private good and the increased politicization of higher education in the state. The book also highlights the threats posed by greater autonomy and continued privatization but recognizes that such changes are necessary in order to preserve Virginia's high-quality higher education system: "Education is not a trivial business, a private good, or a discretionary expenditure. It is a deeply ethical undertaking at which we must succeed if we are to survive as a free people. The founders of this Commonwealth, who were eminent among the founders of this nation, seem to have known this more certainly than we do today. As the millennium approaches, and we engage in introspection, as we inevitably shall, we might ask whether Virginians have the conviction and commitment to make education the single highest priority of government."[7]

Davies's description of the state of affairs in Virginia in the late 1990s is very telling for states and institutions of higher education across the country in the second decade of the twenty-first century. As we step back and think about the role of higher education, it is, truly, a central element of our work as a democratic society and, arguably, should be made the single highest priority of government in the states. Nearly twenty years ago, the forces of privatization had already spurred conversations about whether higher education was a public good or a private good.

The financial and political shift in Virginia was evident through the 1990s, and several legislators and university leaders described this period as the most antagonistic and combative toward higher education. The Commonwealth had already begun to feel the budget pressures of other funding priorities, and higher education had alternative revenues (tuition and philanthropy). The focus began to center on how public universities were serving the needs of the state.

Chichester's 1996 commission frankly admitted that the state was unable to "provide services in the same ways it has provided them," and laid the groundwork for much of the decisive legislation that followed.[8] And in 1997, SCHEV head Gordon Davies, reflecting on changes in his state over the previous decade, lamented that "opportunities remain abundant, but we are struggling to regain a place of grace."[9] Today, both public and private universities are under great scrutiny and appear to be still in search of that long-ago place of grace.

The first steps toward even greater autonomy in Virginia's higher education policy were taken during the 1995–1996 legislative session, which approved dramatic changes to UVA's hospital to remove the liability legislators were facing due to skyrocketing health-care costs. In a solution approved by both the state and the university, the hospitals formed their own private authority over their affairs in return for remaining a state agency. Leonard Sandridge, the former long-time executive vice president at UVA, described the change as *codified autonomy*, which "turned the place around" financially. Greater efficiency, thanks to enormous flexibility with capital outlay and competition with private health care, established UVA Hospitals' codified autonomy as a successful precedent for changes to the entire school, and gave UVA the confidence to move on the initiative.

The last notable events prior to definitive restructuring occurred under Governor James Gilmore, who served from 1998 to 2002. Gilmore was seen by those in the academy as hostile toward higher education, coming into conflict with university leaders and appointing antagonistic members to their boards, refusing to invest in institutional reform in favor of tuition cuts, and weakening SCHEV. Considering the decline in state appropriations in the previous decade and the relative prosperity in the economy, Gilmore in some ways moved the universities two steps back.

Even before Gilmore, it was evident that the relationship between the state and its colleges and universities was showing signs of strain. In the general assembly there was the constant pressure from university leaders, which Senator Chichester described as the "hue and cry for more money and more money and more money for this, that, and the other . . . There remains an unquenchable thirst for more dollars," which legislators could never adequately meet. Senator Warner, who was governor at the time of the restructuring in 2005, saw "an unproductive tension between institutional leaders, who viewed themselves as fully capable of managing their institution's affairs, and central state agency staff, who felt their oversight was both warranted and necessary."

Restructuring the Relationship

The Restructured Higher Education Financial and Administrative Operations Act of 2005 was landmark legislation in the state and the culmination of more than a decade of changes in higher education. The idea sprouted in 2003 as the "Charter University Initiative," with the University of Virginia, Virginia Tech, and William & Mary seeking to create a new relationship with the state that would recognize their special status as selective institutions with a highly professional administration and strong financial position—a determination based on their bond rating—that could manage their own affairs. After a significant slide in public appropriations during the 1990s, the universities sought to make a deal with the state that one university leader expressed this way: "If you can't afford to fund us, then set us free to secure our own destiny." Frank Atkinson, a Richmond lawyer and consultant who represented several major universities during the restructuring, put another spin on his clients' goals: "The conceptual underpinning of the whole restructuring effort was the schools' desire to be accountable for results rather than micro-managed from Richmond. We had reached the point where the schools would say, 'Tell us what you want the outcomes to be—and then give us the tools and the flexibility to go do it.'"

Another early request was the explicitly defined ability of universities to set their own tuition, which was in the domain of the board of visitors, but boards were leery of raising tuition because it was too politically charged. This, however, did not improve much with the legislation, and universities could not escape scrutiny from the general assembly for raising tuition closer to market levels.

The Commonwealth was still experiencing a significant decline in state revenues, with then Governor Warner seeking to increase taxes in order to balance the state budget. At the same time, the other colleges and universities learned of the initiative and sought to have their institutions included as well. Glenn DuBois, chancellor of the Virginia Community College System, was chair of the Council of Presidents in Virginia at the time, and he recalled saying to the presidents of the three universities, "Hey, if it's good enough for you guys, why not include all of us in this effort?" Indeed, it quickly became clear that the legislation would work only if it benefited all public institutions in the state, rather than just the three most selective research universities.

The final legislation was put into action after negotiations that came to be known as the "State Ask," basically to ensure that after restructuring the institutions would still be accountable to the state's educational needs. In concise terms, it gave institutions significant latitude to manage their affairs in a way that was cheaper and more efficient than they could have accomplished as a traditional state agency. One university leader reminded me that public universities should be treated more like MIT and less like the DMV. For example, institutions could hold and control their revenues, rather than sending tuition money to Richmond and then waiting to have it returned, thus earning the interest on those invested dollars. Capital construction projects could also be run locally in a more time- and cost-effective manner. The precise amount of autonomy awarded depended on the universities' demonstration of their level of managerial ability and financial stability. UVA, Virginia Tech, and William & Mary were granted the greatest autonomy—level three—but all other institutions gained some autonomy, at either level one or level two.

What became clear in the years following the passage of the Restructuring Act was that future legislatures were not bound by previous legislative actions, so the autonomy could always be taken away—and several legislators have threatened to do so. Significantly, the ensuing years have proven that while the institutions could have wandered from their public mission, the clarification of the public purposes that the state expects the institutions to serve has actually strengthened the universities' connection to the public good, rather than diminishing their connection to the state.

Funding in Historical Context

The election of Governor Robert McDonnell in 2009 was seen by many as a victory for higher education in Virginia. He was considered to be one of the governors most committed to education since the sixties, described as an "education governor" by many of those interviewed for this book. Two months after taking office, he established the Governor's Commission on Higher Education Reform, Innovation and Investment, with a charge to create "a comprehensive strategy for increased educational attainment, skills development, and lifelong learning that will equip Virginians to succeed at the highest levels of global economic competition," including one hundred thousand new degrees by 2025.[10] Academicians praised his focus on higher education as a solution for economic and employment growth during a monumental recession.

In response to McDonnell's commission, the Virginia General Assembly passed the "Top Jobs" Act. This bill sought to increase funding for higher education in certain targeted and high-need areas and to create something akin to a performance-funding pool to be awarded to institutions that increased enrollment of Virginia students and in high-need fields such as science, technology, engineering, medicine, and health care. The Top Jobs Act helped to create a more stable funding framework for universities on the heels of the Great Recession.

Beyond funding, however, political involvement in higher education in the state remains a major concern. As recently as the summer of 2012, the mood at the state's public institutions was restless when the board at UVA fired—and then rehired—President Teresa Sullivan, and questions were raised about the selection of board members and the role of the board in institutional governance. The relationship between the state and the universities is still evolving after the 2005 restructuring and the 2011 Top Jobs Act. As UVA's former Executive Vice President Sandridge saw it, change in higher education in Virginia could never be "a flash of light that says things are going to be different." Indeed, with continued turnover in the legislature, very few feel bound by the decisions made by their predecessors and within a relatively short period of time, a new legislature could decide to make major changes to higher education policy.

In addition to the political and structural changes in the past twenty years, more and more state money is being diverted away from higher education. Since 1990, items such as Medicaid, prisons, roads, and K–12 programs have crowded out higher education appropriations, which fell from 16 percent of the state budget in 2001 to 11 percent in 2011.[11] As former UVA President John Casteen put it, "the trend in state finance is that almost all public priorities now outweigh educating the young." Figure 5.3 shows that, when adjusted for inflation, the net revenue Virginia universities receive has not improved for decades and is less today than in 1987.

The University of Virginia has obviously not been unaffected by the cuts troubling the state more broadly. Of its $2.4 billion budget in 2011, only about 10 percent of UVA's operating funds come from state appropriations. Figure 5.4 shows the long-term decline in state appropriations for UVA—the total funding today is a little more than half of what it was in 1987. Looking at appropriations from the perspective of per-student funding, the picture is even gloomier. This decline in appropriations and rising tuition at UVA, as evidenced by figure 5.5, has been steady since the 1980s, and the inversion of tuition and appropriations since 2002 does not appear to be turning around any time soon.

FIGURE 5.3   Total Virginia higher education appropriations, 1987–2012 (in constant 2012 dollars)

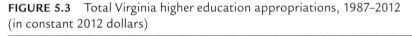

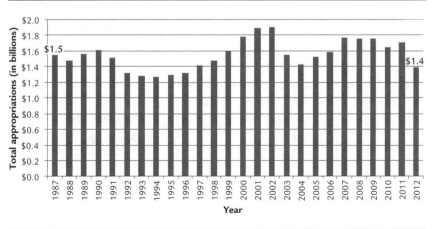

Source: SHEEO, 2013

Note: Constant 2012 dollars adjusted by SHEEO Higher Education Cost Adjustment (HECA). Educational appropriations include ARRA funds.

FIGURE 5.4   Total appropriations to the University of Virginia, 1987–2010 (in constant 2010 dollars)

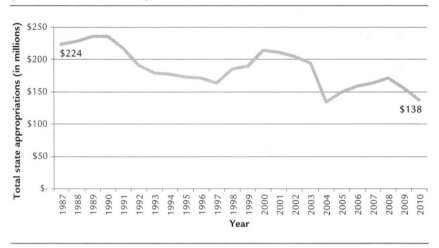

Source: Delta Cost Project dataset, 2012

Decreasing appropriations brings diversification of funding sources. Certainly, tuition, philanthropy, and auxiliary revenues have each made up for portions of UVA's finances that the state traditionally had funded. Tuition has doubled, philanthropy has tripled, and federally funded research has also doubled. Virginia has one of the lowest per-student state funding rates nationally, at twenty-eighth. Perhaps surprisingly for a public institution, despite UVA's strong academic tradition, appropriations haven't held a plurality of the university's per-FTE undergraduate funding since the early 1990s. Figure 5.6 clarifies the interplay of funding sources where private dollars now significantly outweigh public dollars.

Philanthropy, in particular, has been essential for public universities in Virginia. UVA was one of the first public universities to begin aggressively seeking private support with campaigns in the 1980s and 1990s, and it recently completed a $3 billion campaign. Though elite private institutions have conducted such efforts for decades, public colleges have begun doing so only recently. This places the university squarely back in the debate about public *versus* private or public *and* private.

Students experience Virginia's low higher education funding in the form of higher sticker price for tuition (although it is still relatively cheap when compared to sticker prices at private universities). Yet UVA's undergraduate

FIGURE 5.5   Total appropriations and net tuition and fees per FTE student for the University of Virginia, 1987–2010 (in constant 2010 dollars)

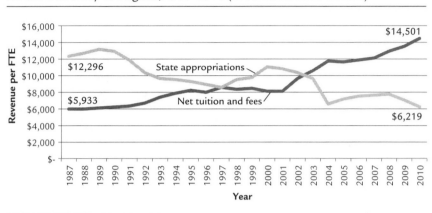

Source: Delta Cost Project dataset, 2012

Note: The fall FTE enrollment was used for FTE calculations. Constant 2010 dollars adjusted by SHEEO Higher Education Cost Adjustment (HECA).

tuition and fees in 2010–2011 totaled $10,836 for in-state residents and $33,782 for out-of-state residents, with tuition accounting for just 31 percent of the university's academic budget. Some might say that, for all the hype UVA and its compatriots' finances receive, tuition is still kept fairly low. Many parents in the state, for example, pay more for preschools than they do for their children's college education. What's more pertinent, though, is that there has been an upward slope—tuition per in-state student in 1990, if adjusted for inflation, was $3,753—three times lower than today. Since 1992, out-of-state students have been required to pay all the cost of their attendance, without any government assistance; in-state students are subsidized for half. Former Virginia Secretary of Finance John Bennett described the rising tuition as a trade-off:

> Virginia is a low-tax, low-spending state. This limits the state funding that is available for higher education. Limited state funding, along with Virginia's commitment to maintain a large, diverse system of colleges and universities, has resulted in relatively high tuition. This was an implicitly recognized policy trade-off for thirty years—Virginia institutions would charge relatively high tuition because a greater policy premium was placed on having low taxes. Senior legislative leaders understood it, and efforts to limit tuition increases or

FIGURE 5.6 Appropriations, tuition, philanthropy, and federally funded research per FTE student at UVA, 1987–2010 (in constant 2010 dollars)

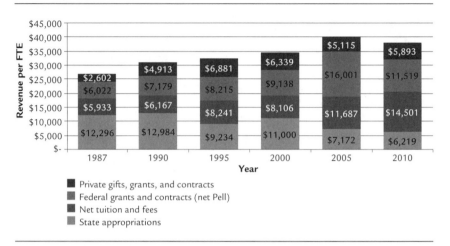

Source: Delta Cost Project dataset, 2012

Note: The fall FTE enrollment was used for FTE calculations. Constant 2010 dollars adjusted by SHEEO Higher Education Cost Adjustment (HECA).

cap tuition legislatively were typically thwarted. Legislators often said they heard very few complaints from constituents about tuition levels. The complaints they did hear, they said, were about students not being able to get into selective institutions.

With all the arguments taken into account, there still exists a strong interplay between rising tuition and enrollment, and declining appropriations trends in the state—shown in figure 5.7—which has the potential to threaten the quality and affordability of higher education in Virginia and its strong public institutions.

Balancing tuition with state needs has always been tricky, and it has certainly been so over the past thirty years in Virginia. Teresa Sullivan, president of UVA, notes that the current reluctance to increase taxes or spending for higher education is not a new phenomenon in Virginia: "In Carr's Hill [the President's House at UVA] there is an original letter by Thomas Jefferson framed under glass, written in 1825, the year before he died, complaining to a friend about how little money the general assembly gives to support the University of Virginia. I think the reason that that letter is there is so that every president understands this is not a new problem. It is not an issue of

FIGURE 5.7   Public FTE student enrollment, educational appropriations, and total educational revenue per FTE student, Virginia, 1987–2012 (in constant 2012 dollars)

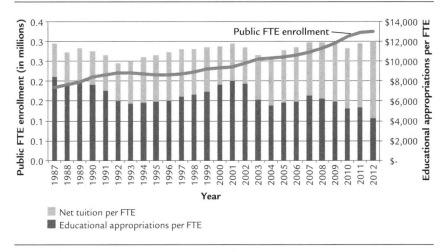

Net tuition per FTE
Educational appropriations per FTE

Source: SHEEO, 2013

Note: Constant 2012 dollars adjusted by SHEEO Higher Education Cost Adjustment (HECA). Educational appropriations include ARRA funds.

twenty years ago. The Commonwealth of Virginia has always been relatively reluctant to support public spending really on just about anything."

The historical and political context is important for understanding the current state of public higher education finance and autonomy in Virginia and why the effects of privatization have been so pervasive at UVA and, increasingly, at other public universities in the state. Nonetheless, reports and commissions in Virginia have continually been dedicated to minimizing it. A blue ribbon commission in 2010 elevated the issue to constitutional importance: "[Thomas Jefferson] spoke of a 'natural aristocracy' based on merit, with education as the means to enlightened citizenship and economic opportunity, not just a privileged few . . . Striking the appropriate balance between the contributions of state taxpayers and tuition-paying students and parents is the recurring challenge. And with the vast majority of Virginians now believing that a college degree rather than a high school diploma is the educational credential required for economic success, it is perhaps time to consider updating the state Constitution to embrace the principle of affordable college access."[12]

Public Mission: Part of the American Narrative

To fully understand the intricacies of Virginia's unique higher education system, we must investigate how and why they developed. Thirty years ago, the system more closely resembled the quintessential, state-reliant public university model, and the years since then have been marked by significant change. However, there has been a constant "commitment to the people" and to the university as a "training ground for all the people, which the people understood in a sense of we the people, the shapers and shareholders of the republic itself." These were the sentiments of an earlier UVA president, Edwin Alderman, and they're very much in line with the university's Jeffersonian spirit.

Virginia's colleges and universities, like any state's, have an intrinsic duty to local citizens. The difference is the degree to which this duty is stressed, and that has a lot to do with other factors. Understandably, UVA has had the opportunity and initiative to stress other commitments as well. In the letter that begins this chapter, Thomas Jefferson establishes a goal for the university to "be a temptation to the youth of other States to come and drink of the cup of knowledge." Often, interestingly, advertising the pursuit of knowledge is not a priority for some universities—higher education today serves broader purposes and specific career interests as well—and, for public universities especially, having a founder who was outspoken about the benefit to other states' students is unheard of. This is a distinguishing feature of higher education throughout Virginia's history. In our interview, former Governor Gerald Baliles reflected on the public mission of higher education as a key component of the American dream.

> The pursuit of public education at all levels is a particularly American idea, especially the conviction that public education should be universally available, and excellence in education should be consistently sought. From my perspective, we had to follow the Jeffersonian notion that men and women—by the sheer force of education—could enlighten themselves to the point that representative government would lead to progress. That is part of the American narrative—by the power of our own minds we could make our society improve and advance into the future.
>
> On the one hand, there are these hopes and aspirations that are idealistic but we have also found a pragmatic means of achieving those ambitions—it is called higher education. If you make a simple, direct assumption that education is good and necessary, that it's a prerequisite for a successful society, then it's necessary to invest heavily to build a public higher education system that aspires to more than mere adequacy.

Governor Baliles spoke to a view of higher education that stretches far beyond local or regional or institutional needs and the assumption that public higher education is a good for the enlightenment of the people. However, since he left office in 1990, many in the state have changed their perspective and focus more on "what have you done for the state lately?" and "how many more students from my district can you enroll?"

Service to the State

The belief in higher education as an important public good for the state does, indeed, require service to the state. For many legislators, that boils down to enrollment and economic development in the state. In the fall of 2011, Virginia public institutions enrolled more than 414,000 college students, 60,000 of them from outside Virginia; this has grown from an enrollment of 326,000 in the fall of 2001. Of the total enrollment at public colleges and universities in the Commonwealth, nearly 24,400 of these students were at UVA, an increase from the more than 22,700 total students enrolled in the fall of 2001.[13] On the whole, however, UVA and the state have upheld their public mission to provide quality education. The six-year graduation rate at UVA is 93 percent, among the best in the country.[14] As far as in-state versus out-of-state enrollment, figure 5.8 shows that UVA has maintained a consistent 65:35 ratio over the last twenty years. The fact that the University of Virginia's commitment to its state's residents hasn't dropped—a popular trend across the country—is reassuring. There are legislators in the state today calling for scaling back to 25 percent as a maximum for out-of-state residents, but there is no clear plan for how the state would account for the loss of revenue coming from out-of-state residents. The truth today is that out-of-state students are helping to subsidize the in-state students by paying closer to market tuition prices. If there were fewer of them and more in-state students, there would be a double hit to the bottom line for public universities unless the state provided significantly more funding—a highly unlikely prospect.

UVA and the other public universities exhibit their commitment to Virginians in ways besides in-state matriculation. The university has been dedicated to initiatives such as economic development and reaching out to rural students. This is manifested by UVA's satellite campus at Wise, in the Appalachian Mountains of Virginia's southwest region. UVA's business, public policy, and medical faculty also spend time working with local leaders, and most state leaders declare that UVA is a better partner now than at any

FIGURE 5.8   Annualized undergraduate FTE student enrollment, UVA, 1993–2012

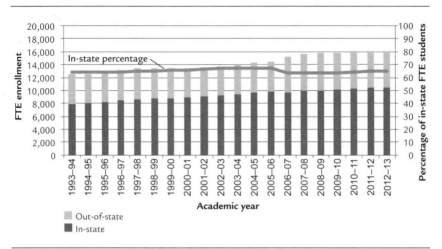

Source: SCHEV, 2013 (reports E05A, E05B, and E05C)

Note: Rounding the FTE calculation to a whole number may yield a variation of +/– 1 total FTE undergraduates in a given year.

point since its founding. Elsewhere in the state, Virginia Tech, William & Mary, and Virginia Commonwealth University have taken responsibility for economic development in a region of the state as one of the conditions of restructuring.

Federal research funding is on the rise at UVA, though at $240 million in 2013 it is low compared to larger flagships in other states.[15] In general, some legislators view increasing the size of UVA's research portfolio as part of the drive toward new funding models stemming from the universities' greater autonomy. In other words, research universities like UVA are focusing more on research than undergraduate education, a familiar refrain from legislators across the country, and a common complaint about privatization. As shown back in figure 5.6, federal grants and contracts—much of it for research funding—now constitute the largest single source of funds for the institution.

The changes in autonomy and funding at UVA and more broadly in the state are certainly strong evidence of privatization in Virginia over several decades, but very few advocate for full privatization of any of the public universities. Robert Sweeney, senior vice president for university advancement at UVA, sees true privatization as contrary to the university's founding goals:

"The idea was that public education was going to be linked to personal free-dom, and democracy was going to need an educated citizenry. So, he [Jef-ferson] believed this notion of 'public' was an absolute—in the initial core element of the DNA of the University of Virginia. There was an absolute rock-solid belief that we did not ever want to be private." Recent state poli-cies have reaffirmed Virginia universities' public responsibility in the context of their autonomy.

Two of the greatest accomplishments legislators and policy makers point to are UVA's increased financial aid commitment—manifested in the Universi-ty's AccessUVa program, which reduces loans for low-income students—and the articulation and transfer agreements with community colleges that re-sulted from the legislation. Preliminary evidence suggests that the increased enrollment of low-income and transfer students into UVA can be attributed in part to this legislation. Transfer rates from two-year to four-year institu-tions in Virginia have increased 50 percent. Glenn Dubois, chancellor of Vir-ginia's Community College System, summarizes Virginia higher education's public value, specifically highlighting these transfer rates: "I think from the state's perspective, UVA and others—in return for certain benefits—have made stronger commitments to the public good, and one is access through transfer. So now, in Virginia, we have a transfer environment that's probably second to none in the country; it's to the point where I can guarantee that any father or mother, wherever they are in the Commonwealth, that if they want their son and daughter to graduate from UVA, I can guarantee it."

The State Ask

As noted earlier in the discussion of the Restructuring Act, when universities drafted the early structural reform proposals, the state countered with what came to be known as the "State Ask." If universities were to be given the au-tonomy to run their own affairs and finances, Virginia legislators needed as-surances that their commitment to the public good would not be interrupted. Then Governor Warner negotiated these eleven requirements (with a twelfth added later). The universities' connection to the state was made clear in goals that included increased access for state residents, connecting the curriculum to the state's needs, strengthening articulation agreements with community colleges and other universities, and working with an underserved region of the state to develop the economy. The twelve elements of the State Ask were:[16]

1. Provide access to higher education for all citizens . . . including underrepresented populations.
2. Ensure that higher education remains affordable, regardless of individual or family income.
3. Offer a broad range of undergraduate and, where appropriate, graduate programs, and address the . . . need for sufficient graduates in particular shortage areas.
4. Ensure that . . . programs maintain high academic standards by undertaking a continuous review and improvement.
5. Improve student retention.
6. Develop articulation agreements that have uniform application to all Virginia community colleges.
7. Stimulate economic development of the Commonwealth and the area in which the institution is located.
8. Consistent with its . . . mission, increase the level of externally funded research and . . . the transfer of technology . . . to private-sector companies.
9. Work cooperatively with elementary and secondary school administrators, teachers, and students to improve student achievement.
10. Prepare a six-year financial plan.
11. Conduct the institution's business affairs in a manner that maximizes operational efficiencies and economies.
12. Promote the safety of the campus and students [added later after the passage of the Restructuring Act].

The State Ask and the Restructuring Act, despite granting unprecedented privileges to universities, were not seen as too much autonomy. In my interviews with the state and institutional leaders at the time of the Restructuring Act's passage, all of them focused on the need for clarity around what the state expected of higher education and, in reverse, what higher education needed from the state. Then Secretary of Finance John Bennett sums up this expectation in reflecting on the Act: "I don't think that it was a feeling that higher ed would ever stray from its public purpose . . . it was the first time that the state had explicitly set out in statute what its expectations were. So that was the trade-off. The state, in return for this grant of authority and a path toward greater operational autonomy, would require the institutions to commit themselves formally to the expectations the state set out. That was the 'to whom much is given, much is expected' agreement."

UVA's Robert Sweeney went even further, citing the bill as part of Virginia's redefinition of "public university." The idea that Virginia was moving toward more of a public-private partnership had some detractors, but most saw this as the next logical step in a two-hundred-year progression.

> We reframed our argument to be the first privately financed public university that maintained its public mandate. Our argument held that we were going to be public and that instead of beating up on the Commonwealth of Virginia about abdicating responsibility, we were going to reframe it, which is to say that no state can afford to fully fund the aspirations of a great, internationally acclaimed, global institution that would be among the elite in the world. If we were going to do that, it would have to be a partnership between the Commonwealth and the university. Part of what played out was that if we were going to keep this mandate of public being truly public, the core element of that was access.

Since the major events of 2005, the business community of Virginia has taken a larger role in higher education. Though the Virginia Business Higher Education Council has existed since 1994, since the last recession businesses have supported higher education quite formally in lobbying. The Council's "Grow by Degrees" initiative persuaded Governor McDonnell to embrace higher education as an economic good to be helped by business. The business community very readily embraced the notion of the public-private partnership in the state because it needed a talented and trained work force in order to keep its businesses strong. One business leader told me the reason he keeps his business in the state instead of moving to a lower-tax state is because the supply of highly educated workers is so much stronger than many other southern states. While the business community was advocating for higher education, it was also looking out for its bottom line—finding the most talented employees. Virginia higher education attorney Frank Atkinson explains: "We've been moving away from the traditional idea of a public system of higher education to one that relies more heavily on private support, on collaboration with private enterprises, and even on private decision making to some degree—it is really true of higher education governance and financing across the board."

The other trend has been slightly increased appropriations for higher education since the late 2000s. After the "renaissance" of the 1980s, with all the turmoil and uncertainty in colleges, public support had reached a low point. But then in 2002 the general assembly passed a $1 billion bond for higher

education that required voter approval. In 2009, the general assembly ratified another large bond for higher education.[17] For a traditionally low-tax and
low-spending state, this recent support for higher education has been quite
impressive. However, the recent recession and a resurgence of loud voices
calling for higher enrollment and lower tuition (featuring the Tea Party
movement) threaten this support, and it is highly unlikely that state support
will ever rise above the levels seen decades ago.

Despite all the threats to higher education, legislators have found it important to look forward. Governor McDonnell's 2011 Commission on Higher
Education Reform, Innovation and Investment is an example of this. The
commission focused on the most pertinent issue of the time—the economy
and higher education's role in solving major social issues—and how higher
education can and must remain intimately involved with the most pressing
needs of the state.

> We think that colleges and universities should become more involved in the
> pressing issues of the day. We are concerned that higher education could be-
> come merely a support service for industry, economic development, or gov-
> ernment. But it is better that the university be engaged than disengaged,
> better to risk involvement than irrelevance.
>
> The women and men who work in colleges and universities are not uniquely
> qualified to solve the major social problems of our time. But they do bring to
> such problems a vast array of knowledge and analytic and technical skills that
> few others command. They come, moreover, from institutions in which free
> and ordered competition among ideas is especially valued.[18]

During tough times such as these, such foresight may be crucial to better
prospects ahead. Harkening back to Gordon Davies's suggestion earlier in
this chapter about making higher education the top priority of state government, that does not seem plausible; but keeping it as a priority *at all* is viewed
as a success in this state.

The 2011 Commission and the Restructuring Act were the most recent
steps in a more than thirty-year history in Virginia that has produced highly
autonomous public universities while providing a clear vision for how those
institutions—independent as they may be—should also remain connected to
and focused on the needs and goals of the Commonwealth. In other words,
public institutions are intended to serve public purposes regardless of their
funding sources and managerial autonomy. The early evidence in Virginia

seems to point clearly to a balance between the institutional autonomy and service to the public good.

Evaluating Virginia's Public-Private Partnership

The public universities had already moved toward a public-private partnership (or were, in some ways, born that way), but the restructuring legislation solidified their public mission as being firmly rooted in Virginia, no matter whether the state contributed 50 percent or 5 percent of an institution's operating budget. It is still too early to assess the long-term impacts of this legislation on either the Commonwealth or UVA, but less than a decade after implementation, the early results, according to most of the people I interviewed for this book, seemed to be pointing to a grade of B+: strong marks on the operational and managerial flexibility, strong marks on the commitment and connection to the state's needs, but low marks on the ever-challenging issues of tuition, stable funding, and out-of-state enrollment. Senator Warner reflected on the outcomes of the Restructuring Act, which passed when he was governor: "When the Act was passed, it was clear that it was a work in progress and that careful monitoring and refinement would be necessary over time. Nevertheless, the Act for the first time in decades redefined the state's fundamental relationship with its colleges and universities. It set out in state law the Commonwealth's expectations for its institutions of higher education. It traded outcome-based accountability for transaction-based state oversight. And for the first time, it aligned state and institutional priorities to ensure that our higher education system as a whole is meeting the needs of Virginians."

The frequent claim by some legislators that Virginia is moving toward privatizing education—in a purely private sense—seems to have been debunked. Teresa Sullivan, UVA's president, says that rather than privatization, what has happened is a reevaluation of the public university. "What makes this institution public is public mission. It is in our DNA. It is what Mr. Jefferson designed us to be." Sullivan also emphasized that *public* is not solely defined by dollars—it is first and always about mission and history.

Legislators and university leaders almost unanimously agreed that the legislation has been helpful both in granting greater autonomy to the institutions and in keeping them focused on the state's needs. Sandridge described the effects of restructuring as a "wonderful articulation of what we [the state and higher education] expected of each other." Over and again, university leaders have proclaimed they just wanted to know what was expected of them as public institutions, and this legislation clarified greatly the accountability expected by the state. However, many do see room for improvement. Tuition is the most frustrating factor expressed by both the state and the institutional leaders—legislators wanting lower tuition and university leaders seeking greater control. Another significant challenge is the legislative turnover every two years, meaning that new legislators must constantly be educated about the legislation's goals and outcomes—and the fact that one legislature cannot bind future legislatures.

Overall, interviewees consistently believed that Virginia's public universities have not, in any significant way, walked away from their Jeffersonian heritage as institutions serving larger public goals and that the legislation has, in fact, strengthened the university's public mission. State Senator Janet Howell said, "The Act hit it just right. We may tweak it over the years, but it is a very good contract between the universities and the state. We have a much better idea of what our responsibilities are on both sides." Above all, given the increased operational efficiency and the money saved thereby, UVA has maintained strong support for the public purposes most sought by the state—articulation, access, and assistance with economic development.

In 2008, the Joint Legislative Audit and Review Commission conducted a review of the first two years of the restructuring management agreements and the performance of the institutions, as mandated by the original legislation. The essential findings of the report were that, so far as could be measured, the management agreements were working; the institutions were meeting the State Ask; and, with the exception of the tuition control at the institutional level, both the universities and state agencies were generally pleased with the new relationship. Moreover, the state's Jeffersonian goals, as interviewees attested, were not in jeopardy: "The greatest benefit of the Restructuring Act and management agreements may be in the State's ability to more effectively lead the institutions toward meeting established goals and expectations. For the first time, the State's goals for higher education have been codified with financial and regulatory incentives for the institutions to meet these goals. The Restructuring Act created changes in how the institutions conduct their financial and administrative operations, but these operations are all done in support of their core academic missions."[19]

While Virginia's public colleges and universities continue to thrive under their more autonomous structure, leaders and legislators in other states

should not look too longingly at Virginia as the model for their state's institutions. As has been discussed throughout this book, one state's history, mission, and culture are quite different from others and play a large part in how
privatization takes shape in that state. Moving south from Virginia, we'll
look next at North Carolina, which serves as another case study of privatization with very different history, circumstances, and outcomes.

CHAPTER SIX

The People's University

The General Assembly shall maintain a public system of higher education, comprising The University of North Carolina and such other institutions of higher education as the General Assembly may deem wise . . . The General Assembly shall provide that the benefits of The University of North Carolina and other public institutions of higher education, as far as practicable, be extended to the people of the State free of expense.

—North Carolina state constitution[1]

We're the university of "both—and": both academic prominence and a commitment to our state.

—Holden Thorp[2]

WHAT IS THE OLDEST public university in the United States? It depends on how you define *oldest* and *public*. While the College of William & Mary is today the oldest public university in the United States, it was not founded as a public university; the University of Georgia was the first university to receive a state charter, but it opened its doors several years after the University of North Carolina.

North Carolina takes great pride in having the nation's first state university—founded with public dollars, public support, and a public charter. Today, the state maintains that strong tradition in the University of North Carolina at Chapel Hill (UNC-CH), the first campus of its successful multicampus system. For more than two centuries, North Carolina has maintained one of the strongest and deepest commitments to public higher education in the United States, perhaps because of its constitutional provision mandating that, "as far as practicable," higher education be free. However, as the political and economic environment begins to shift in the second decade of the twenty-first century, North Carolina is beginning to feel the earliest effects of privatization as funding shrinks and legislative priorities shift. This case study reveals again that a state's connection to its history is at the core of an institution's public mission and that any discussion of privatization must first begin with this state context.

North Carolina has a system of public higher education that is among the finest in the nation. This is a result of strong state funding that has survived economic downturns, its loyal support among legislators and citizens who consider it to be a public mandate, its unified system of governance, and its historic focus on serving the people and needs of the state. Long described by those in the state as the "people's university," UNC-CH and the broader UNC system have weathered the same twenty-year storm of withering state funding and public support that most states have faced, but with less impact on funding, legislative enthusiasm, or popular support among the state's citizens. While some of this was due to legislative, gubernatorial, and university leaders who were unflinchingly supportive of the university, there was also a mutual dependence between the university and the state, which leads many legislators today to describe support for higher education as being in the state's DNA.

A Valley of Humility Between Two Mountains of Conceit

In 1789, the North Carolina General Assembly ratified a charter for a public university, which, just half a decade later in 1795, became the first such institution to open its doors. Over two centuries, the University of North Carolina withstood civil war, Reconstruction, and social unrest to consolidate its reputation as one of the most beloved public institutions of higher education in the country. It fostered an admiration for education that manifested itself in an entire system of public colleges and universities. But as a tightly budgeted, tightly monitored future looms for all universities, North Carolina's higher education legacy is being threatened, and questions inevitably arise as to how the university can continue to effectively serve the Old North State's proud sons and daughters.

Before 1776, the thirteen colonies featured only nine colleges; none were in North Carolina, and only one—the College of Philadelphia, now the University of Pennsylvania—was not a religious institution. The privileged sons of North Carolina's wealthy planters most often traveled to study at the College of New Jersey (now Princeton University). After the start of the Revolutionary War, visionary men from North Carolina who attended the state's Fifth Provincial Congress, in Halifax in December 1776, wrote a new constitution that created a state government for North Carolina. Article XLI of the 1776 North Carolina state constitution provided: "That a school or schools shall be established by the Legislature, for the convenient Instruction of youth, with such salaries to the masters, paid by the public, as may enable them to instruct at low Prices; and all useful learning shall be duly encouraged and promoted in one or more Universities."[3]

The University of North Carolina grew out of that gathering and the constitution it created because, as one historian has noted, the delegates "recognized the importance of an educated citizenry that would support the government and provide trained officeholders."[4] William Richardson Davie's bill to charter a university passed the North Carolina General Assembly on December 11, 1789, shortly after Davie returned from the Constitutional Convention in Philadelphia and mere weeks after the U.S. Constitution was ratified by North Carolina's legislature.

The precedent for North Carolina's academic growth had been set. The university received a charter, a board of trustees, and a donation of twenty thousand acres in 1790, and UNC opened its doors in 1795 as the nation's first public university. It was the only public university to graduate students in the eighteenth century, beginning with its first graduating students in 1798.

A state constitutional mandate for public K–12 education is fairly common in the United States and is one reason why K–12 education is seen as a "right" for citizens, whereas higher education is sometimes seen as a "privilege." Certainly, one element of the changing value that states place on higher education is based upon a shifting belief that higher education today is more of a private benefit than a public good that serves the state more broadly. The fact that North Carolina, in its earliest days as a colony and then on through some challenging financial crises in the twentieth and twenty-first centuries, has maintained a commitment to higher education is noteworthy, as is its constitutional mandate for higher education.

After the university's founding, the next century of North Carolina history came to be dominated by the Civil War and Reconstruction. The state faced great destruction in Sherman's devastating march through the South, and although 60 percent of UNC's student body took up arms in the 1860s to defend their state, the university never closed.[5] The university continued its commitment to educating North Carolinians throughout Reconstruction and into the twentieth century as a beacon for higher education.

As a side note, it was remarkable how nearly every legislator interviewed for this book referenced Reconstruction at some point during our conversation. The period following the Civil War left such an indelible mark on the state's citizens that one hundred fifty years later it is still part of the conversation as to why higher education matters in the state. Later, while conducting interviews in California, I mentioned this to a legislator there, who suggested that the significant difference in the value of education between the South and the West is based upon the effects of Reconstruction and the long-term feeling of education as the great escape. In other words, education came to be seen almost as an entitlement in the West, whereas it was seen as an escape from the past in the South.

In its earliest years, the University of North Carolina did not see itself as a college for rich planters' sons. Its students, sons of tobacco planters or textile workers, came from small towns and small farms far removed from a large port, a river, or the railroads of the North. Opportunity was scarce, and as former Senate Majority Leader Anthony "Tony" Rand says, the university was the way out. He, like so many other legislators I interviewed, sees the university as something deeply rooted in the state's history and something that has always worked to the state's betterment. "North Carolina has often been described as a valley of humility between two mountains of conceit. We are a state of small towns, mainly agrarian, but people put significant stock in education. We have always been somehow different from the other southern states, and I have always believed that it was the university that led us out of the wilderness." Former North Carolina senator and Senate Appropriations Committee co-chair Richard Stevens espoused similar pride in North Carolina's humble origins: "We used to talk about being the valley of humility between the two mountains of conceit, Virginia and South Carolina, in the land of the aristocracies. This was a farming state, a poor state of immigrants, and so to latch on to something like the university was significantly important to help pull ourselves up. I will say to you that there is not a more significant institution than [UNC] Chapel Hill in pulling the state up." UNC opened the door for thousands of poor families' youth (only sons at first) to break from their backgrounds and become leading figures in the nineteenth and early twentieth centuries. The state did not diversify its economy until after the Second World War, but for generations, UNC offered a promise of advancement in a region where otherwise there was little.[6]

The role of UNC as a hearth and home for the state's struggling youth was fostered by a fundamental—and in the U.S., unique—constitutional provision. It graces the beginning of this chapter not only because it allowed the University of North Carolina at Chapel Hill—affectionately called "Carolina"—to establish a character especially intertwined with the society surrounding it, but also because the resulting public reputation has remained the university's foremost marker. No matter how relevant or "practicable" it is, the principle that UNC and all other public institutions will provide the benefits of higher education "to the people of the State, free of expense" runs deep in North Carolinians. Andy Willis, former state budget director, exemplifies the state's faith: "I grew up in poor, rural North Carolina, and teachers preached to us that if you work hard enough and study, you can go to college for close to free. If you get accepted and don't have the means, that won't stop you in this state." Having so many leaders in senior government positions in the state who know about and believe in the constitutional provision helps mightily to ensure that public higher education remains a priority in North Carolina. The constitutional provision is indelibly connected to the foundation of the public aura that came to be associated with public higher education.

The People's University

"Each of the campuses [has] unique roles, but generally it is to promote the public good." These words from Angela Bryant, a member of several educational committees in the North Carolina House of Representatives, could not be truer. She could have gone further, however, by clarifying that the beneficiaries of this good are largely North Carolinians. Because of the state's support, as well as a handful of powerful figures in both the government and the university, tuition has been kept low and funding kept high, both relative to national trends. Underlying all this, as expressed by almost everyone I spoke to, is a commitment to North Carolina, to its college youth, and to its prosperity. Analyzing these forces in UNC's development, within the conceptual model of the foundations of privatization (introduced in chapter 1), offers perspective on the rationale behind the resistance to privatization in higher education politics. For until the turn of this century, it was this overwhelming solidarity that continuously pulled North Carolina from its agrarian origins, and for that reason the state hesitates to deviate from it.

Structure and Leadership: "The Most Beautifully Balanced System in the Country"

One of UNC's greatest achievements is its development into a system of public universities chiefly "dedicated to the service of North Carolina and its people."[7] Being so close to the citizenry has also brought the UNC system close to the legislature, which plays a famous role in the university's prosperity. The strong connection between the state and the university system was characterized by one of its best-known presidents, the late Dr. Bill Friday, who strengthened this feeling of mutual responsibility between the state and the university during his thirty-year presidency from 1956 to 1986. In our interview shortly before he died, he stressed time and again the importance of a focus on the people and needs of the state and how privileged those were who had the chance to attend a UNC campus. He once famously reminded students of the weight of that responsibility, stating, "A million North Carolinians living in poverty pay taxes to support your education. I want to know what you're going to do to pay it back."

It wasn't until 1931 that North Carolina affixed its name and authority to any other institutions besides UNC–Chapel Hill. That year, however, was historic: under UNC's administration were added two more institutions: State College, the state's land-grant institution focusing on agricultural and mechanical studies (now called North Carolina State University), and the state's women's college, which has become the University of North Carolina at Greensboro. The newly formed UNC system significantly contributed to uncovering opportunities for stable state-sponsored education, regardless of gender or desired career outlet. The system continued to grow, and in 1971 the general assembly passed the Higher Education Reorganization Act to create the University of North Carolina system as the overarching governance of a sixteen-campus system (since then, a seventeenth campus has been added). The general assembly charged the unified system with a new mission: "to foster the development of a well-planned and coordinated system of higher education, to improve the quality of education, to extend its benefits, and to encourage an economical use of the state's resources."[8] *US News & World Report* ranks four of the UNC campuses among the top 200 universities in the nation, with several more ranking highly in the regional university rankings, and together the system enrolls an estimated 215,000 students.

UNC-CH's place in this relationship is interesting. It was the first and has been the biggest and most highly endowed of the UNC institutions. When people mention "Carolina" or "UNC," more often than not they mean the Chapel Hill campus, and one legislator even jokingly told me that the system "stole Chapel Hill's name." However, for the public mission of North Carolina to succeed, and for the principle of high access to be maintained, UNC-CH is to be a leader by example. Then UNC-CH Chancellor Holden Thorp made clear in our interview the commitment that the Chapel Hill campus has to its sister institutions as well as the state. Rarely during my travels through North Carolina did I hear a university administrator or legislator speak about the primacy of one campus over another; rather, they spoke about the strength of the overall system. Therefore, though this chapter focuses heavily on the flagship campus, it is useful to understand the scope of the UNC system and its legacy, which is shared by all the state's public four-year institutions.

In creating the UNC system, the general assembly established an overarching board of governors. Appointed by the general assembly, the board of governors is the main policy-making body, but each of the campuses has a board of trustees responsible for some on-campus operations, along with the chancellor of each campus, who reports to the president of the UNC system. Overall, North Carolina has a very strong central operation in higher education where the president and the board of governors are empowered to make policy, financial, and administrative decisions.

While North Carolina's system of higher education is considered strong and unified, no single body coordinates all of higher education; the private and independent colleges and universities, as well as the North Carolina Community College System, are all independent of the UNC system and have their own governing boards. As a result, coordination and articulation is not as strong as it might be, but is still quite good. Hannah Gage, former chair of the UNC Board of Governors, described the system as the "most beautifully balanced system of higher education in the country."

However, the figure of power in the university system—certainly historically—is the president, and the most iconic of them was Bill Friday. The UNC system president, besides keeping each of the seventeen campuses focused on the public mission, is the primary lobbyist for North Carolina higher education in the state capitol. Several of the chancellors are happy with this arrangement, because it allows them to stay more focused on their campus and avoid fussing with legislators (it also prevents the campuses from separately fighting for dollars in competition with one another, as is the case in other states). For three decades, Bill Friday held this position, and he integrated the system with the state and held off the pressure to surrender any of its public character. Through one of the most turbulent and progressive periods for college campuses in the United States, Friday stuck to the credo that UNC's success lay in the system's strength, and for decades after his presidency ended in 1986 he remained influential in state higher education politics.

Low Tuition, High Support

The UNC system's finances followed the same path of development as everything else. Its structure further expresses the centrality, in the state's ideology, of the system above any individual campus. UNC was one of the later public universities to focus heavily on philanthropy and tuition for major operating funding, and the strategy worked for a long time. With overwhelming support in Raleigh, tuition was kept low and programs continually improved, even while other states experienced wandering public missions and faltering state support. From the 1960s through the 1990s, as UNC built up its reputation among both public and private universities, little more was needed to justify a tidal wave of money than a link to the university roots—the constitutional article pledging that "as far as practicable, [higher education] be extended to the people of the state free of expense."

UNC-CH consistently ranks among the most generously funded public universities in the United States. Even today, despite recent budget cuts, North Carolina appropriates about $20,000 per student at UNC-CH, more than the $14,000 per student at the University of California, Berkeley, and three times more than the Virginia General Assembly's appropriation of about $6,000 per student at UVA.[9] System funding is similarly generous, accounting for 12 percent of the state's operating budget. Figure 6.1 captures the increase in state funding for all of higher education, which, on a per-student basis, is close to the highest in the nation, having nearly doubled in twenty-five years. Like UNC system funding, it has been in an almost perpetual growth pattern, and was continually well supported throughout the late twentieth century. While all states have grown their appropriations on a real dollar basis over time, almost none have grown on an inflation-adjusted

FIGURE 6.1   Total North Carolina higher education appropriations, 1987–2012 (in constant 2012 dollars)

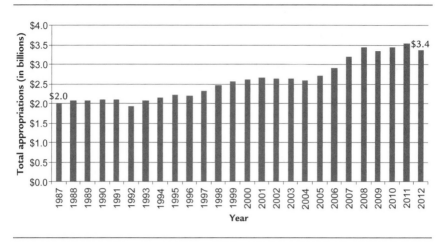

Source: SHEEO, 2013

Notes: Constant 2012 dollars adjusted by SHEEO Higher Education Cost Adjustment (HECA). Educational appropriations include ARRA funds.

basis as is seen in North Carolina. This is significant among the fifty states, where the trend has almost always been flat or declining appropriations on an inflation-adjusted basis.

Tuition at UNC campuses is a major point of pride, having earned them a spot on more than a handful of "best value" university rankings.[10] UNC's annual tuition, on average across all campuses, is roughly $6,000 for in-state students and $18,000 for out-of-state students (but closer to $30,000 for out-of-state students at Chapel Hill). Maintaining low tuition is one of the proudest achievements of the university, and the reason grateful residents so cherish the constitutional provision. Former State Senator Tony Rand, one of the most steadfast and influential defenders of low tuition in North Carolina, offered a sentiment repeatedly expressed by state legislators. "[The N.C. constitution] says to me that our universities will be available without regard to a person's economic situation and condition—the university is there for our people. If you can get in, by God, you can go there."

This *free provision* has been drawn upon in the North Carolina legislative chamber for decades. During the early 1990s recession, many public universities saw the state/university relationship begin to weaken. In North Carolina, according to Hannah Gage, this "was never even an option." Though "the legislature would have loved to raise tuition and take some of the pressure off them," she says, "our constitution says that you've got to offer tuition as low as possible." Former Senator Rand bluntly describes another concern: "Be careful, you don't want to get sued—don't try to put that tuition too high!" This consistent focus on low tuition backed up by high state appropriations is unique among the states. No matter how you look at the cost, $6,000 tuition is extremely low, particularly when coupled with financial aid options.

A large share of the credit for the pro-UNC attitude among legislators in the state actually goes to Rand, as well as fellow senator and former President Pro Tempore Marc Basnight. They worked closely to ensure that UNC overall and Chapel Hill in particular were funded generously and given the flexibility to thrive and grow. Though Rand was a Chapel Hill graduate and a successful lawyer, Basnight held only a high school degree. But he came to appreciate higher education over time and saw its value for the state's prosperity.

The university was a favored child in the general assembly for many years, but it required the sheer force of will and the personality of these men to ensure that it survived the cuts seen in other states during the past two decades. Almost every legislator of both parties acknowledged this reality. As one example of the significant legislative support for UNC, near the end of his service in the senate, Basnight pushed for a cancer research fund at the UNC-CH Hospital and helped to create a near-perpetual appropriation of $50 million for the university's cancer research center, funded by legal settlements with tobacco companies.[11]

In most states, higher education funding is a discretionary expense—something that is nice to spend money on but not necessarily mandatory in the same way as K–12 and Medicare. Legislators in other states reminded me often that higher education has the ability to raise revenues, whereas most state agencies do not. In other words, higher education is usually a "below the line" appropriation, meaning it comes after everything else that is required. Basnight and Rand changed the perception of higher education funding, raising it to a status where it was essentially viewed as an "above the line," almost mandatory appropriation. They fought any and all threats to funding for higher education. One legislator recalled his clashes with Senator Basnight over higher education appropriations: "Those two men [Basnight and Rand] almost singlehandedly saw to it that higher education was protected. For a man with no higher education [Basnight], he really believed in it. I raised possible cuts at times with him, and he would tell me to shut up; I knew I didn't have any chance in hell of getting anything past him. He wouldn't want to talk about anything that would take money from higher education; you couldn't even get him to consider the option."

Influential legislators were joined in solidarity by strong and stable leadership in the governor's mansion. Two of the state's most influential governors—Terry Sanford (1961–1965) and Jim Hunt (1977–1985 and 1993–2001)—shared a similar attitude and held education as a priority. Sanford oversaw the consolidation of the UNC system and the foundation of the state's community college network, and Hunt worked with Friday, Rand, and Basnight to usher in an era of prestige and generous support for North Carolina higher education in the final two decades of the millennium. North Carolina's system of higher education was unique, Hunt postulated when we spoke, because the citizens valued higher education so greatly.

> It wasn't just me and Marc [Basnight] and Tony [Rand], but we reflected what people thought. There was no question that the people were behind the strong financial support that we provided for the university; the people understood the university's importance to our state and to the fueling of our economy.
>
> The people of this state saw their future and that of their children in having good public education that ought to be made available to people across the board in the most economical way possible. That's been a strong thread in the political life of this state.

What is so remarkable about Governor Hunt's focus on higher education is not only his own belief in its importance, but also the belief of the citizenry—something not often found across the country, where competing priorities have won out over higher education recently. Higher education seems to be fighting constant criticism about efficiency, productivity, and relevance, but Hunt's optimism epitomizes what I heard broadly about public higher education in North Carolina, and does much to explain the long-term affection and support in the state.

Aspiring Globally, Serving Locally

The UNC vision has been reflected by a number of powerful trends in the past half-century, the most prominent being its commitment to accessible education and success. The state has been a pioneer in creating options for its potential students, and the university has thrown off many restrictions on their opportunity to develop intellectually. Governor Hunt, among others, referred to the university as "a gift to the people." Through UNC's iconic support for its state's interests, and through all of its programs for the state's well-being, the university has become among the most respected anywhere in the country.

One way UNC supports the state is manifested in the proportion of in-state students it enrolls. While many of the very best public universities have 30–50 percent out-of-state enrollment, the UNC system's board of governors has established a cap of 18 percent out-of-state students that has stood since 1994. Former UNC-CH Board of Trustees Chairman Robert Winston sees this as a quintessential North Carolina feature: "We have a cap on the number of out-of-staters, so we feel more in-state, we feel more publicly owned, and so we're not this elitist kind of thing that some people think we are. Maybe we're kidding ourselves, but we do feel this publicness. And I do believe that's in the core of what we are, of who we are, and I think we'll always want to do that. I think even the people who believe, like myself, we need to raise tuition want to be real, real careful about still staying very low and making sure that the citizens of the state of North Carolina have access to this university." The commitment to access for North Carolinians is overwhelming. As the enrollment trends in figure 6.2 show, UNC has maintained the focus on educating North Carolinians consistently through the years.

FIGURE 6.2   Fall undergraduate FTE student enrollment, UNC-CH, 1987–2012

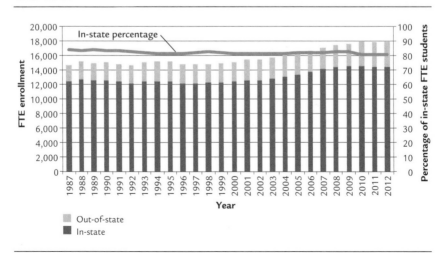

Source: University of North Carolina, fall enrollment reports, 1990–2012

The university's commitment to the state does not stop at the composition of the student body. There were, no doubt, countless individuals in the state who opposed desegregation and the civil rights movement, but over the years North Carolina institutions and their faculty and staff have been central to promoting students' rights. One such case is the famous Greensboro sit-in of 1960 by students from North Carolina Agricultural and Technical University (NC A&T), a UNC campus. A group of black students sat at a whites-only drugstore counter and ordered food, sparking a wave of such sit-ins across the segregated South and prompting an impressive student movement on campus, incorporating professors and students of all races. Such progressive support for the students' civil liberties in North Carolina was not isolated. Legendary UNC-CH basketball coach Dean Smith recruited the ACC conference's first black player in 1966, when desegregation was still a dirty word in the South. UNC President Friday called segregation "the greatest social issue we have faced in generations" and supported a number of Carolina-borne programs to encourage desegregation.[12]

Later in the 1960s, Friday supported a student movement at UNC against a policy that banned alleged communists from speaking on campus.[13] This classification, used loosely, often extended to such groups as the NAACP, all of whose members were also banned from working in the UNC system by a general assembly bill. The legislature's passage of the ban elicited a remarkable reaction; not only did students protest en masse, but speeches were held on the edge of a stone wall delineating the border of campus. Bill Friday took up the fight for an open forum on campus. The ban was lifted within the decade, thanks in no small part to the spirit and vision of UNC and its leaders. These events—from the speaker ban to the sit-in to the success of Dean Smith's recruitment policy—contributed to the atmosphere of a university of the people as much as anything else.

Higher Education Broadly in North Carolina

Unlike Virginia, where the public sector constitutes the overwhelming majority of the higher education system, the UNC campuses are not the only source of access to higher education in North Carolina. North Carolina is home to a number of renowned private institutions that educate an estimated ninety thousand students and greatly influence global research and academics (more than fifty thousand of those students are North Carolina citizens). Duke University, Wake Forest University, and Davidson College are among the most selective educational institutions in America. North

Carolina higher education has also been marked by a high degree of coop-eration between the public and private sectors, especially in research, which has only improved the state's fortune.

North Carolina's public university system has also benefited citizens who are not directly involved—one of the central tenets of higher education's claim as a public good. While the state certainly trains great researchers, its universities have found creative ways to keep them in the state. In a bold act of private-public partnership, Duke, UNC-CH, and NC State created the Research Triangle Park (RTP) in 1959, which now employs almost forty thousand state residents at preeminent STEM corporations and laboratories, such as GlaxoSmithKline and Cisco Systems. Citing the Research Triangle Park as an example, UNC President Tom Ross says North Carolinians have long shown a "clear recognition of the linkage between strong universities and economic development." Former UNC-CH Chancellor Holden Thorp points out that university research alone contributes over $1.6 billion to the state's economy. As discussed in chapter 3, economic impact studies are not always the best measure, but they do tell something about overall connection to the state. One economic impact study found that the UNC system overall contributes $8.7 billion ($10.4 billion with multiplier effects).[14]

In addition to the vision that all of North Carolina's citizens would find a higher education within reach, the research mission has also been an impor-tant element in the state's system of higher education. In 2013, UNC-CH secured $548 million in federal research funding, placing it highly among all research universities, public and private. The growth in federally funded research and development expenditures as compared to the changes in state appropriations at UNC-CH has been significant and illustrates how research has become a more prominent element in the university's three-part mission of teaching, research, and service. Using constant 2010 dollars, at UNC-CH in 1987, research funding was about $9,000 per FTE student and grew to about $22,000 per FTE student in 2010. State appropriations over the same time period shrank from $22,000 to $20,000 per FTE student.

North Carolina is also home to a large network of community colleges, which served eight hundred forty thousand students in 2011—about one in nine of the state's citizens under twenty-five years of age. The system was created on the heels of a study conducted by the general assembly in 1957, and by 1979 it operated under an independent state board with the ability to implement policy. As with the UNC Board of Governors, the governor and the general assembly appoint members to this board, which also includes the state treasurer, lieutenant governor, and a student representative. Today, fifty-eight campuses are spread out across the state so that a community college education in North Carolina can always be within a thirty-minute drive of its citizens.[15]

Though it undoubtedly focuses on a public agenda, the community college system faces demands that are quite distinct from those on UNC. These institutions exist to train and educate the work force to help them earn a sustainable living, but serve an integral role in a state where, again, the goal has been broad-based education and training. Community college programs such as North Carolina BioNetwork, which runs online and in-person programs with STEM, agricultural, and industrial institutions, help meet this demand.

The community college system's student body is largely nontraditional, with an average student age, for instance, of twenty-eight. A report prepared for the NC Tomorrow Commission, which attempted to ascertain the most pressing concerns of the state's universities, noted that from 1990 to 2005, the state's Hispanic population grew by almost 600 percent and the Asian population by almost 200 percent.[16] The educational needs for some of these groups are being met by the community colleges, through minority mentoring and professional development guidance. As the primary educators of North Carolina's college students, community colleges play a disproportionate role in the state's prosperity.

A full picture of North Carolina's higher education system would not be complete without also exploring its African American college legacy. Historically black colleges and universities (HBCUs) have deep historical roots in North Carolina—for example, NC A&T, whose students sparked the aforementioned sit-in protest, was founded in 1890 in Greensboro. It has become a leading producer of engineering, accounting, and agricultural degrees for African Americans in the nation. In fact, one-fourth of the *US News & World Report*'s top twenty HBCUs are in North Carolina; other prominent examples include Shaw and North Carolina Central University (NCCU). NCCU and NC A&T are also members of the UNC system, along with three other successful HBCUs and UNC Pembroke, an institution originally targeted toward Native Americans. While they are now open to students of all backgrounds, HBCUs have historically served traditionally underserved populations in North Carolina.

The very essence of North Carolina has been imbued into its educational systems. For years, the mutual respect between the universities and its patrons, championed by university and state leaders alike, gave rise to the quintessential public university system. And though secondary and other tertiary institutions played an important part, the heart of policy provision and conversation in the legislature lies in the UNC system. It was immune, practically until the end of the century, to elements of privatization as have been defined and discussed in this book. But the twenty-first century has caught up with North Carolina, and some of those deeply ingrained beliefs are being publicly reconsidered for the first time.

Changing of the Guard

While the Great Recession brought privatization to the fore, forces had been pushing in that direction for years. But UNC-CH and the broader UNC system survived the shrinking state funding and public support faced by most states with little impact on its finances, legislative enthusiasm, and popular support among the state's citizens. Strong leadership and the interdependence of government and university kept this in check. But with a new generation of state leaders and severe economic disruption, things are changing in North Carolina. In the legislative conflict between North Carolina's educational heritage and the twenty-first century, there is no easy victory.

Structurally, the UNC system has retained its centralized, government-defined parameters for the past several decades. The most significant changes have been in leadership. The iconic leadership that built up UNC has turned over. Governor Jim Hunt's last term ended in 2001; Marc Basnight and Tony Rand stepped down from the general assembly in 2009 and 2011, respectively. President Friday and Coach Smith have been gone for at least fifteen years, and their protégés have had successors of their own. It is a new era for North Carolina politics, and with a new generation of legislators and governors, the time is ripe for change, or so it seems.

Without its historical context, the decision to vote out an elected administration at a time of economic turmoil may seem logical; it is the trend. North Carolina is a southern state and, in presidential elections at least, it usually votes with its southern neighbors. But there is a difference. North Carolina has had only four Republican governorships since Reconstruction, and the Democrats have solidly held both legislative chambers until recently. UNC has relied on this largely single-party control and solidarity; almost all of the influential politicians mentioned have been Democrats. Carolina education has become the state's "DNA," as legislators put it, because overwhelming popular support put pro-centralization Democrats who opposed cuts to higher education into power.

The Democratic control all changed in 2010. First the general assembly and then the governorship were swept by Republicans, amid corruption scandals and the struggling economy. While this change will undoubtedly bring new ideas, some fear—perhaps without reason—that it will destabilize everything that has been built over decades in public higher education. The new officeholders express strong support for higher education, but many Democrats in the general assembly are afraid of what the historic shift in power will mean for the "People's University." There has been more discussion of autonomy and flexibility on managerial matters, but this should not be construed as a certain premonition that the system will be dismantled. The ideologies of Hunt, Rand, and Basnight echo yet in the legislative chambers in Raleigh.

Free . . . "So Far as Practicable"

Changes to UNC finances have become a major focal point in North Carolina's privatization conversation. We can split this into two trends: changes in appropriations and changes in nonstate government income. Previously, with Carolina's insistence on public service, appropriations were paramount and nonstate government income more superfluous. Tuition and philanthropy were never a dominant element in university funding, on a relative basis. Now the traditions have begun to be reworked, and the brute outcome is a drop in state support that UNC is having a hard time supplementing from other sources, both fiscally and ideologically. President Tom Ross and North Carolina Senate President Pro Tempore Philip Berger, respectively, argue the following:

> I believe that those who would support [a shift toward high tuition and low state support] lack a full understanding of the reach of the University system—or how broadly it touches and impacts North Carolina. But it also makes an invalid assumption that it's only the users who benefit, because I'm one who believes there is a wider public good that our public universities provide. I don't know that we have a lot of hard evidence that such a philosophical shift has occurred in the state. Obviously, tuition has gone up, but the relative ratio between tuition and state funding hadn't changed too dramatically in our state until the last few years when we've taken substantial budget cuts. But it's still too early to tell whether that's driven by the downturn in the

economy alone or whether it's a combination of that and a shifting philosophy about how to fund higher education. [Ross]

As we move forward, the push for greater autonomy will continue. The budget situation will not get any better, so the leveling of tuition will come a little closer to those peers. The goal that most legislators have is that we would aspire to continue to be the best public university in the country—we think we're there and we want to stay there. [Berger]

The significance of the statements by these two leaders is their uncertainty about the future. Certainly, no one can predict the future, but North Carolina is in new territory and is not familiar with the possibility that tuition might rise or autonomy might grow.

But despite the recent drastic cuts, small indicators of diminishing support have been apparent for several decades. For one, priority has shifted away from education in terms of proportion of state budget. In 1990, 16 percent of the state budget went to UNC, while Health and Human Services (HHS) received 15 percent. By 2010, UNC received about 12 percent of the state budget and HHS's proportion had swelled to 24 percent.[17] At the same time, the proportion of the UNC budget that comes from state appropriations has fallen. Total appropriations for the UNC system (calculated in 2010 dollars) were $1.1 billion in 1990 (45 percent of the system's operating budget), $2.4 billion in 2000 (37 percent of the system's operating budget), and $2.6 billion in 2010 (31 percent of the system's operating budget).

The UNC-CH campus has seen a similar pattern, with withering percentages despite growing brute appropriations. Although tuition has risen over the past few decades, the state appropriations have remained a much stronger portion of the overall revenue model at UNC-CH than most public universities across the country, as shown in figure 6.3. Clearly, tuition has grown and appropriations have declined, but compare this to the trends in Virginia and California: the difference is stark. Figure 6.4 displays the modestly growing appropriations in the state overall during the same period, which bucks the national trend of declining state appropriations over that period. Most public institutions today would consider a flat line to be a major victory, so to see appropriations actually rise over the past twenty-five years is significant.

These facts can be taken either as a glass-half-empty or glass-half-full perception. Robert Winston, former chairman of the UNC-CH Board of Trustees, tends toward the optimistic side: "[Total state] funding has gone down as a percentage, but the magnitude of the numbers is huge. The state of North

FIGURE 6.3 Total appropriations and net tuition and fees per FTE student for the University of North Carolina–Chapel Hill, 1987–2010 (in constant 2010 dollars)

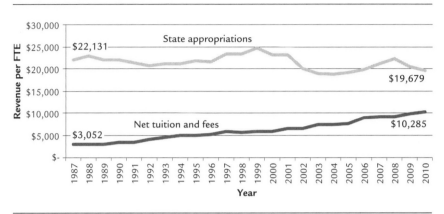

Source: Delta Cost Project dataset, 2012

Note: The fall FTE enrollment was used for FTE calculations. Constant 2010 dollars adjusted by SHEEO Higher Education Cost Adjustment (HECA).

Carolina can't keep up with our budget, my God. So that's the rallying cry, 'Oh, they don't care about us,' but when you really look at the size of the dollars and the amount of what it costs the state, I think the state has done an incredible job." Winston's portrayal of the reaction from most universities is accurate and a good reminder that higher education has seen strong support for many years in this state—it's the growth in the overall budget that very few (if any) states can keep up with over time. University leaders in other states have pointed to the recession of the early 1990s as the turning point in their universities' relationship with the state, from which point the state/university relationship changed permanently. Today, leaders in North Carolina—both in the general assembly and at UNC—are quietly wondering whether the Great Recession was the beginning of North Carolina's slide into diminished state support for public higher education.

The way forward has been debated on both ends of this relationship. One legislator told me that the general assembly isn't necessarily lessening its focus on higher education, but is shifting toward the community college system, which is seen by legislators (and many policy experts across the country) as more important to the economic well-being of the state and its people. It has also historically received far less per-student funding than the UNC system.

FIGURE 6.4   Total appropriations to the University of North Carolina–Chapel Hill, 1987–2010 (in constant 2010 dollars)

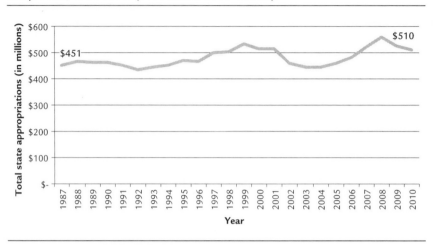

Source: Delta Cost Project dataset, 2012

Note: Constant 2010 dollars adjusted by SHEEO Higher Education Cost Adjustment (HECA).

Others assume that UNC will come under the same scrutiny as other agencies of government because its longtime protectors—Hunt, Basnight, and Rand, among others—are no longer in power, and the budget situation is severe enough that all expenses have to be carefully examined. Pat McCrory, who became governor in 2013, did not mince words when he envisioned cutting liberal arts spending to focus on degrees with immediate prospects for lucrative jobs. In 2013, he said: "If you want to take gender studies, that's fine, go to a private school and take it, but I don't want to subsidize that if that's not going to get someone a job."[18] In a state where higher education was always given preferential treatment, many saw this as a shot across the bow.

The cumulative impact on quality is now being debated at Chapel Hill, where after several years with no raises, faculty have had only slight raises in the past several years, and class sizes are increasing. And though many professors scoffed at Governor McCrory's belittling of humanities fields, the UNC system's budget proposal clearly favored STEM and agricultural fields that can produce graduates who are immediately employable in industries crucial to the state.[19] Calls from legislators for performance benchmarks and accountability are more common in the general assembly than ever before, and block funding will be more closely scrutinized.

Tuition is rising as the university has been forced to turn to the students to pay a larger share of the cost of education. UNC has had one of the lowest tuition rates of any American higher education institution, and even if tuition rises, it would still be the lowest among the top public universities, including UVA, Michigan, Berkeley, and UCLA. Tuition and fees remain tenth lowest in the country and well below the national average of $8,655. Low tuition is clearly understood as a part of the university's heritage across the state. None of the legislators or board members I interviewed advocated for anything other than low tuition (as you would expect from elected officials), and those who sought to increase it slightly added that financial aid should rise at the same rate. Of the proposed increases in tuition in recent years by the UNC-CH Board of Trustees, a considerable portion was to be allocated to the Carolina Covenant financial aid plan, which many legislators also cited as indispensable.

The main obstacle to raising tuition, however, remains the constitutional clause declaring that higher education must be free, "as far as practicable." This clause, as former State Senator Rand points out, actually guarded the university against tuition hikes two centuries after its creation: "The constitutional provision means you better not mess with tuition or you'll end up in court. On the other hand, the legislature can't try to strangle the university. The provision can be a sword or a shield, which is what's frightening." Senator Rand was always colorful, but his recognition of the either/or proposition facing public universities is better than that of most legislators, who either refused to acknowledge or failed to see how declining appropriations are usually the reason for rising tuition. However, the "free" clause is not a literal barrier against charging money for college; rather, it expresses a goal to strive for in the state.

Many legislators expressed to me that their seriousness about state support was a key factor stopping UNC from following other elite public universities in moving toward what they saw as more of a private model. Figures 6.5 and 6.6 show the changes over a decade to appropriations per FTE student and to in-state tuition and fees at the state's two- and four-year colleges and universities. The privatization effects seem more muted in North Carolina than in most states, but there is clear movement over a decade from the lower-right quadrant to the upper-left quadrant—one of the telltale signs of privatization and shifting financial models.

Intriguingly, when I interviewed them, several legislators attempted to clarify the North Carolina constitution's grammar. The most common, practical

FIGURE 6.5A   North Carolina public, two-year institutions, 2001 (in constant 2011 dollars)

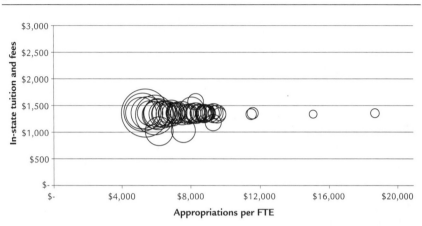

FIGURE 6.5B   North Carolina public, two-year institutions, 2011 (in constant 2011 dollars)

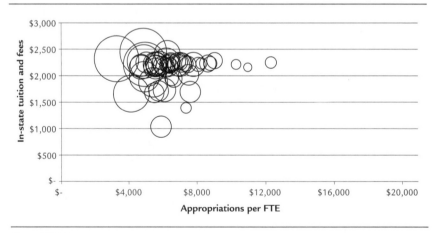

Source: IPEDS, 2012

Note: Appropriations per FTE were calculated using state appropriations divided by fall FTE enrollment. Inflation-adjusted totals were calculated using 2011 HECA. Bubble size reflects fall FTE enrollment.

FIGURE 6.6A   North Carolina public, four-year institutions, 2001 (in constant 2011 dollars)

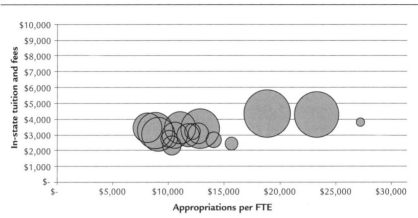

FIGURE 6.6B   North Carolina public, four-year institutions, 2011 (in constant 2011 dollars)

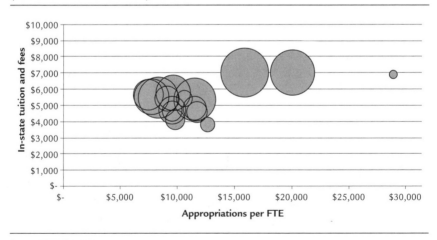

Source: IPEDS, 2012

Note: Appropriations per FTE were calculated using state appropriations divided by fall FTE enrollment. Inflation-adjusted totals were calculated using 2011 HECA. Bubble size reflects fall FTE enrollment.

understanding was that the state wants to keep tuition in the bottom quartile among its public peers. Because of the high state appropriations on a per-student basis, particularly when compared to other states, North Carolina is able to ensure low tuition, and since 2006, the board of governors has capped increases at all the UNC campuses at 6.5 percent. Exceptions to this policy are allowed only if the general assembly directs a greater increase or if an institution can "demonstrate significant unfunded need."[20] Efforts to demonstrate such unfunded needs will certainly be central to future debates about this policy.

Looking Beyond Appropriations

Funding sources other than appropriations compose a greater share of the operating budget at UNC-CH today. As figure 6.7 demonstrates, state appropriations, at least at Chapel Hill, have shrunk slightly, and now that federal research grants, tuition, and philanthropy are making an impact, fewer projects will hinge solely on what the Senate and House do in Raleigh. In 1987, tuition, philanthropy, and federally funded research together constituted about 40 percent of the institution's operating budget, and today those three make up two-thirds of the budget.

FIGURE 6.7   Appropriations, tuition, philanthropy, and federally funded research per FTE student at UNC-CH, 1987–2010 (in constant 2010 dollars)

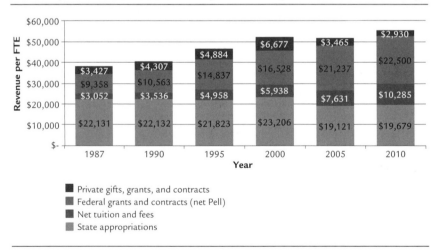

Source: Delta Cost Project dataset, 2012

Note: The fall FTE enrollment was used for FTE calculations. Constant 2010 dollars adjusted by SHEEO Higher Education Cost Adjustment (HECA).

While tuition, philanthropy, and research grants have become a larger share of the funding model for North Carolina's public institutions, appropriations remain a critical component for survival. As it recognized that the financial crisis might endure, and that the state might not restore its appropriations in the short term, UNC-CH, like many other universities, began to examine cost-cutting efforts aimed at increased efficiency and productivity. Former Chancellor Thorp, in an effort to gain the confidence of legislators who were wary of university spending and to refocus more of the operating budget on the academic core of the university, engaged Bain & Company to conduct an efficiency study, which became the "Carolina Counts" initiative. The efforts have seemingly been successful and have since been replicated at many other universities. Returning to our discussion in chapter 4 of the "business of the business," UNC-CH was able to reduce operating expenses on the administrative side in order to support the academic core.

The North Carolina public still appears to be quite supportive of higher education, regardless of the current economic or political situation. What I found in North Carolina—far more so than in Virginia or California—was a close and effective working relationship between the legislative staffers and the universities. Universities are still beloved by the people in the state, and they are very good with public relations.

As one example of the widespread support in the state, in 2011 when the newly elected legislature proposed letting expire a one-cent sales tax that would support education, in a statewide poll a whopping 78 percent of North Carolinians expressed their support for keeping the tax (the legislature let the tax expire later that year anyway).[21] And in 2001, a $3.1 billion education bond referendum passed unanimously in all one hundred North Carolina counties. Senator Fletcher Hartsell and former Senator Tony Rand both emphasized the people's overwhelming support for the bond referendum in our interviews and how a bond of that magnitude is a remarkable sign of support. Then UNC President Molly Corbett Broad felt it epitomized the Carolina legacy: "The biggest bond campaign ever in the history of American higher education passed in all one hundred counties, with three out of four voters approving it. What it did was tap into this belief on the part of the citizens that they had a great university that they wanted to continue to nurture and support, and they wanted their children and their grandchildren to have the opportunity that most of them never had."

Though North Carolina has seen a shift in higher education funding over the past twenty-plus years, the level of state funding has been so high that the "wave chart" for North Carolina (see figure 6.8) demonstrates that the volatility of state appropriations over time has been more muted in North Carolina than in many other states, and shows the state's commitment to keeping tuition low. The kind of consistency this chart illustrates is something the old guard of highly government-sponsored higher education holds on to. One such leader, former Governor Hunt, defends the state's past and issues a warning for revolutionaries: "We've had ups and downs as every state has, but the idea of being able to economically attend the state university has been very deep in the fabric of this state, and the idea of trying to change the nature of those universities so they can easily raise tuition arouses strong opposition." ·

Access: A Vision for All in the State

UNC is epitomized by longtime president Frank Porter Graham's hope that it "would light up the heavens of the commonwealth . . . for the poorest youth . . . an outpost of light and liberty among all the frontiers of mankind."[22] Continuing widespread access to public higher education in North

FIGURE 6.8 Public FTE student enrollment, educational appropriations, and total educational revenue per FTE student, North Carolina, fiscal years 1987–2012 (in constant 2012 dollars)

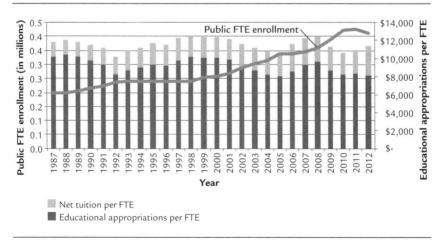

Net tuition per FTE

Educational appropriations per FTE

Source: SHEEO, 2013

Note: Constant 2012 dollars adjusted by SHEEO Higher Education Cost Adjustment (HECA). Educational appropriations include ARRA funds.

Carolina is closely tied to the financial and demographic situations. Until recently, funding was not a serious problem, and State Representative Rick Glazier suggests that it was taken for granted by some in the state: "The commitment was across party lines, and it was just unshakable—both at the executive level and at the legislative level. The debates were never what the universities were going to get."

Former UNC President Erskine Bowles and the UNC Board of Governors undertook a statewide tour in 2007 to listen to the state's citizens and to ensure both that the university remained a central priority for the state and that it remained connected to the state's needs. A state commission of institutional leaders, as well as business, government, and other education and nonprofit leaders—called the UNC Tomorrow Commission—was charged with "learning what the people of North Carolina need from their University and making relevant recommendations to the UNC Board of Governors."[23] The commission offered an opportunity for even deeper input from across the state about the future of the system, and, in turn, each campus, including Chapel Hill.

The commission's findings fell into seven major categories: global readiness, access, improving K–12 education, economic development, health, the environment, and outreach and engagement by each of the seventeen UNC campuses—their local, regional, and statewide connections. After the commission presented its findings to the UNC Board of Governors, each campus had an opportunity to consider how it might best respond to the challenges presented in the commission's report. Rather than isolating themselves in the ivory tower, the leaders of UNC have continually reached out not only to the state legislature, but also to the citizens of the state, time and again.

In more recent years, however, reaching out to the citizens of the state has to be done in the context of immediate revenue needs. One recent proposal was to make the 18 percent out-of-state enrollment cap a systemwide average rather than a mandate for each campus, which would allow Chapel Hill to increase revenue with out-of-state enrollment. Counting international students as in-state residents has also been an idea suggested toward the same end. Unsurprisingly, though, these proposals have been met coldly by legislators. UNC's historic state priorities are in conflict here with the globalizing nature of higher education because public higher education is seen first and foremost as helping to educate the state's citizens.

The reality is that North Carolina is facing the same pressures as Virginia and California and the same effects of shifting appropriations that other public universities have been grappling with for more than twenty years. But interestingly, North Carolina's history of a strong commitment to higher education has supported an unusually optimistic outlook by university leaders, who are seldom publicly critical of their state government (not a single university leader offered the familiar "we used to get x percent of our budget from the state, but now we only get y percent"). One UNC Board of Governors member qualified the recent downturn in state appropriations in the general assembly as "more of an adjustment and cost reduction than a long-term change in the commitment to higher education." Nobody dared compare the privatization trend to that in Virginia, California, or other states, and many legislators seem to believe that as soon as the economy turns around, funding for UNC will return to historic levels, because that is the will of the people. One legislator suggested that the crisis has "actually gotten [the system] more connected to the state." Maybe and maybe not, but the forces that built up North Carolina's system of higher education are hard to ignore.

Public Mission and the Public Good in North Carolina

When the University of North Carolina graduated its first students in 1798, its mission and vision were clear; it aspired to educate North Carolina's sons (and later daughters) and to ensure that the enlightened spirit that began with the American Revolution would continue to pervade the state. More than two hundred years later, the campus in Chapel Hill and the larger system of higher education across the state maintain a central focus on serving the original public mission, even though higher education is no longer quite as "free" as it once was. As the twenty-first century brings new challenges for public universities across the country, North Carolina must grapple anew with what it means to focus on the needs and interests of the state and its people. It must also aggressively identify new ways to finance its colleges and universities. Whether these two priorities can be balanced in the years ahead will determine how the forces of privatization affect North Carolina.

There are many fears among those in the state that the treasured university, held in such high esteem by so many in the legislature and broadly in the state, may not continue to flourish if it receives consistently lower levels of funding. There are several paths that other states with great public universities have taken, and North Carolina will have to find its own way of balancing institutional needs, system goals, and the public mission to serve the wider public good. Gene Nichol, director of the UNC Center on Poverty,

Work & Opportunity, makes the case that North Carolina is different and must be different if it is to remain true to its public mission:

> Our commitment to public obligation is, of course, contested. It is contested at home—on many parts of the campus. It is contested nationally—as many of our strongest competitors opt to emulate the privates. It is even contested in national rankings—which penalize universities that keep tuition low, favor resident students, and match their research efforts to the pressing demands of their communities. But unless we are to abandon the charge of democracy, and assume, like much of the rest of the academy, that real opportunity lies only for the already privileged, the need for great public universities is stronger now than at any time in our history.

Nichol, who is also a former dean of the UNC Law School, emphasized strongly the need to stay focused on issues where the public university—even more so than private peers—has a mission and charge to maintain in support of the state's and nation's core interests, such as democracy, access, and opportunity.

In the rush toward national and international exposure in higher education, there is always a temptation to lose sight of the public mission that great public universities are called upon to serve. At his inauguration, UNC-CH Chancellor Holden Thorp spoke of the balance between local and global as a prerequisite for national and international success: "Throughout our history, our leaders have held true to a concept so bold, so audacious, and so challenging—to aspire to global academic eminence while focusing our teaching and our service on North Carolina's students and people. We're the university of 'both—and': both academic prominence and a commitment to our state."[24] The description Thorp uses of "both—and" summarizes so well how public higher education in North Carolina has always faced, and seemingly balanced, the tension between national and global interests with local needs.

The long-term impacts and effects of privatization will not be known for many years, particularly because the commitment to public universities has been so strong for so long in North Carolina. There are certainly elements of concern for many lawmakers, but there is no evidence of any diminution of the public agenda for higher education in the state. In my interview with President Friday, he concluded that it is precisely the conditions that North Carolina has created that lead to a continued strong union between the state and higher education, and he believed increased privatization would be a tough sell in the state:

Ever since the founding of the place, there has been this constant effort to relate the institution to the well-being of the people, in the interest of the people. For example, after World War II, we had the highest rate of rejection of servicemen in the U.S. for poor health. That led to the Good Health Movement, which was a statewide organization that mobilized the university family. That resulted in building a school of medicine, nursing, and public health. The institution is positioned in the hearts of the citizens.

I don't believe this university will ever move away from the benefits and connection to the citizens of the state. When you have a system that reaches from the mountains to the sea, you've got a strong base where everyone in the state is affected by the university. They see the face of the institution in the life of the state. I don't think anyone would dare advocate to further privatize our university.

President Friday's description of the way the citizens see the "face of the institution in the life of the state" is the essence of a public mission, yet I tried (unsuccessfully) to explain to him how elements of privatization do not have to change that bond because a public-private partnership can still maintain the same focus.

The state of North Carolina has built a strong history of public institutions serving the public good, including access and low tuition—but more broadly than just that constitutional definition. There are those who would aim to achieve the level of autonomy at other great public universities—especially while facing similar challenges in funding its future success—but the circumstances, leaders, and history are quite different from other states. UNC-CH demonstrates how a rise to prominence and early effects of privatization can have little impact on its public mission in any meaningful way, at least in the short term. As they navigate increased privatization together, UNC-CH and the state of North Carolina continue their long history and mutual commitment to meet each other's needs and to serve the public good. Once again, the history and state context in North Carolina prove more powerful than forces of autonomy and finance.

Next, we move across the country to explore California's system of public higher education and the impacts of privatization in the Golden State.

CHAPTER SEVEN

The Master Plan Meets Privatization

The tax which will be paid for [the] purpose [of education] is not more than the thousandth part of what will be paid to kings, priests and nobles who will rise up among us if we leave the people in ignorance.

—Thomas Jefferson[1]

The best investment that any society makes is in the education of its young people, and this shouldn't basically be looked upon myopically as a "cost"; it should be looked upon as the best investment that any society can make.

—Clark Kerr[2]

LANDING IN SACRAMENTO late on an August afternoon, I wanted desperately to get to my hotel and go to sleep. My flight had been delayed several hours at Dulles Airport in Washington, and the five hours I'd spent in the middle seat had proven to be the extent of my patience. I had scheduled twenty-five interviews with legislators and staff over the course of three days, and I needed every minute of sleep to maintain my energy through the marathon meetings. I finally made my way through the airport to the taxi stand and collapsed into the back seat of a cab, asking in my nicest voice to be taken to the Marriott downtown and hoping my facial expression was clear: *I really don't have the energy to talk with you, so please just drive me to my hotel.* But the message was not delivered, apparently.

"First time to California?" asked the driver. I politely said no, I had been to California many times, though this was my first trip to Sacramento. He proceeded to tell me many virtuous and fine features of the city and clearly didn't pick up on my exhaustion, so I decided to give up and be a bit friendlier. He asked why I had come to town, and I gave him the short answer (by this point I had learned that very few people were interested in the long answer about privatization in higher education and its impacts on the public good). "I'm writing a book about higher education and how legislators see the future for colleges and universities."

"Really?" said the driver, moderately more excited now that I was engaging in conversation. "I came here from Mexico twenty-two years ago and went to Sacramento City College [a community college] and paid just a few bucks per class. I have two kids now in third and sixth grades, and I send them to private schools because the public schools are so bad. I'm really worried about what the colleges will be like when they are older." At this point, I put my researcher's hat firmly on my head and started inquiring a bit more. It didn't take more than one question to get him talking about the "useless" legislators in California who "just can't get their act together. If they don't do something soon, the whole state will be in the tank." Welcome to California and all its complexity.

California is the largest, most diverse, and, I would argue, most complex state in the union, and when California catches a cold, the rest of the country sneezes. My initial goal in focusing on three states in-depth was to pick states with vast differences, and California is as different from Virginia and North Carolina as one can imagine—geographically, politically, and historically. The story of higher education in California is relatively short, but it holds great influence on what is happening across the nation.

The history of higher education in California has been well documented, and I will not attempt to retell it. For well-researched and well-written background, you can start with Patrick M. Callan, longtime policy leader and president of the Higher Education Policy Institute, and John Aubrey Douglass, the renowned UC Berkeley professor and historian of California higher education.[3] Instead, I will focus on California today and how broader policy decisions have impacted the future of higher education in the state. From the legislative perspective, this is an extremely complex state, and the politics of California's funding model require deeper exploration because it speaks to how higher education is coming to be seen as more of a private good than a public one. Privatization is relatively new in the lexicon of California legislators, but the state is facing the same financial and political pressures as the rest of the country, and the relationship with its universities is necessarily beginning to evolve—particularly at the flagship University of California, Berkeley.

The California Master Plan: Fifty Years Later, Much Has Changed

The University of California was one of the many offspring created from the sale of lands given to the state by the federal government through the 1862 Morrill Act. In 1879, at the state's constitutional convention, the California higher education system was reorganized. Due to the fear of corrupt legislators, the California higher education system was written into the new constitution, autonomous from the legislature. This allowed the university to craft a unique and differentiated mission for its various institutions. "The California Idea" had its roots in the Progressive era—the idea was that higher education was no longer a privilege, but a right for every citizen. During the 1920s, California became the first state to pass community college legislation, and the tripartite division of the three segments of higher education was created.[4]

With a widely dispersed population, the higher education system grew slowly at first, but by the 1930s, it had become clear that a state as large and populous as California would need greater coordination. In 1932, the state legislature commissioned a study by the Carnegie Foundation for the Advancement of Teaching that found great dysfunction and a lack of clear policy in a state that was largely driven by local interests and politicians: "There is a lack of articulation among the various units of the educational system. This has resulted in vigorous controversies over admission requirements, transfer regulations, and curricula. These controversies are aggravated by regional rivalries and local ambitions."[5]

The end of World War II, the GI Bill, and significant in-migration to California further exacerbated the uncoordinated growth of higher education in the state. Without an overarching policy framework, the dysfunction continued because the only policy tools were legislative studies (not unlike Virginia). In 1957, Clark Kerr took over as president of the University of California and recognized that the state was facing a "tidal wave of students."[6] He urged the legislature to take up the issue of coordination. Assemblywoman Dorothy Donahoe seized on the issue and helped to instigate the commission that would lead to the creation of the Master Plan. Though today it would likely take years and hundreds of hearings, a small commission of leaders from public and private higher education hammered out the Master Plan in six months and presented it to the legislature in 1960 for approval. In April 1960, Governor Edmund "Pat" Brown Sr. (father of the current Governor Edmund "Jerry" Brown Jr.) signed the legislation, the California Master Plan for Higher Education. California's accomplishment was truly ground-breaking, as Pat Callan explains: "The true genius of the Master Plan was that California was the first state and really the first government entity anywhere in the world to promise access to higher education to any adult who could benefit from it. That sounds kind of tame now, but no one had ever done that before."

Clark Kerr is given much of the credit for the Master Plan, but in reality he was only one of many players involved in shaping it. John Douglass describes the unique goals of the Master Plan as the "California Idea." The Master Plan set out to do something no other state had been able to accomplish: create broad access so that higher education was within the reach of *every* citizen (not just the privileged few), maintain clearly differentiated missions for three levels of higher education, and create a very high-quality system of higher education that was affordable and expandable as the population grew.[7] Community colleges were to be spread across the state and to provide a first opportunity for entry into higher education. They were perceived as "democracy colleges," because they spread education to students who would normally not have that opportunity.[8]

The differentiation between missions allowed for clarity of roles, and articulation and transfer agreements between the segments allowed for a true "system" of higher education, very rare in the United States. Other states had been successful with one or two of these goals, but never accomplished all of them. Most states had been unable to overcome the turf wars between colleges and universities, and getting to true mission differentiation seemed impossible. High-quality education and broad access were rarely seen as compatible goals, and this made California unusual in its approach. While the focus of this chapter is largely about higher education in the state and the flagship campus of the University of California, Berkeley, the campus, the UC system, and the three segments of higher education have been intertwined for quite some time and are not easily separated in discussing public policy and finance.

Very few remember the full title of the Master Plan—*A Master Plan for Higher Education in California, 1960–1975*—which was intended to be a fifteen-year view of the higher education system, not an eternal document.

Steve Weiner, the late education activist who held senior roles at Stanford, UC Berkeley, and the UC system, emphasized the Master Plan's limits: "I believe the Master Plan was a good thing, but it shouldn't be glorified. It was a political deal. We get these students, you get those students, we get the doctorate, you don't get the doctorate. That's what it was and, again, the state only had so many resources so it needed to be smarter with them. It couldn't build a university in every state senator's district." The importance of Weiner's view on the Master Plan is that the deal, so to speak, was not divine; it was crafted by policy makers and administrators with a goal of coordinating something that was uncoordinated. During my travels through California, however, every legislator would quote the Master Plan as a guiding light, the North Star, the foundation of any discussion about higher education. Over time, I came to see that very few truly understood what was included in the Master Plan or really appreciated what its creators thought was necessary for it to succeed. Like North Carolina legislators describing the constitutional mandate, California legislators would look to the Master Plan as the Gospel and Clark Kerr as a disciple.

What would be required, however, to maintain this extraordinary system over the generations were two elements that could not be guaranteed forever: significant resources and political commitment to the goals laid out at inception. Indeed, California's last decade has seen one of the most dramatic economic transformations of any state in the union, and the fortunes of higher education have dramatically shifted. When I asked what has changed the most in the last two decades in California, no legislator or university administrator would discuss policy; instead, they all would point to the shift in funding. Figure 7.1 shows the historic funding in the state for higher education, which has been significant over time but recently took a nosedive; likewise, figure 7.2 shows the historic funding for UC Berkeley, which has been a roller coaster over the past twenty-five years, particularly the most recent few years. Beyond just a problem of money, I will explain in this chapter how the policy that underlies the funding change—and other elements of privatization—is largely a result of the people's decisions using the proposition voting system in the state.

The Laws of Unintended Consequences

In California, in addition to electing their state legislators, voters can also propose laws that can be voted on directly by the electorate, essentially bypassing the legislature. The state created a referendum system in its constitution in

FIGURE 7.1   Total California higher education appropriations, 1987–2012 (in constant 2012 dollars)

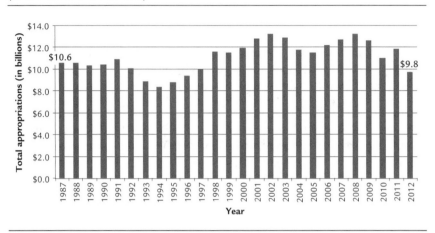

Source: SHEEO, 2013

Note: Constant 2012 dollars adjusted by SHEEO Higher Education Cost Adjustment (HECA). Education appropriations include ARRA funds.

1849, and the ballot initiative system (best known for the "proposition" initiatives) was introduced in 1911.

The beauty of such a system is that the voters can take their issues directly to the people and avoid some of the mess of democracy, where issues are debated endlessly and sometimes the majority party won't bring an item up for a vote. Depending on your disposition toward representative government, the challenge of such a system is that issues can be brought to the voters that significantly alter the revenue base available to the legislature. California voters have now enacted so many changes in their laws that it is difficult to find good, overarching public policy that focuses on the broad issues facing the state and its citizenry. In some ways, the story of California's system of higher education is one of unintended consequences and benign neglect. California Assemblywoman Susan Bonilla describes how a series of ballot initiatives have led to unintended consequences for one of the country's greatest systems of higher education: "Sometimes it's hard to see everything in context when it's just an individual ballot initiative. So you're not seeing how it is interplaying with everything else you already voted for and what are going to be the consequences. So there's certainly an irony, but I think it's not uncommon that when you reach a place and time where people begin to take for granted something like our university system and our community college system that

FIGURE 7.2   Total appropriations to the University of California, Berkeley, 1987–2010 (in constant 2010 dollars)

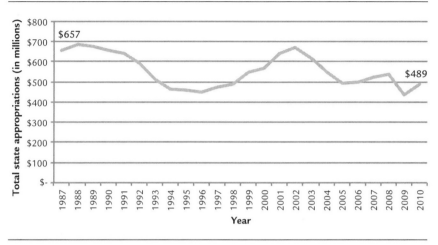

Source: Delta Cost Project dataset, 2012

Note: Constant 2010 dollars adjusted by SHEEO Higher Education Cost Adjustment (HECA).

has such incredible access that when it's taken for granted you deprioritize it, whether through deliberate action or through kind of an apathy or just by neglect." Assemblywoman Bonilla speaks to a significant underlying problem in California—higher education has been "deprioritized" and when that happens, it doesn't matter if it was deliberate or by accident.

Proposition 13 (1978)

California's state constitution focuses extensively on public K–12 education and higher education—unlike the U.S. Constitution, which makes no mention of education whatsoever. Article IX of the California constitution provides very clear information about education at all levels. It begins: "A general diffusion of knowledge and intelligence being essential to the preservation of the rights and liberties of the people, the Legislature shall encourage by all suitable means the promotion of intellectual, scientific, moral, and agricultural improvement." This almost Jeffersonian description of the need for a widely educated population gives a strong framework for educational funding and support—so long as it remains a priority.

In the late 1960s, a California citizen brought a lawsuit against the state, alleging that the method of funding public K–12 education failed to meet the requirements of the equal protection clause of the Fourteenth Amendment of the United States Constitution and the California constitution. Because the financing of school districts depended on local property taxes, John Serrano, the parent of a Los Angeles public school student, sued Ivy Baker Priest, the state treasurer, noting that some parents would have to pay a higher tax rate than those in other school districts if they wanted their children to get an equal education.

Serrano v. Priest essentially argued that, in California, an education is a fundamental constitutional right set forth in the California constitution, unlike in the U.S. Constitution and most other state constitutions. If it is a fundamental constitutional right, then is it a denial of equal protection under the law when a student in one community gets a dramatically different allocation of funding to support his education than a similarly situated student in the community right next door, with the only difference being the level of property tax wealth in the second community? In 1971, the California courts said yes. Joe Simitian, a former state senator who left office in 2012 due to term limits, explains the impact of *Serrano v. Priest*—and, later, Propositions 13 and 98—on education in the state: "That means, then, that the state has to step in and play a role in terms of equalizing. So the word *equalization* is a big one in California school finance, 'step in and equalize.' Couple that with Prop 13, that pushes down the whole level of funding availability. Put the two together, and California as a state is much more involved in financing K–12 instruction than other states might be." Senator Simitian's description of "equalizing" is an important concept in the history of state funding for education and was another step in the history of finance and public policy in the state.

Following *Serrano v. Priest*, the antitax revolution of the late 1970s and early 1980s that swept President Reagan into office was quite active in California.[9] In 1978, Californians amended their constitution through the initiative process by passing Proposition 13, officially named the *People's Initiative to Limit Property Taxation*. Prop 13, as it came to be called, lowered property taxes by setting property values at their 1975 value and then restricting annual increases of assessed value to an inflation factor that was not to exceed 2 percent per year. The only circumstances under which a new baseline value could be created were a change in ownership or completion of new construction. Prop 13 required adherence to the legislative mandate to equalize school taxes and funds. With equalization, wealthier communities would have lost out in property value, while poorer districts would have gained.[10] Similar propositions had sprung up in 1968 and 1972, but both failed; one major contributing factor in the passage of Prop 13 was the verdict in the *Serrano* case.[11]

The citizens of California, particularly older voters who had lived in their homes for a long time, voted overwhelmingly to pass the ballot initiative. These voters believed they should not be priced out of their homes by high taxes. Assemblyman Tim Donnelly, who rode the 2010 Tea Party wave into the state assembly, agreed with those voters and shared with me his perspective on why Prop 13 was a good thing for homeowners and the state: "Prop 13 limited how much property tax you could steal from people. And I say 'steal from people' because when Prop 13 was instituted, there were people who were paying unbelievable rates because it was a progressive rate, and it was confiscatory. And all it did was limit it to what almost every other state has. But the problem is, they always tie it to higher education. The problem is not that we don't have revenues. The problem is we're chasing that increment of growth that we used to have." Assemblyman Donnelly's perspective is important because he vocalizes what I heard from many of the newly elected legislators, who see the problem as one of the state spending too much rather than not having enough revenue.

Just as the Taxpayer's Bill of Rights (TABOR) in Colorado (described in chapter 4) fundamentally altered the tax base and financial support for higher education, so, too, did Prop 13 in California. In addition to decreasing property taxes, the initiative also required a two-thirds majority in both legislative houses for future increases of any state tax rates or amounts of revenue collected, including income taxes. It is nearly impossible in any legislature or the federal government to get a two-thirds majority in the polarized political state we are in today.

Former Assemblywoman Dion Aroner, who represented Berkeley until 2003 when term limits forced her out of the state assembly, talked about how Prop 13 took power away from local districts and placed it in the hands of the state assembly:

> Many public policy makers trace the beginning of the state's fiscal problems all the way back to Proposition 13. Everything pretty much does go back to that because a reversal took place then in regards to property taxes. Something that the voters at that time no more understood than a hole in the wall was they gave all the power to the state legislature, as opposed to local jurisdictions, over K–12 and local governments' financing. Everybody thought that they were voting to simply protect senior homeowners who wanted to be

assured they would not be pushed out of their homes by rising property taxes reflecting rising property values. They had no idea what was in the rest of the ballot measure. Specifically, that it required a two-thirds vote of the legislature to raise taxes. Our educational system in this state has never recovered from Prop 13.

Assemblywoman Aroner points again to the law of unintended consequences where, as you might imagine, voters were not thinking about the impact on social services or higher education in voting to hold down property tax increases, but that is exactly what happened. Privatization is almost never the result of intentional decisions to go down that path, and California's recent history shows how the unintended consequences of legislative and citizen-led actions can have a long-term deleterious effect on higher education. Proposition 13 diminished one of the state's primary revenue sources, the property tax, and that had an immediate impact on funding for many statewide interests.

Perceived government inefficiency and waste, not a desire to limit government services, drove the passage of Prop 13. By the late 1970s, the state had accumulated a surplus that would have reached $10 billion if Prop 13 had not passed, but state and local governments did not cut taxes, so the voters took matters into their own hands. Prior to the 1978 vote on Prop 13, 38 percent of the California electorate believed that the state and local governments could absorb a 40 percent cut in tax revenue without cutting services. People did not vote for a cut in services, but this quickly became the result, and user fees for various government services increased substantially.[12]

During the course of the research for this book, when I asked whether the state had changed its prioritization of higher education or whether there was just a money problem, nearly every person believed that if the state had more money, it would put it back into funding higher education. Many legislators believe, as Aroner articulated, that Prop 13 was the beginning of the end for California's Golden Era. Charles Reed, the longtime chancellor of the California State University system, believes that "California made a fatal mistake in its passage of Prop 13. And mentally, I think, the political leadership and the people of California thought that you could get something for nothing." Those who work in the three segments of higher education in the state often used this phrase in describing what has happened to support for higher education, and they often ended by stating that there is no free ride with education. The California "wave chart" (figure 7.3) shows that the changes over

FIGURE 7.3 Public FTE student enrollment, educational appropriations, and total educational revenue per FTE student, California, 1987–2012 (in constant 2012 dollars)

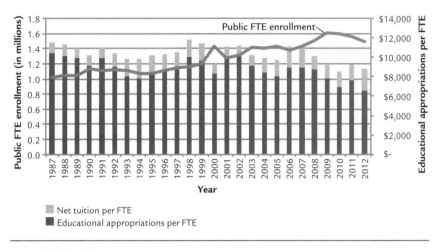

Net tuition per FTE
Educational appropriations per FTE

Source: SHEEO, 2013

Note: Constant 2012 dollars adjusted by SHEEO Higher Education Cost Adjustment (HECA). Educational appropriations include ARRA funds.

twenty-five years in appropriations for higher education, tuition, and enrollment have not been a pretty picture for the state's system of public higher education and funding has not kept pace with the significant increase in enrollment.

There is, however, strong political support for higher education among the state assembly members in California stretching back to the Master Plan's inception. Very few legislators I met during the course of interviews actually wanted to roll support for higher education further back. But there is a real conundrum in the state. One legislative analyst said, "Legislators seem to have a universal feeling that they want to support higher education and they believe in higher education. What Prop 13 did, at least to a large extent, was took away some of their ability to fund the discretionary elements of the budget—particularly higher education." Here, as in Virginia and North Carolina, as a discretionary item in the budget, higher education often loses out to the mandatory expenses.

The essential function of any legislature, however, is to set priorities for spending, and while it is easy to blame every one of California's budget woes on Prop 13, some legislators believe that they have not done their duty. Politicians across the country are seeing their approval ratings declining (one poll shows them lower than cockroaches!) and a major reason cited is that they are not working together to solve problems and make hard decisions. Assemblywoman Kristin Olsen puts much of the responsibility on her fellow legislators to set those priorities and get things done.

> I think it's so easy to point fingers at Prop 13, the budget crisis, the economic decline, and the job market as reasons or excuses as to why we can no longer fund education. But the fact of the matter is we have x number of resources, and it's our job as legislators to decide how we're going to spend that pot of money. Whether it's $10 or $10 million, how are we going to spend that pot of money? It's about setting priorities.
>
> While Prop 13 certainly relates to the resources we may or may not have in the general fund, the fact is it's been lost since 1978, and it's only more recently that we have scaled back in a significant way our investment in public universities. So I think to say that it's because of Prop 13 is a red herring.

Assemblywoman Olsen is correct that even after the passage of Prop 13, public funding for higher education remained high, far above that of most of the other states. Over time, however, Prop 13 has taken a toll on social services across the state and had a dramatic impact on higher education. And a decade later, another proposition would change the available funding sources for colleges and universities.

Proposition 98 (1988)

As I researched this book, I occasionally confronted a decision or action taken by a legislator, a legislature, a governor, a university, or a state and scratched my head, because it seemed so clearly not to be in the interest of the public good. I kept a sticky note on my desk with the words, "All politics is local," to remind me that not every decision is made in the interests of the common good—and that visions of the common good quite often clash. There are many instances of such decisions in this book, but it bears reminding again in the case of California. Proposition 13 succeeded in holding down property taxes, but it had a significantly deleterious effect on local public schools, which relied on those property taxes for funding. In an attempt to remedy this situation, the people brought forth and voted on a ballot initiative, but they again created consequential changes to higher education funding.

Proposition 98, the Classroom Instructional Improvement and Account-ability Act, was passed in 1988. It was a direct result of Proposition 13, and it required that a minimum percentage of the state budget be spent on K–12 education and guaranteed an annual increase for K–12 education in the Cal-ifornia budget based on three tests, rough economic barometers used to dic-tate funding increases. The first test, in the early years, required spending on education to constitute 39 percent of the state budget. During years of strong economic growth, Prop 98 requires that spending on education equal the previous year's spending plus an adjustment for per capita growth and stu-dent enrollment. In years of weak economic growth, Prop 98 guarantees the prior year's spending plus an adjustment for enrollment growth, increases for any changes in per capita general fund revenues, and an increase of 0.5 per-cent in state general funds.

A primary goal of the California Master Plan was to create more seamless coordination between the three higher education segments and to more ef-fectively differentiate the segments' missions. One of the major regrets that legislators expressed to me was higher education's lack of coordination with the K–12 system, and some had hoped that Prop 98 might create closer con-nections with the higher education system—or, at the very least, between the K–12 system and the community colleges. Gary K. Hart, a former state sena-tor and secretary of education, shared, "I've always felt there is a huge gap be-tween higher education and K–12—especially concerning sharing of student data, curriculum, and effective teaching practices. Coordination on these critical subjects is missing and compromises our ability to improve student performance especially in K–12." Unfortunately, one impact of both Prop 13 and Prop 98 was to put the K–12 and higher education segments in direct competition with one another for resources. The more that was dictated for K–12, the less discretionary funding there was available for higher education.

More than one legislator said—off the record—that every single member of the state assembly has a K–12 school in his or her district, but not all of them have a college or university, so it is much easier to support Prop 98 in theory. Because, after all, who is against schools? But higher education is seen as an easy target because it's easier to raise tuition than raise taxes. Figure 7.4 shows how tuition at UC Berkeley has risen over the past twenty-five years as state appropriations have declined, and the two are now almost equal. Prop 98, by definition, mandates how nearly half of the state budget is to be spent each year before legislators even begin discussing priorities.

FIGURE 7.4   Total appropriations and net tuition and fees per FTE student for UC-Berkeley, 1987–2010 (in constant 2010 dollars)

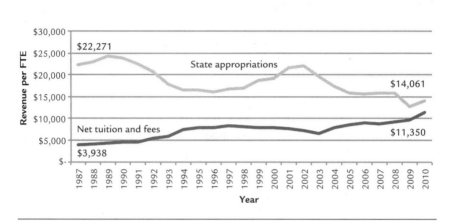

Source: Delta Cost Project dataset, 2012

Note: The fall FTE enrollment was used for FTE calculations. Constant 2010 dollars adjusted by SHEEO Higher Education Cost Adjustment (HECA).

Proposition 98 underfunded community colleges by $2.7 billion during the decade from 1990 to 2000. It was supposed to create a minimum funding level for K–12 schools and community colleges (specifically, 10.93 percent of all Prop 98 funds were supposed to go to community colleges). However, since the money has dried up, the legislators suspend that portion of the education code in most years and shift the reduced funds to K–12 districts. This creates a rivalry between the K–12 and community college sectors (which is true in a growing number of states, but particularly severe in California because of these laws). In 2001, community colleges served 1.6 million students a year—70 percent of the total number of college students in California—and a good majority of these students are low income or minority, and are primarily Hispanic and African American. Since 2008, the total budget reduction for community colleges stands at 12 percent, or $809 million.[13]

One way of conceiving of the effects of privatization is the shift on the continuum from public to private financial support. Figures 7.5 and 7.6 show the changes in one decade for the community colleges and the four-year institutions in California. Over that decade, you can see the move toward less funding per student and more tuition. Because of the unique funding model in California, the community colleges have fared far better than the

FIGURE 7.5A   California public, two-year institutions, 2001 (in constant 2011 dollars)

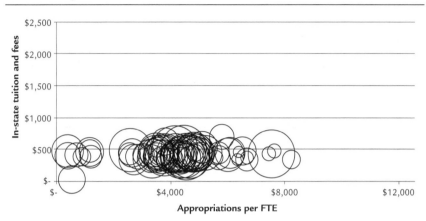

FIGURE 7.5B   California public, two-year institutions, 2011 (in constant 2011 dollars)

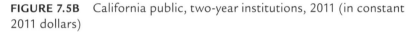

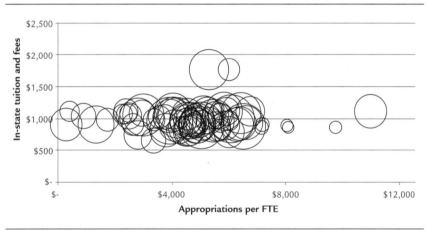

Source: IPEDS, 2012

Note: Appropriations per FTE were calculated using state appropriations divided by fall FTE enrollment. Inflation-adjusted totals were calculated using 2011 HECA. Bubble size reflects fall FTE enrollment.

FIGURE 7.6A California public, four-year institutions, 2001 (in constant 2011 dollars)

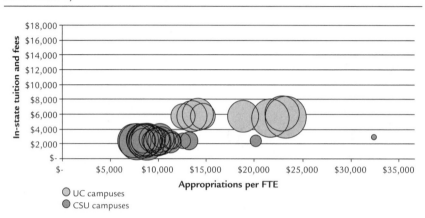

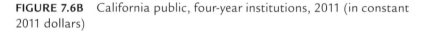

FIGURE 7.6B California public, four-year institutions, 2011 (in constant 2011 dollars)

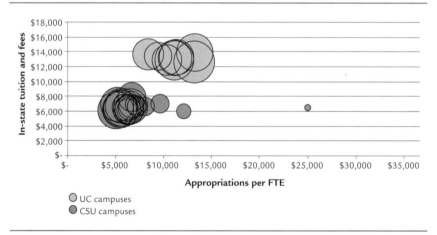

Source: IPEDS, 2012

Note: Appropriations per FTE were calculated using state appropriations divided by fall FTE enrollment. Inflation-adjusted totals were calculated using 2011 HECA. Bubble size reflects fall FTE enrollment.

four-year institutions, and both have done better than many other states where the cuts have been even more dramatic. These figures also show how affordable the California institutions are relative to the two other case studies presented in this book. Nonetheless, the movement on the scale is still noticeable from higher appropriations and lower tuition toward higher tuition and lower appropriations.

Once again, a ballot initiative achieved a very popular goal that the voters had championed and approved, thus altering the state constitution. However, because it mandated levels of spending on K–12 public education, the legislature had less flexibility in determining spending levels for all its other priorities. Subsequent legislative and initiative actions would continue to limit the levels of funding available for higher education, which is discretionary spending in most states, including California. One final example of unintended consequences in the state focuses not on taxes, but on prisons.

Three Strikes Law (1994)

In 1974, Texas enacted mandatory life sentences for repeat criminals, and by the early 1990s, a number of states decided to follow suit. Most states require one or more of three felony convictions to be for violent crimes in order for the mandatory sentence to be pronounced. In 1994, California enacted a three strikes law and mandated a minimum sentence of twenty-five years to life if the first two felonies were deemed to be either "serious" or "violent." But California did not require the third "strike" to be serious or violent to qualify for a life sentence, and people could easily be given this enhanced sentence for minor infractions. And in California, more crimes qualified as serious or violent than in other states. There are differing opinions about the effectiveness of the law, but overall, violent crimes decreased, and the crime rate was significantly lower than it was before the law was enacted.[14]

Once again, voters believed they had solved a significant problem. Because the three strikes law prescribed mandatory sentences, however, by definition it mandated more funding for incarceration. Just as Proposition 98 had done, this law further restricted the pool of funding available for higher education. Today, the state's corrections budget exceeds its higher education spending.[15] From 2000 to 2010, the University of California's appropriation has decreased from $2.25 billion to $1.6 billion. The allocation to prisons, on the other hand, has increased from $5 billion to $11 billion. California spends $50,000 per year per prisoner and less than one-tenth that amount on university students.[16]

Term Limits: "Get Me Off This Dog!"

California's is one of just ten state legislatures that the National Conference of State Legislatures classifies as full-time. These states require the most time of legislators, usually 80 percent or more of a full-time job (even though part-time legislatures still work significant hours outside of session). In these states, legislators have large staffs, and they are paid enough to make a living without outside income. These legislatures are more similar to the U.S. Congress than are the other state legislatures where legislators tend to have other, full-time employment and do not spend the entire year in the state capitol.

Some idealistic versions of the founding fathers' views of the "citizen legislator" recount that the founders preferred those working in government to still have a day job, so they never become too entrenched in power. I found many California legislators (and scholars, too) that interpret the Federalist Papers to mean that the founders preferred term limits, so no man could become king—George Washington, after all, stepped down as president after his second four-year term. Today, fifteen states have imposed term limits on state legislators, but only three of the ten with full-time legislatures have done so—including California. Term limits were spurred by another voter initiative in 1990, and in 2012 voters approved Proposition 28, which now allows legislators to serve a total of twelve years, regardless of whether the years are served in the assembly or state senate. Previously, legislators were limited to six years in the assembly and eight years in the senate. In addition to limiting the knowledge base about areas such as higher education with legislative turnover, several legislative staffers and university administrators noted the decline in the quality of those in the legislature. One university administrator described the change in California's legislature in less than glowing terms: "Twenty-five years ago, most of the people in the legislature were citizen legislators, they were part-timers, and they weren't doing this for a career. They were doing it as citizens for public service. And that changed when they started to pay legislators a lot more. It's the best job some of those people could ever get, and all they think about is hanging on to their job because of the pay and perks they get. So you don't get the same committed visionary citizens."

For higher education, term limits are generally viewed as bad, because higher education requires a long-term view and deep knowledge to understand the nuances of funding (as do other aspects of state government). No legislature can bind the next one, and if a legislator won't be around for the long term, he or she can't be held accountable for the effects of past decisions. Further, legislators who face term limits almost immediately start running for their next office because they can't stay in their current office for long. One senior administration official explains the effect: "Across the board, it's [term limits] had a dramatic effect on the historical knowledge that elected officials have and their ability to hold people accountable when a commitment is made. If they make a promise to you now, who is going to be there five years from now to make sure that it is still made?" Legislative and gubernatorial staffers spoke frequently of great legislators who "termed out," taking with them all the knowledge gained during their time in office. One staffer summed up what I heard from almost all of them: "I've had three bosses [committee chairs] in the five years I've worked here. Every year and a half, we're educating a new person, and we're a staff frustrated trying to get them up to speed because we're battling against lobbyists who are not term-bound, you know, agencies who have the ability to retain their bosses and their directors for however long they want." Another experienced legislative staffer has seen the dramatic change in legislators as a result of term limits. "They've reduced the legislator's ability to move forward with an understanding of the past . . . Many legislators that had a real good understanding of what the Master Plan really was about are gone now." Loss of knowledge is one issue, but time is, perhaps, even more important. Assemblywoman Bonilla explains from a legislator's perspective how term limits have severely damaged legislators' ability to think long-term about big issues in the state:

> How do you implement a long-range strategic plan when you don't have the people that have the passion for it after six or eight years? The short time the legislators are here makes it hard to ever gain the influence to be able to effect a real shift in policy. To me, that's the main issue. It's not that you can't get the knowledge. You can get the knowledge, but you don't have time to do anything about it. We're all aware of how critical some of these big issues are, but how do you build the relationship and gain the influence that would actually be able to move something as huge and important as funding for higher education?
>
> You can get things done, but you're honestly managing in crisis mode, and what it means is that the will of other stakeholders is far more sustainable than the will of the legislature, because they're going to be here when you're gone. You're the one that's temporary. So that's a difficult place to bring leadership from and so that the result of term limits has actually empowered every other stakeholder group more than the legislature itself.

State Senator Ted Lieu provides a stark contrast in comparing legislators with the leadership of a private sector company: "We would never run most institutions, private or public, this way, where every two years you take a third of your leadership and fire them whether they've done brilliant jobs or bad jobs."

In each state where I interviewed legislators, there were a faithful few who relentlessly supported higher education funding, fighting in the face of even the most dramatic recessions to preserve funding for the colleges and universities, and their longevity was central to maintenance of that support. In California, I met several such legislators, too, including Ira Ruskin and John Vasconcellos, who served for nearly four decades in the California legislature. Like many others, both had been termed out, and with them went their understanding of the issues. These giants in the legislature were known for their deep knowledge and steadfast support, but now are long gone from the halls of the capitol.

Legislators who remember the years after the passage of the Master Plan recall that the education committees in both chambers were once the most respected and sought after. With the passage of time and the unintended consequences of the compounding ballot initiatives and laws limiting spending on higher education, more and more legislators began avoiding those committees. One legislative analyst said, "The education committees used to be the power committees. They were the places where you wanted to be, and now it's essentially the dog. They don't want to be there because there's no money there." One of the most senior legislators in the California State Assembly summed up the sad state of affairs related to education committees this way:

> I sat on higher education [committee] for two years, and one of the problems in a term-limited environment is we have to raise money all the time. There is no money to be raised in higher education. The lobbyists don't give money, so the people who are on the education committees are really the wonks and the people who are on the school board and the community college board. They're the true believers. Everybody else says, "Get me off of this dog, I can't change much and I can't raise much."
>
> You've either got to get press or you've got to raise money from something; otherwise, what's the point? In the short-term environment, that's the mentality of most people.

The significance of this legislator's summary of the steep hill facing higher education runs far beyond California, but is especially acute in this state—

namely, lobbyists are far stronger in other areas of government spending. Because they are always in campaign mode, legislators remain focused on where they can get funding for their next election. Sadly, the trends are similar in other states around the country where higher education institutions—and the educational system as a whole—are forced to behave like market actors when there is limited funding for education.

The Unwinding of the Master Plan: Financial or Philosophical?

One of the central goals of the Master Plan was to avoid mission creep and politicization as the state's higher education segments expanded. By the mid-2000s, just before the fiftieth anniversary, the system had begun to show signs of cracking. For example, several of the Cal State universities began offering doctoral degrees in education, even though doctoral education was intended to be the province of the UC system. Cal State system leaders argue that the UC system declined to focus on education (particularly the EdD degree), and so Cal State was helping to fill a gap. But politics had also begun to enter into the expansion of the segments and where campuses were located. One legislative staffer, somewhat exasperated, said of the current situation in California: "A big chunk of the problem is California doesn't have a public agenda. It doesn't have a vision of what it wants higher education to achieve." Indeed, the public agenda, or larger vision for the state, seems to be somewhat absent in the current conversation about what legislators want from their system of higher education.

One question I asked all the legislators was whether they knew what they were "buying" when they funded higher education. Granted, that's not an easy question to answer—on the record, at least—but it is a valid and important question when you consider the significance of the resources being put into higher education in California and around the country. The answer: most legislators don't have a clue where the money goes, how it's used, or toward what agenda. The legislative staffer who said the state lacks a vision had good reason to be frustrated. The state truly doesn't seem to have a clear agenda for what it wants to accomplish today, more than fifty years after the Master Plan was adopted.

In the years leading up to the passage of the Master Plan, several dozen bills were introduced in the state assembly to create new college and university campuses. With the baby boomers coming in the years ahead, the state's leaders knew they would have to expand the educational pipeline. But the question was where and how to expand, and the Master Plan created a less politicized order to how and where new campuses would be created. Over fifty years, however, politics has crept back into the process. In 2005, the University of California opened its tenth campus—UC Merced—in an area that made very little sense to some legislators and policy analysts because of the lack of population density compared to other parts of the state with rapidly growing populations. Pat Callan believes the last thing California needed was another research-focused UC campus (instead of more community colleges and Cal State campuses, which serve larger portions of the population growth), and many legislators I met agreed with him.

> The worst thing of all was Merced. That's 1960s thinking. This is a university that is eroding the quality of its own excellence by expanding further than there's any chance that the state can support. So if you don't want campus proliferation, if you don't want pork barrel politics running the higher education system, you have to have something more sensible. Even the legislature realized that it was going to bankrupt the state.
>
> So we went from 1960 until 1990, when the CSU built the Monterey Bay campus, without ever adding a campus—for all of California's reputation for flakiness, it was very disciplined about that. You had to have demographic rationale. The legislature said if the State Higher Education Commission didn't certify that there was one, they wouldn't put a campus there. So it took the issue out of politics. That is, any legislator, when its constituents said, "We want a campus because we're building a neat shopping center or housing development," they'd say, "We can't do that."

As the Master Plan begins its sixth decade, most of that policy discipline seems to be eroding, as each of the three segments finds its way in a new world order and faces elements of privatization. A staffer who has worked in both chambers of the legislature described today's situation as quintessential local politics—"what's in it for my district, and where's mine?" His recollection of the creation of the UC Merced campus highlights the erosion of the original intent of the Master Plan in creating new campuses: "A lot of them were Central Valley guys that gained power in the legislature, and they were like, 'Hey, where's my campus? We don't have anything here.' When you think about Merced, I think that was brutal politics at play—Central Valley guys going, 'Hey, where's ours now? We need something to motivate our voters,' and they were hoping that this was the thing that was going to do it.

Politicians are smart—they know they can bring jobs and prestige to their district if they get a UC campus." Charles Reed, the former Cal State chancellor, was even more blunt when he talked about how the Merced campus came to be: "You can never take politics out of higher education. That's just the way it is. And that was politics at its worst. That was a waste of money." Others point to the growth in the state population over time and note the need—in the long run—for another UC campus, but most believe politics ruled the day.

The "Impotent" Legislature

Beyond the financial challenges the state has faced in the last decade, many legislators do truly feel as though they don't have any control or options as a result of the legislation passed over decades that mandates state funding for specific purposes. Robert Birgeneau, former chancellor of UC Berkeley, saw firsthand the impact as legislators would often shrug and say their hands were tied: "What strikes me, particularly in California, is that the legislators almost seem like impotent members of this process because of Prop 13 and because of their limited ability to fund higher education with discretionary dollars. It's a story that has to be seen in the context of the state's operations overall. The legislator does not have much flexibility at all." His use of the word *impotent* is particularly strong, but illustrates how legislators have few options even if they want to support higher education. Not only was funding for K–12 and corrections mandated, it was also more politically palatable to cut higher education than to cut most other areas of state government. Ira Ruskin, who served in the state assembly and chaired a special committee on the Master Plan, explained the political realities of California education spending: "From a legislator's point of view, there's a big difference between cutting higher ed and cutting K–12. K–12 means cuts right to the heart of each community, not just the college-going students. And it affects them at the community level, it affects the district boards, it affects the neighborhoods, whereas the college will affect just those going to college. I think it's fair to say that you could tell neighborhoods or the local constituencies you are forced to cut higher ed budgets and get less rancor than if you said you are forced to cut your primary schools and your high schools. People felt they could perhaps cut higher ed with some amount of impunity, an impunity they didn't have in cutting K–12."

The citizens were directly responsible for the passage of Propositions 13 and 98. In essence, they mandated a change in the state's focus on higher education set forth in the Master Plan. High-quality, affordable, and accessible higher education were the goals of the Master Plan, but these things required significant political and financial support. Former State Senator Simitian said that citizens sometimes seem unable to connect the dots between diminishing revenues and fewer unrestricted dollars for discretionary spending (including for higher education):

> I have a very distinct memory of a constituent who came up to me at a community meeting and said she was so delighted that Governor Schwarzenegger had rolled back the vehicle license fee and she really appreciated the relief it provided, but she was concerned and wanted to talk to me about the fact that the fees for her kids at UC were going up. I tried very politely to say that there is a relationship between those two events. When the State of California no longer has the revenue that was provided by the vehicle license fee, then we're no longer able to support our UC system the way we once did, and that means that higher fees are charged to you and your kids.
>
>   She said, "Oh, I hadn't thought about that."

Funding or Philosophy?

One theme I heard often in my California interviews from those who have served the state through the decades is a belief that Californians in general still hold higher education in high regard, and that the shift has been less philosophical than financial. Jack Scott, a long-serving state legislator and then chancellor of the community college system, said, "I would say most of the people of the State of California still believe in the idea that higher education should be available to everyone. The thing that has constrained us in fulfilling that is not so much a philosophical shift but the fact that we don't have the money to do it anymore."

While Scott and others believe this is a money problem, two former legislators separately raised an interesting hypothesis. Both compared education generally and higher education specifically in the South versus the West. Both pointed out the hardships faced by southern states, particularly after the Civil War: the extreme poverty faced by their people, their agrarian economies, and, in general, their struggle to survive for many years. Education became a way out for the people, and it was held in the highest regard (some scholarship has been written about this topic, which is an important area for further exploration).[17]

In contrast, California's relatively shorter history has been one of abundance—natural, economic, and, as a result, educational. There have always been enough resources, enough land and sunshine, and enough raw talent for California to be highly successful in the educational arena and to fund higher education at a very high level. Each of these two legislators noted that Californians have taken their educational system for granted because, like the sunshine, water, and air, it has always been good and plentiful. But today there is scarcity, and we are seeing how the state and its citizens react. In the words of one of these legislators: "I have a sense that southern states have struggled more economically than California. Historically, they don't have the economic resources, they don't have the natural resources, and they're not as attractive in terms of weather as California. They've got to figure out how they're going to survive and thrive. They've worked a lot harder and they've put aside some of the bureaucratic obstacles. I don't think that's happened in California. Now, of course, with California having serious economic problems, it ought to be our turn to kind of put some of these differences aside and work closely together. Why don't we? It seems to me it is a struggle of leadership." Senator Simitian echoed the notion that California takes its educational system for granted and doesn't match rhetoric with funding. "This is perhaps the great irony of the debate today. I think almost everyone is aware of the importance of the [higher education] system to California's role in the world economy, but that awareness does not translate into support, for whatever reason."

The lack of leadership described here and in many other interviews may stem from the partisanship in the legislature, but also the lack, historically, of an "education governor" in California—someone who really cares about and prioritizes education in the state. In a state where the governor has great budget and veto power, that does not bode well for education. Interestingly, the two governors who, according to interviewees, showed at least some interest in higher education, were Arnold Schwarzenegger (who took English classes at a community college when he came to California) and Pat Brown (who skipped college but attended law school at night and signed the Master Plan into law in 1960). The struggle also refers to the challenges of term limits in terms of historical knowledge and willingness to deal with something as complex as higher education that could take decades to tackle. With just twelve years per legislator, most have more immediate issues with greater payoff.

The Tension Between Coordination and Autonomy

With the Master Plan in place in 1960, California had a clearly differentiated system of higher education with defined roles for each of the three segments.

The University of California system would enroll the top 12.5 percent of under-graduate students, as well as lead doctoral education in the state. The Califor-nia State University system would enroll the top third of students in the state, and the community colleges would be open-access institutions for all students. Nearly fifteen years after the passage of the Master Plan, it was already evident that better coordination and planning would be required. In 1974, the legisla-ture created the California Postsecondary Education Commission (CPEC) to integrate the functions of the three segments and "to assure the effective utili-zation of public postsecondary education resources, thereby eliminating waste and unnecessary duplication, and to promote diversity, innovation, and respon-siveness to student and societal needs through planning and coordination."[18]

Pat Callan was at the helm of CPEC from 1978 to 1986, and legislators and university leaders alike saw him as a significant leader in coordinating Cali-fornia's growing system of higher education. Over time, however, CPEC lost credibility in the state and was seen as toothless in coordinating higher educa-tion policy in the state. In 2011, Governor Jerry Brown eliminated CPEC by vetoing its entire appropriation, calling the commission "ineffective." At the same time, the state had no secretary of education, a role that had been created and eliminated by several governors since the 1960s. Taken together, the lack of CPEC and the secretary left a vacuum of coordination and central leader-ship in the state, frustrating some legislators and most legislative staffers, but providing much greater autonomy and flexibility to the higher education in-stitutions. As one of the last strong leaders of CPEC in the state, Pat Callan reflects on the evolution of the coordinating body and its role:

[At the time it was eliminated], it was ineffective. I would've abolished it, too. The only difference between me and them is I would've put something in its place. For the last fifteen years it just had almost no impact, and those kinds of bodies are not doing very well in the country generally. That is, they're either being pushed into the governor's cabinet or they're being wiped out completely. They're hard jobs because you have no real political constituency. You've got to live by your wits and build coalitions around issues. And at the same time, you've got to run the thing on the basis of good public policy.

There's nobody that represents the principle that the whole is greater than the sum of the parts here. The result is that the institutions have enormous ca-pacity to pursue their own self-interests.

Callan pointed out another critical challenge today for central agencies—the lack of funding to compete in hiring talent with the institutions themselves. Nonetheless, the lack of a public agenda is the primary issue that requires attention. Gary K. Hart, former legislator and secretary of education, concurs that CPEC had grown ineffective, but notes that the entire state has lost its coordination. While the Master Plan may be viewed as sacred in the state, Hart notes that it is also responsible in part for the lack of coordination today: "For example, while the Master Plan clearly defines the mission for each higher education segment, it has also contributed to a silo effect where effective collaboration among the segments is lacking. With a state as large as California with regional labor markets, we need regional coordination in higher education and with K–12, and I think the Master Plan is an obstacle to that type of planning and collaboration. I believe some type of regional higher education governance structure is long overdue in California."

The leaders of the three segments at the time of my research—Charles Reed (CSU), Mark Yudof (UC), and Jack Scott (community colleges)—all retired in 2013. Each of them said that CPEC had outgrown its usefulness long before Governor Brown eliminated it, but each also said that he had a strong relationship with his two counterparts and the three of them would talk by phone or meet quite frequently. They saw the differences among their respective segments, but they also saw areas where they could work together fruitfully. They said that CPEC at some point transitioned from focusing on public policy and coordination to focusing on management and operations; once that transition occurred, CPEC was unable to return to helping create good public policy, and the three leaders didn't believe any central agency could effectively help them with management and operations of their system.

With significant cuts taken from the budgets of all three segments in the last decade, Governor Brown decided to give more autonomy to the systems to manage the cuts in a way they saw as most beneficial to preserving their core functions. In essence, he allowed those managing the institutions to decide where to make the cuts in the least harmful fashion. In an era of sequestration and automatic cuts in the federal government that allow little flexibility to affected agencies, the governor at least helped to minimize the pain in this one way. One of the outcomes of privatization in many states has been to give greater autonomy to the institutions to manage their own affairs—when you can't give money, many states give autonomy.

California's institutions have far less autonomy than Virginia's, for instance, but this move by the governor was seen as a big step forward and was much appreciated by the system and university leaders. The one slight exception is the University of California, which enjoys constitutional autonomy, giving its board of regents the sole authority to make governance decisions. However, its regents still receive their budget from the legislature, so they don't have complete autonomy. The legislators I interviewed seemed to support giving more autonomy to the leaders of the systems and the institutions, with many recognizing the transient nature of the legislature relative to the longevity of faculty and administration. The overall budget at most UC campuses is now far more diverse than a decade ago, with philanthropy, tuition, and federal research funding composing as much or more than the state appropriation. Figure 7.7 shows the history of revenue sources at UC Berkeley, where appropriations no longer constitute a majority (or plurality) of funding for the institution.

The problems identified by legislators and university leaders alike point to a challenge in reasserting public purpose. The primacy of the public agenda seems to have been somewhat lost in California, but it is clear that the public purpose cannot be reinstated without strong leadership at the legislative, system, and campus levels. Berkeley is the flagship and original campus, but, as was the case in North Carolina, differentiating that campus in a discussion

FIGURE 7.7   Appropriations, tuition, philanthropy, and federally funded research per FTE student at UC-Berkeley, 1987–2010 (in constant 2010 dollars)

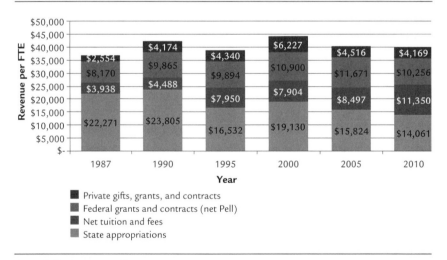

Source: Delta Cost Project dataset, 2012

Note: The fall FTE enrollment was used for FTE calculations. Constant 2010 dollars adjusted by SHEEO Higher Education Cost Adjustment (HECA).

with legislators about higher education in the state was quite difficult. However, some legislators spoke openly of abolishing the Office of the President at the University of California, which, at one time, had a budget of nearly $500 million and an enormous staff. Abolishing the Office of the President sounds like rearranging the deck chairs on the *Titanic* to most policy leaders. Campuses need sufficient autonomy to make good decisions, but first there needs to be a reassertion of the public purposes as the focus for the larger system of higher education by those directing public policy in the state—namely, legislators and the governor. There must be a stronger match between the state's interests and the institution's interests, both of which seem unclear at the moment.

Public Mission Maintained: The "Opportunity Factory"

As was the case in North Carolina and Virginia, there has been no significant alteration of the public mission for UC Berkeley, the entire UC system, or the three segments of higher education overall as a result of the elements of privatization in the state. I heard time and again from legislators and staffers, as well as university administrators, that the definition of *public* extends far beyond dollars and cents and focuses instead on mission, access, and the people of the state. In this last element—focusing on the people—community colleges and the Cal State system clearly have a stronger focus on local and regional interests, whereas the UC system takes a more national and global view of research and education. Nevertheless, there is a clear belief throughout the state that higher education remains vital to meeting the needs of the people—educationally, economically, and, more broadly, with the system of social services provided directly and indirectly by graduates and research.

Water, Air, and Education—Defining "Public"

When asked what defines the public mission today, legislators gave a variety of answers. But many focused on the commitment to access that stretches back to the original goal of the Master Plan—any student who desires higher education should be able to access it. One senior legislative analyst offered his opinion about the public mission and focus, which sums up what I heard from many staffers: "Is there a tipping point when public is no longer public? No. There is no bright line. I think that there are some people who think that even if the state provided no funding any longer that UC and CSU would still be public institutions. They're chartered with a public mission. They're on public land. Their buildings have been built with public dollars. You can still make that argument that even though the state doesn't provide financial support they're still public." What is particularly striking in this description of public higher education is, once again, the mission and history rather than finance as defining features of *public*. But it also speaks to the evolution—privatization—as not taking away from that focus. Once again, privatization has changed and altered the relationship between higher education and the state, but not in a way that has lessened that central focus. U.S. Representative Julia Brownley, who has since been elected to Congress, was still in the California legislature when I interviewed her, and she discussed the potential impacts of privatization on the public good and described the differing views among the parties:

> For me, the "P" word [privatization] is very, very important. I think the nature of a public university system for California has been unique, one of the best public university systems in the country, so I think it is extremely important. But there are other legislators who believe that there's no reason why we can't follow other models, like the Michigan or Virginia model, which is just to say, they have become, in my mind, more private than public, their student base just continues to grow with out-of-state students.
>
> I think legislators generally think that the public university piece is really important, and want to get back to a place where we are making a much larger investment out of our state budget. "Public" to me means affordable and accessible, and it means that the preponderance of students there are students from California, and that the quality of education is high, and the cost of education is low. That's what it means to me.

Representative Brownley's description of public higher education exemplifies that there are no two ways to define or understand public higher education—it means different things to different people.

Some legislators were puzzled when asked to describe what public higher education means to them and what it means to the state, unsure how to put into words something that is as ubiquitous as air or water. Others, once they warmed up, began to really reflect on how they view the system of higher education—with great affection—and have high hopes for the state overall. Assemblyman Roger Dickinson began by talking about the same notions of access and affordability as the others, and then reflected more deeply: "I think the University of California is important because it represents the potential of the people of the state. It is a reflection of saying, 'California is a place where we have the best and the brightest.' It's okay to say that California is a place where people come, and they're dreamers, they're creators, they're innovators, and we've got public institutions of higher education that are the best in the country and among the best in the world because, in California, we see ourselves as being the best. And I don't mean that in a way of dismissing other people or being condescending; it's just more of a pioneer spirit of, 'By God, California. We're gonna make it all happen.'" Dickinson's description of the entrepreneurial spirit and faith in the people of California is a beautiful encapsulation of the mission of higher education—teaching, research, and service. I quite often found this same spirit among California legislators; they wanted to recapture the pioneer spirit that brought the state to prominence in the nineteenth century with the massive move westward and again in the twentieth century with technology and entertainment. California has been an innovation laboratory for the rest of the country (and world). These legislators—not all, but many—recognize that the innovation and ingenuity they desire in the state will come from their universities. Although funding has diminished significantly from the original goals set out by the Master Plan, legislative leaders are proud of the system of higher education, have high ambitions for it, and have not seen negative effects from the growing privatization trend.

Strains on the System of Higher Education

How can the system of higher education adhere to the principles of the Master Plan under the circumstances they are facing today? By 2009, the UC system could not accommodate the top 12.5 percent of California students. The rejected students put increasing pressure on the CSU system, and the rejected students from the CSU system put pressure on an already burdened community college system (beginning in 2010, thousands of students were denied entrance to community colleges). The three-tiered system, whose mission was high-quality, low-cost, and accessible education, may become increasingly stratified—the elite universities will continue to prosper and the lesser ones may falter. If the universities' mission is still public and extends beyond dollars and cents—which I argue that it does—but the state continually underfunds the segments of higher education, then the social contract between the state and higher education has changed, even if just in small ways. Christopher Newfield has described this as the "assault" on the middle class, which is not accidental and has been at play for quite some time.[19]

Enrollment limitations have been one way of dealing with declining resources in both the UC and CSU systems. The state produced roughly two hundred thirty thousand associate's and bachelor's degrees in 2009; if it were to help the United States reach President Obama's achievement goals by 2020, it would need to graduate four hundred thousand students per year, but the current projection for 2020 is only two hundred fifty thousand. Current progress might indicate this is increasingly becoming a distant dream.[20] The focus on in-state enrollment and solving the state's most pressing needs was just beneath the surface with most legislators. Figure 7.8 shows the enrollment history at UC Berkeley, where the vast majority have historically been in-state students, but the trend is moving quickly toward more out-of-state students in the past decade—since 2008, out-of-state students have doubled at Berkeley.

Many legislators spoke about the accessibility and financial issues surrounding privatization and the definition of a public university, but very few spoke about the broader goals of civic education and engagement—preparing the next generation of society's leaders, training young people to be active participants in government and society. Legislators weren't able to articulate what it meant to have institutions focused on California students, although—historically, at least—this focus was always a significant component of the Master Plan, which made available *some* form of higher education to *every* citizen.

FIGURE 7.8   Fall undergraduate FTE student enrollment, UC-Berkeley, 1999–2012

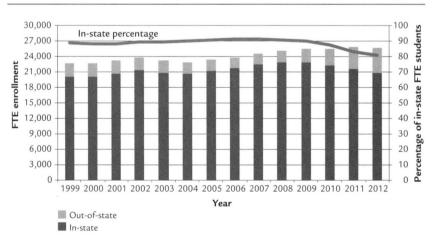

Source: Institutional research, University of California Office of the President, 2013

Pat Callan voiced the underlying message that I was hearing from many legislators—a public university still has inherent public purposes that are worthy of preservation: "I guess that's one reason why I don't like privatization. I don't like the word. If you ask me how I would judge how successful or unsuccessful we're being, it's, 'Are we educating the people of the country? Are we educating the people of California? Are we producing research that's internationally recognized in fields related to the economy, that's internationally competitive, and that supports our needs?' So I think there are public purposes here and, to a large extent, the privatizers aren't very interested in those public purposes." Public purposes can be found at public universities, to be sure, but one legislator noted that public universities don't have a monopoly on public purposes—for example, corporations can have public purposes, and private universities can and do have public purposes. Public universities, however, have public purposes in their founding mission.

California is large and diverse and the state's population is still booming, with most of the growth in its Hispanic and African American populations, which traditionally have been less represented in the UC system than in the Cal State and community college systems. Even so, the UC system is more diverse—racially and socioeconomically—than most other top-twenty-five private or public universities. Charles Reed, former chancellor of the Cal State University system, describes the demographic future: "This huge, huge wave of brown people are coming, and it's getting bigger and bigger. Seventy percent of the public school children in California are brown. I don't think the legislature feels they need to educate them, and that's reflective in their commitment." Pat Callan explains the demographic challenges ahead for the state, guided by its Master Plan:

> The biggest innovation in the Master Plan was the broad access. And that's where we've made our biggest compromises. The second is the demographic change. So this was a system that was built for white, middle-class Californians. I think the critical thing is, what are we going to do about this demographic change? That's the core issue in education. The answer to that question is that we need to keep the universities strong and vibrant but limited in scope so we can support it. The critical decisions are really going to be about the broad-access institutions—the CSUs, the community colleges, and the for-profits too, I think. They're either going to make or break it. This demographic clock is ticking. Every year the proportion of elementary and secondary kids is more Latino, more immigrant, more first-generation families—we have to figure out how to get them to higher ed.

California is a unique state in many respects, but is perhaps most unique in the way that legislators are uncomfortable with the diminishing level of support for higher education. Some legislators in California seem shy about demanding that institutions focus on the state because they know funding has been severely cut. In a way that was very different from Virginia and to a lesser extent North Carolina, California legislators weren't used to the role of apologetic "owner," who was sorry he or she hadn't funded the colleges and universities as generously as they had grown accustomed to over time. Virginia's legislators seem to have grown quite comfortable in their role of demanding overseer, with little regard for the fact that they are funding a diminishing minority of the institutions' operating budgets. Assemblywoman Bonilla asked a question that was on the minds of several legislators: "Are we going be able to maintain the portion of public influence that we have? I think a strong interest of the legislature is to not get completely squeezed out and ultimately have no role in determining what direction, what priorities, what place our residents take within these institutions." I found her question fascinating because it really speaks to the unknown future ahead after so many decades of optimism and connection. Though legislators wonder about Assemblywoman Bonilla's question, she also noted the role of the legislature: "They [the universities] have their own board and they govern themselves. But we're here to hold them accountable—we're here to create that tension." Though accountability for the state's resources invested in higher education is a high priority for many legislators, for Californians, granting greater freedoms to colleges and universities and confronting the forces of privatization is still very unfamiliar. Having met with hundreds of legislators, however, I am fairly certain that California legislators will soon grow more comfortable.

Even so, public higher education is held in special regard in this state, and that is perhaps why legislators are uncomfortable with diminishing support for their institutions. Steve Weiner, who worked both at Stanford and the UC system, reminded me that the California universities are "a sacred thing to many people, and their memories of the university are sacred and their aspirations for the university, even if never realized, are sacred." Truly, I did find a certain level of sacredness to the feelings about higher education in this state that were very similar to the high regard North Carolinian legislators have for their institutions. These are viewed as engines of opportunity and possibility for the state. Mark Yudof, the former president of the University of California system, captured the essence quite nicely:

We're an opportunity factory. Berkeley or UCLA have more low-income kids than the whole Ivy League. You need social economic mobility; so moving families through the higher education system and hopefully getting better jobs, lower unemployment rates, participating in democracy, creating more beautiful oil paintings, writing poems, and so forth are all good things. We have 40 percent low-income kids; Cal State is 47 percent.

What you see in California is the combination of serving the low-income, serving the first to go to college in the family, and all the rest, and being a very powerful research engine doing $5 billion worth of research a year. Doing $10 billion of medical care, medical procedures, clinical visits, and so forth, it's a rare combination.

What I am saying is in terms of mission, this idea that if you raise tuition $500 you have lost your public purpose is complete nonsense.

As I said in chapter 3, the nonmonetary benefits of higher education (public goods) in addition to the benefits to the students (private goods) are significant in California. This state, which pioneered high-quality, low-cost, and very accessible education, stands at an important juncture and will require strong leadership, continued vision and creativity, and the same focus on public mission that has been a hallmark of the state for many decades.

CHAPTER EIGHT

The Foundations of Privatization

Higher education is the engine driving America to a better future for all its citizens—not a consumer good, but a public investment—and a public good. It is the single most important driver of opportunity and prosperity at home, and for American influence and idealism abroad.

—Robert M. Gates[1]

ONE CENTRAL FOCUS of this book is to examine the macro and micro forces in American society that have led to significant (and sometimes unintended) changes in the system of higher education. Beyond changes, however, I have sought to understand how privatization has affected (or not) the focus these institutions have on the public good and how the institutions are viewed by those charged with developing and funding higher education policy. Many public universities have experienced for several decades some of the effects of privatization, while others are just beginning to feel the changes resulting from the shifting political, economic, and social forces in their respective states and in the nation. The history, trends, and case studies in this book provide some evidence for the longer- and shorter-term effects of greater autonomy and legislative action (or inaction) in higher education.

Privatization is often viewed as an agenda being pushed by a university seeking to gain more autonomy, but at many colleges and universities, forces are at work at both the institutional and state levels. The universities are, indeed, pushing for more autonomy to set their enrollment mix and tuition level, and for other freedoms to compete in the marketplace, but many legislators and governors are also pushing them to identify alternative revenue sources, become more efficient, and operate differently from the rest of government.

At the same time, some of these universities are being pulled toward national and international prominence, which requires a significantly greater focus on research—much of it federally funded—and a decrease in the traditional focus on teaching as the university's primary domain. In addition, the new knowledge economy, driven by globalization, requires institutions to focus on economic development in wholly new ways. In other words, the universities, the states, and the federal government, as well as larger global economic forces, are all complicit in the privatization of public colleges and universities, which now find themselves on a continuum between public *and* private institutions, rather than public *or* private.

Marketplace economics was an umbrella description that some legislators used to summarize the push and pull and all the drivers and effects of privatization. Quite simply, many public universities are seen as competing in a national marketplace for students, faculty, and funding; and, especially at the higher end of the academic continuum, they may compete more with private peers than with other public universities. Some legislators saw the need for autonomy to allow universities to compete in that marketplace, but only if those institutions could do so without diminishing their focus on the state. Often, legislators would lament the impacts of privatization as blind ambition or a desire to be preeminent (usually defined as achieving "top twenty-five" status in some ranking), and under those circumstances, they were quick to criticize higher education.

Perhaps the most significant finding of this research study is that autonomy and finance are critical factors in understanding what drives privatization and how it affects institutions, but they are not the only factors. The state context—the understanding of a public mission, the institutional focus, and the overall historical connections between a public university and the state—is a dominant element. This finding serves as the framework for the new model for understanding privatization (*foundations of privatization*— refer back to figure 1.3) and will also guide the findings and analysis in this chapter. This model was introduced in chapter 1 as a guide to the many changes being discussed throughout the book, and now we can review how these effects played out in some of the institutions and states examined in the preceding pages.

Foundations of Privatization: Making Sense of Change

Virginia, North Carolina, and California feature three of the finest systems of higher education in the world, even though they are very different. The state context is vitally important to understanding what has happened over time at their public institutions and why their approaches to meeting their respective missions appear to be so different. California's and North Carolina's were historically very highly coordinated and managed systems, and Virginia's is very loosely coordinated and more autonomous. California and North Carolina historically had very high per-student state funding, while Virginia historically had very low state funding. Today, each university is facing greater pressures to achieve autonomy and stable funding amid economic and political uncertainty and to define what *public* means for them. Significantly, the three flagship universities examined in these states are also meeting important public policy objectives, even while they are forced to seek greater autonomy.

The State Context: Mission, History, and Culture

As the first and most important foundation of privatization, the state context is one element not fully accounted for in the scholarly literature.[2] The state context is central to understanding the differences between a mission that is avowedly public and one that is more focused on students as consumers. However, mission, history, and culture define the state context in which an institution exists and are always in the background when institutional leaders or legislators contemplate or articulate elements of privatization. An institution must answer the question, "where did we come from?" before it can set a clear plan for where it is going.

The differences between Virginia, North Carolina, and California are particularly evident when we examine the flagship institution in each state. UVA's founder envisioned it as an institution that would have national appeal to students outside of Virginia and that would be something of a national public university. The state prided itself on maintaining an autonomous environment for the institution, and that history is central to understanding how current autonomy proposals were born and why the financial model today is a true public-private partnership. UNC-CH, on the other hand, was born out of the state's need to educate its own sons; its vision has always been, first and foremost, focused on meeting the needs of the people of North Carolina. Autonomy has never been a significant issue because there was such strong central governance and a financial model (based on a constitutional mandate) that dictated strong public financial support and low tuition. California's significant political and financial support for a centralized system of higher education—which the Master Plan differentiated and the citizens supported as high-quality, low-cost, accessible education for every citizen— is the important context for what is happening there today and why the changes in the state are so difficult. California, like North Carolina, focused on the needs of its citizens, so it built and invested in a system of public education designed to meet the varied needs of the population.

In every state, mission, history, and culture are at the core of understanding what drives privatization and how it plays out. This was one of my most significant findings because most discussions of privatization focus quickly or solely on the financial aspects or the elements of autonomy. The history of these institutions is so deeply rooted in the state that it is not possible to talk about loosening that relationship without first acknowledging the depth and importance of state context. It also makes it extremely difficult for one state to say, "we want what Virginia has" or "this state has never been as generous to higher education as California."

Defining the Public Mission in an Era of Privatization

An important component of my research agenda for this book was to come to a better understanding of the public mission, a key factor in how privatization affects public universities and their connection to the public good. In other words, who or what defines the public mission today? Is it the demands of the marketplace, the ambitions of the institution, the state legislature, federal agencies? For so many of these colleges and universities, the historic public mission remains a guiding force for navigating the privatization waters, yet it is challenging to define it.

Legislators are pulled in many directions, and public higher education is but one constituency—described on occasion as "another mouth at the trough"—albeit a crucial constituency for achieving the country's and the state's social, civic, and economic goals. Every legislator I interviewed for this study proclaimed a firm belief in the primacy of the public mission, even amid diminishing state resources, but very few could define what that public mission meant today; most described it, in essence, as something that you know when you see it.

Access for state residents, low tuition, and service to the state are the most common definitions of public mission, but these leave out a broader conversation about the desired public purposes of public higher education. Virginia's Restructuring Act attempted to spell out the public mission with the State Ask, but few legislators could remember what was included, and many were too new to the legislature to have been a part of the act's passage, so they had only vague knowledge of it. North Carolina's legislators spoke with passion about how the public mandate and the overt public mission were completely in concert with the state, yet legislators most often connected it to the constitutional mandate for low tuition. California's legislators could all cite the Master Plan, but few knew what it meant in a modern context (considering that it is now more than fifty years old). In all three states, this study revealed that legislators had a shallow reservoir of knowledge or insight about the public mission and, therefore, a lack of clarity about whether higher education is maintaining a clear focus on that public mission in an era of privatization.

Higher education insiders often trace the public mission of public universities back to the Morrill Act of 1862, with its goals of providing broader access for citizens as well as knowledge useful for progress in the states—particularly in the agricultural, technical, and mechanical fields. But, historically, there was also an inherent focus in the United States on creating an educated citizenry. Many land-grant colleges feature passages engraved on buildings that describe the search for knowledge and its connection to civic duty. Thomas Jefferson, founder of UVA, described public education as the "salvation" of free people. But when I interviewed legislators, very few discussed the democratic education of the state's citizens for civic life. Robert Berdahl, former president of the American Association of Universities, who also served as president of several institutions, laments the shift in discussions about public mission: "The whole issue of creating educated citizens has been lost. That, of course, was the fundamental reason for public higher education. You'll find statements that go back to the founding of the university about the purpose of a state university is to create an educated citizen. That's almost completely absent from the discussion now, but the primary public mission was historically to increase the quality of civic life, to create social cohesion. But the word *citizen* never appears on a legislator's list today."

In the discourse about public mission, there is wide divergence among the thousands of public colleges and universities. Different states necessarily have different public agendas, and I found many concrete examples of the institutions meeting the public agenda. The rare legislator who was deeply knowledgeable about higher education would note how the colleges and universities were intertwined with the state's fortunes. One aptly described it by saying, "As goes our university, so goes our state. If you look back at the history of our state, it's almost impossible to distinguish the evolution and whether it was led by the state or the university." Understanding the public mission and who (or what) defines it provides insight into how a state approaches privatization.

In the quest to understand how privatization affects public colleges and universities, it is clear that the public mission is defined differently depending on whom you ask. Legislators increasingly want to see their university focus definitively on the state's people and needs; that means high-quality and low-cost education for the state's citizens, as well as the economic development that comes from having the best students educated by the best faculty, creating national and global economic competitiveness. The expectations are significant and growing, even while state funding is diminishing. Many public universities face a challenging balancing act of pursuing two sometimes-competing missions: to serve the state and to achieve national and international prominence. Though the two missions do not inherently conflict, and one can bolster the other, legislators see and feel the tension.

State context, the first foundation of privatization, focuses the conversation on the origins of an institution, primarily rooted in its mission but also in the long history and entrenched culture of the state. By understanding the roots of the state and an institution, one can begin to see a longer-term trajectory and understand why it is highly unlikely that an institution will ever fully sever its ties with the state—they have usually been inextricably intertwined over centuries. Public universities and their states are certainly linked in more ways than just finance and autonomy.

Vision and Focus

The second foundation of privatization centers on the vision and focus of the institution and asks the essential questions, "Who are we serving? Who are our 'publics'?" As we've seen, public institutions in Virginia, North Carolina, and California have a clear history of who formed the student body, which was rooted in the circumstances of their states and in the goals of their founders. UNC-CH's earliest focus was on serving people from the local region and the state, because the state saw a need to educate students closer to home. At UVA, Jefferson's vision was not only to serve his native state of Virginia but also to entice the brightest students and faculty from other states to join him ("come and drink of the cup of knowledge . . . with us"). UC

Berkeley has been a mix of the two in a state far more diverse and larger. To-day, as public and private universities around the country shift from a local or state focus to a more national and global focus, new questions have arisen about which "publics" the institution should serve.

Because of the vastly different history, mission, and culture of each state, the vision and focus of these universities also differs greatly. The *foundations of privatization* model shows how institutional vision and focus constitute the second foundation of privatization, influenced by the state context. Impor-tantly, these are more central to discussions of privatization than are finance, autonomy, enrollment, and tuition, which are more frequently discussed.

Focus on the state   In his inaugural address in 2008, former Chancellor Holden Thorp spoke about the connections between UNC-CH and the state of North Carolina and cited the need for increased interdependence with the state, even as faculty and students sought to impact the broader world. Legis-lators feel and express this commitment so frequently and with such intensity that it is surely a critical component of the public mission at many universities across the nation. Public universities' (particularly land-grant colleges') focus on their states has historically differentiated them from private universities. But the differences are shrinking between the premier public and private uni-versities today. Both private and public universities receive support from the state and federal governments, and tuition, philanthropy, and research fund-ing makes up a significant portion of the operating budgets at both.

One potential result of privatization is for a university to shift its focus from serving the needs of the state toward a broader national and interna-tional approach; this is more likely to happen in some states than others, but legislators across the country are leery. A primary difference among the three states I examined is the significance and strength of the connection to the state in North Carolina and, to a lesser extent, California, and the perceived lack of strong connection in Virginia. Though leaders at UVA proudly de-clare their connection to and focus on the people of the Commonwealth, legislators simply do not see or feel this connection in the way legislators in North Carolina do. As a qualitative researcher, I could sense this quickly dur-ing my interviews in the three states—spending immense time in each of the state capitols produced quite a contrast in comparing the three.

Within and beyond the borders of the state   Though access to higher edu-cation for state residents and the need to focus on and educate the state's citizens were consistent themes among legislators, a few of them recognized that knowledge today has no boundaries, and that the work force of the twenty-first century stretches far beyond state lines. The subtle distinction between public mission and location causes heated debates in all states, but, at some point, we must recognize the diminishing importance of state lines in a borderless world. Simon Marginson and Gary Rhoades have written about the global-national-local, or "glonacal," conception of policy and events; this certainly holds true for education as well.[3]

The glonacal heuristic is a way to envision the increasing interconnectedness of the world. As privatization of higher education increasingly becomes the norm, this glonacal perspective must be taken into account. Since the Morrill Act of 1862, there has been a "contract" between public higher education institutions and their states. Institutions were supposed to serve their states and states were supposed to adequately fund their institutions, yet localities, states, and even nations are no longer isolated entities. Rather, localities are tied to state, regional, national, and global interests through a complex network of interconnections. The research produced by UVA, UC Berkeley, and UNC-CH, for instance, does not just benefit the home state. Instead, the research benefits those states and, through communication and transportation networks and channels, really benefits the entire world. Privatization must take into account these growing connections and how the evolution of higher education in a global world will affect institutions and states.

Though the understanding and definition of the public mission have shifted over time, some of the core elements have remained prominent in the perceptions of legislators, governors, and other policy makers. The university's role in economic and work force development is near the top of the list for many legislators in all three states when they describe the public mission of higher education today and, most often, when they talk about an institution's role in the life of its region and the state.

University leaders have learned to adjust and modify how they describe the university's role to the external world, particularly to legislators, and they talk about the university's impact on the state's economy in terms of dollars and jobs. Legislators—even critics of public universities—praise the university's role in growing and sustaining the state's economy and training the future work force during a significant economic recession.

Former governors described the strength and prominence of public universities as a recruitment tool to use when they encourage businesses to move to their state, because of the high-quality graduates these institutions produce.

The governors also described the active role that the universities and faculty specialists play in working directly with companies to recruit them to the state and then to help with their business development and work force needs.

Though some university leaders lament that they have been forced to define their university's value in economic terms, most understand that to secure state funding, they must make the case—particularly during a recession—that the university is an economic engine for the state. Molly Corbett Broad, president of the American Council on Education and former president of UNC, describes the challenges brought about by the inability of higher education institutions to adequately articulate the economic development that they create: "There can be not a doubt about the beneficial impact of a university to a healthy economy and a strong democratic society—both in the short run and the long run. Universities do not typically tout or advertise the day-to-day accomplishments of faculty and students. We seem stuck on using the old formula of tallying total expenditures and then using an economic multiplier to capture the impact of the university on the community or region. That is not a strong or comprehensive way to measure the full impact."

An institution's answer to the question, "who are you serving?" speaks volumes to the shift from local and state to broader audiences on a national and global stage. This is not to say that it's wrong to focus on issues affecting broader populations than those within a state's borders, but it does signal, fundamentally, a transition on the privatization continuum.

Autonomy

My research commenced with a deep focus on the elements of finance and autonomy and largely defined privatization in terms of how a given university was funded (percentage of operating dollars from the state) and how free it was to pursue an agenda to increase its external funding. Once I immersed myself more deeply in the states, it became clear I could discuss autonomy and finance only after providing a fuller understanding of the states' context and the institutions' vision and focus.

For public universities, privatization cannot be defined solely by financial models or degrees of freedom from the state. Instead, it must be understood through the many layers of the public agenda for higher education. The essential question defining the third foundation of privatization, autonomy, is "who 'owns' us?" The question seems simple to answer on the surface, but it becomes more complicated and nuanced once mission, history, culture, vision, and focus are factored in.

The "owners" of the university and the public mission   Some Virginia legislators spoke of higher education in terms of ownership, as in "we own the universities, so they will never be private," while others expressed harsh feelings
of animosity or were downright patronizing. One Virginia legislator, James P.
Massie III, described the relationship between the state and the university as
a parent-child relationship. But he also spoke to the much larger notion that
the state is pushing the university toward privatization and greater autonomy,
just as much as the institution is pulling away.

> In that spectrum of schools, UVA is the most mature child. They have the
> largest endowment; they have the largest national and international recogni-
> tion, and it is an extremely well-run operation, so the demand for their ser-
> vices is extremely high. So we treat our more mature educational children
> differently than we treat our less mature. Just like at home, when you get ma-
> ture you are expected to go out and take care of yourself, especially when you
> are able to take care of yourself.
>
> I think it is the appropriate thing to say to them, "Hey, you are a very ma-
> ture child. You have a large endowment, there is tremendous demand in the
> marketplace for your educational services, and you need to start taking care
> of yourself more." Then we are going to reallocate some of those dollars on
> operating basis toward our less mature children and help them get stronger,
> because they don't have the advantages that you have. They are still in the
> nest. And then we take those resources and allocate them to our less mature
> children.

Delegate Massie touches on an important note in privatization that has often been put forth by university leaders, which is that in exchange for greater
autonomy, the state should take some of the appropriations from the flagship
and use it for the community colleges or the comprehensive universities. Stability and autonomy to raise revenues from tuition, these university administrators offer, is more valuable than what they see as diminishing support
from the state over time.

The notion of ownership that characterized some Virginia legislators' perspectives was colored as a reaction to what they often saw as uncoordinated or
combative relations with university leaders in the state. Legislators often called
the universities' definition of state support misleading, because some university officials would describe state support as a percentage of the overall university operating budget, including the graduate programs, medical centers, and

auxiliary revenues, even though state support is usually earmarked only for undergraduate programs. Presidents or chancellors, in speeches and in print, often said something along the lines of, "We used to get x% of our budget from the state, but now we only get y%." In these examples, x was always a significant number and y was puny—the trends were true enough, but the actual results were somewhat skewed by the growth of the rest of the budget. State legislators often lamented that university leaders did not show enough appreciation for past support, easing the way for political attacks by opponents of increased spending on higher education.

By contrast, North Carolina legislators were overwhelmingly proud of the UNC system and the Chapel Hill campus, and nearly flowery in their praise. The term *ownership* was used to describe the university, as it was in Virginia and to a certain extent in California, but with a completely different meaning. North Carolina legislators talked about the broad public ownership by the citizens of the state and thought of the university as their own. In California, the same sense of pride that exists in North Carolina came through in an appreciation for what Californians had created with the Master Plan, becoming the first state to really focus on education for *every* citizen, but I would characterize ownership in the state as one of benign neglect. Several legislators and university administrators used those actual words, and noted that the state had taken for granted its public institutions over time.

The historic public mission also influences ownership, which, in turn, affects where the mission is defined. Though legislators in each of these states knew that their public institutions had lost state revenues over time, they held a strong belief that whether the university receives 5 percent or 50 percent of its revenues from the state, it is still owned by the state, accountable to the state's residents, and public in its mission to serve the people and the needs of the state.

It is important to note that none of these universities has ever sought to privatize in the sense of becoming a truly private entity. However, legislators went out of their way to make clear that the level of public funding is not what determines the public mission; instead, ownership is the defining factor.

Legislators in Virginia spoke proudly of the local, broad definition of public mission and the mission differentiation that has been encouraged by having a loosely organized system of higher education—quite a different approach than in North Carolina and California. Each institution has been free to pursue its mission because of the autonomy granted to the institution and its board of visitors. But, because of that autonomy, a few legislators complained about the loss of anything resembling a coherent public policy toward higher education in the state.

In North Carolina—perhaps because of the more explicit connections between the UNC system, including the Chapel Hill campus, and the state—legislators articulated a clearer sense of public mission that rose above ownership and the role of the board of governors. Moreover, the definition they offered was almost the same, word for word, as that offered by university leaders. Truly, North Carolina and California legislators passionately expressed a deeply felt sense of the duty higher education has to the state—a duty they believed the public institutions had fulfilled beyond all expectations over the past two centuries. In answering the guiding question of "who 'owns' us?" legislators and university leaders alike in California and North Carolina pointed to the collective "people" of the state.

System comparison   Each of the three states studied for this book has internationally recognized universities, which are ranked among the very best in the world. So, when comparing the three systems of higher education (*systems* defined broadly as all public higher education in the state), we must first acknowledge that there is no one way to create a top-tier system of higher education. However, each of the three systems has virtues and flaws that may not be replicable elsewhere because of the history and culture of that state.

Virginia prides itself on very loose coordination of its public universities. Legislators and institutional leaders alike point to the system's autonomy as its greatest strength, allowing individual missions to evolve and develop in the marketplace and to create the conditions that will allow the individual institutions to thrive. North Carolina, on the other hand, prides itself on a strongly coordinated and managed system that seeks to prevent duplication of efforts, ensures that all regions of the state are served, and aims to create a more fair distribution of resources among sister institutions. California's leaders still believe after fifty years that the Master Plan effectively differentiated the state's institutions while also assuring that not only the elite, but all citizens who wanted one, would have access to an education.

Harvey Morgan, a former Virginia legislator, reflects on the balancing of freedoms and coordination: "Virginia carefully expanded the autonomy of several of its larger universities to the apparent benefit of all concerned. While too much authority could create a disincentive for cooperation, I believe the Virginia plan demonstrates that appropriate independence is desirable." Though

Virginia, in theory, would seem to have a less defined vision for the public purposes it seeks from its public universities because they are so much more autonomous than North Carolina's and California's, quite the opposite is true. The Restructuring Act created clarity around exactly what the state sought from each of its public institutions of higher education, such as access, accountability, and economic development. Virginia has been a test case for the effects of greater autonomy, and it has proven that coupling of autonomy with accountability can have a positive impact on the state's public policy objectives. Virginia's public institutions may not gain all the freedoms that they sought, such as control over tuition and enrollment, but the connections between the state and the institution seem to have strengthened.

UNC-CH, which began as a single campus and then grew into a statewide system over time, has always had a much stronger connection to its state, in part because of the significant funding that the system and each campus received, and in part because a highly engaged legislature and board of governors have been involved in establishing policy objectives. Since its founding, the UNC system has been led by strong presidents and presented a united front among the sister campuses, so there was never a threat to unity like other states, such as Wisconsin and Oregon (discussed in chapter 4), have seen. UNC-CH's historic role within the system helped anchor the institution to the state's mission, and its loyal support in the general assembly further bolstered its connections to the system and the state. Only in the past few years has UNC-CH—facing budget cuts due to economic and political challenges—begun to contemplate a more independent approach to sensitive issues such as tuition and enrollment.

In California, UC Berkeley was the first campus of what would grow into the multicampus University of California system. The Master Plan helped to clarify the mission, role, and each segment's place in the larger system of higher education, and state legislators also preserved UC Berkeley's place in the state's hierarchy for funding, enrollment, and research primacy. For the past fifty years, the campus has been a willing partner in the larger system, but today I sense greater anxiety in the legislature about the campus's role in the UC system and, more broadly, in the three segments of higher education. Berkeley's leaders recognize that other UC system campuses are not at the same prestigious level in terms of research and enrollment, and that some of the newer campuses are pulling support away from Berkeley. Nonetheless, the UC system and the larger system have been held together with remarkable unity over several decades.

The unifying feature of all three state systems of higher education has been an understanding that strong flagship institutions that are both highly selective and highly ranked, such as UVA, UNC-CH, and UC Berkeley, require some degree of differential treatment. Many legislative and higher education leaders acknowledged the need for additional funding and freedom, noting the cost of education at these institutions is higher than at some other public institutions because of the level and cost of research conducted, the additional focus on graduate education, the caliber and salaries of the faculty recruited to campus, and the public mission responsibilities each institution carries. Highly successful institutions could not maintain their selectivity if other institutions in the state didn't meet the broader public access mission. This is clearly part of what has made California's system so great—the premier institutions have partners serving the other segments of the population, so the pressure on them is somewhat relieved. Virginia and North Carolina don't have the same clear definitions for two-year versus four-year institutions.

Politics, governance, and the executive branch   In addition to the broadly outlined systems of higher education in the states, the governing boards for the system and the individual institutions are increasingly seen as political tools to be used by governors and legislators. Understanding autonomy as a foundation of privatization requires an understanding of the politics involved in public higher education governance, including the executive branch, the legislative branch, and the interaction between the two and with the system of higher education and individual institutions. State legislators often couple autonomy with accountability, and both are essential elements of privatization. States and public institutions have sought differing degrees of freedom and made differing trade-offs with their respective efforts.

Governance is one area where the legislative and executive branches come into conflict over the desire for greater autonomy. In Virginia, where each institution has a separate governing board of visitors, many appointments to the boards must be approved each year, and legislators were intimately aware of the politics involved in who is nominated by the governor. John Casteen describes the evolution of politics in the appointments of Virginia's boards of visitors: "One thing that changed is that our governors now appoint campaign donors to governing boards. What that meant was that the relationship between the governing boards and governor changed. The change occurred in the early 1990s with the first round of appointments Governor Wilder made, and he made the changes because he realized, first of all, that the boards were not in line with his attitude toward the universities, and second, that he had the capacity to reward friends and punish enemies by manipulating the appointments. Subsequent governors almost took that to be the way it always was, but it wasn't." The appointments to boards of public universities in most states have some political nature to them, but the significance of Casteen's analysis is that just within the past twenty years have governors really taken this as the way to do business. In our interviews, legislators offered suggestions ranging from taking away the governor's power to nominate board members and giving it to the legislature, which several states already do, to making board members stand for statewide election, as in states like Michigan.

The unfortunate incident at UVA in the summer of 2012 when President Teresa Sullivan was fired (and rehired) was one several legislators and university leaders pointed to—quietly—as an example of the need to change the way boards are appointed and whom those boards comprise. The two most glaring issues cited are that sunshine laws and open public records laws essentially prevent the board from ever having a substantive conversation in closed session; reporters are almost always in the room, and the result is that board members have side conversations rather than discussing issues as a full body. The second issue is that most members are leaders in business and law and aside from their own college experience, they know very little of the inner workings of higher education and faculty governance.

Beyond the governance of individual institutions, political stability and continuity of legislators and governors, as well as the role and strength of the governor, is critically important in understanding long-term support for higher education. Virginia prohibits its governor from serving consecutive terms, so governors rush to accomplish as much as possible very quickly. The Restructuring Act, for example, pushed through during Mark Warner's term, didn't come fully to fruition until his successor, Timothy Kaine, was in office, and many legislators described Kaine's administration as being disinterested in it because it was "Mark's thing." Nonetheless, the governor has fairly broad powers and is responsible for drafting the budget and presenting it to the general assembly.

North Carolina, on the other hand, does not have as strong an executive branch, and the state constitution did not allow consecutive terms until 1971; now a governor can serve two consecutive terms before leaving office but can then return again for two more consecutive terms (as Governor Jim Hunt did across the span of three decades, serving four terms from the 1970s through the 2000s). Similarly, until 1996, the state constitution prevented the governor from vetoing legislation. Though the governor in North Carolina is also responsible for drafting the budget and presenting it to the general assembly, North Carolina has one of the constitutionally weaker executive branches among the states.

California's governor historically had great power, but the ballot initiative process has removed much power from the governor and the legislature in the past several decades. Decisions that affect revenues and spending obligations are taken out of the hands of the executive and legislative branches and placed directly into the hands of the voters.

Legislative insight (or lack thereof)   The third foundation of privatization focuses on institutional autonomy, but the question of ownership centers on the state and the legislature. After interviewing nearly one hundred fifty state legislators, I found that they are, at once, the most important "owners" of these public institutions while at the same time the least knowledgeable about higher education and the public agenda. The contrast in support for public higher education—politically, at least—among the fifty state legislatures is dramatic. Some show almost unquestioned financial and political support, and others show increasing animosity and criticism to go along with diminished appropriations. But, at the end of the day, the legislators interviewed for this study in each of the three states believe their public institutions are meeting the needs of the state and serving the public good effectively. With three such different states, that is a significant finding that privatization has not diminished institutions' focus on the public good.

University leaders and policy makers are all keenly aware that the future of public higher education rests in the hands of the legislators, at least so long as the state remains a partial funder and full "owner" of the institutions. Higher education is a significant line item in the budgets of most states, a discretionary item that is generally one of the largest in the budget. However, legislators have very limited knowledge of the workings of higher education. Even those most knowledgeable sometimes have only the scantest understanding of higher education finance, or the public purposes that the state wants to achieve with its institutions. Legislative insight—or lack thereof—is a significant factor in these legislators' perspectives on higher education.

California is one of the few states with a full-time legislative body, and both Virginia and North Carolina have part-time legislatures, whose members have, for the most part, other full-time jobs that demand a large share of their attention. The volume of legislation is significant, and legislators described a need to have a few experts or specialists in the House and Senate who could inform the other members. In Virginia, a few legislators joked that it would be generous to say half a dozen members understood higher education, while North Carolina legislators estimated that perhaps fifteen did so. Everyone in California purports to be knowledgeable about higher education, but very few actually wanted to serve on those committees because there's no money available from lobbyists.

Though several committees deal with higher education, it is really the "money committees"—Appropriations and Finance—that have the deepest knowledge and understanding of the inner workings of higher education and the clearest sense of how privatization has impacted the three flagship universities. For example, major decisions, such as Virginia's Restructuring Act, were handled almost entirely within Appropriations and Finance, and the Education Committee saw the legislation only at its very latest stage. California legislators on money committees expressed slightly deeper knowledge of higher education than those in the other two states, but they also have much bigger financial issues demanding their attention in a state that has been facing significant deficits.

U.S. Representative Julia Brownley, who was in the California State Assembly when we met, explained why California legislators have limited knowledge, making it hard for them to know what they are "buying" when they fund higher education:

> There's certainly different degrees of awareness. And always when you get to education, every legislator would probably say they know a lot about it because they've experienced it: either their own experiences or their children's experiences.
>
> Just the one example of the middle-class squeeze—I don't think a lot of legislators are aware of that. They might hear a speech on the floor when we're dealing with a particular issue, but are they aware of that and are they following up on that and trying to figure out what the real data is behind that? I don't think so.
>
> There are a lot of subject areas that I know very little about. And we tend to pursue an area or two, and in the short period of time that we have, try to become a little bit of an expert in it and move on. I didn't get the sense from people who were peripherally involved in education that they had a deep sense for what they wanted to accomplish with their $2 billion that they're putting into the University of California, for instance. And we haven't, as a body, we really haven't wrestled with that kind of question at all.

There are so many issues facing legislators, and higher education is but one voice in a sea of needs. California Assemblyman Richard Gordon joins Representative Brownley in explaining the lack of awareness most legislators have about higher education funding. For some legislators, funding of higher education is about trust based on their own experiences as students.

> I don't think we know truly what we're buying. For the most part, what we're funding is our memory of our college experience. I think what we're sort of buying is if something positive happened for us—it helped us to advance in life, so it must be good, because it was good for us. So I think what we're paying for is that. I don't think we really know what we're paying for. I don't know how it is used when we give these huge lumps of money—I mean, is that going to faculty members, is it going to administrators, is it going to a classroom? I don't really know the specifics of what we're buying. But I'm trusting, based on my own personal experience, that it's going to be okay.

Throughout my interviews, many did reflect on their own educational experiences or those of their children, but very few were highly knowledgeable about the issues facing higher education, how the financial model works, or what the public agenda should be.

With legislators pulled in multiple directions, with very little staff support, and with short legislative sessions in many states, the focus on higher education is minimal. In most states, one of the impacts has been a larger role for the legislative staff, particularly in presenting analysis and making recommendations to the members. The staffs working with the money and education committees present data and options to members, and because they are full-time staff, they provide long-term memory and continuity. They also have great sway. This is one reason why university leaders emphasized that they must spend more time with the legislative staffs and lobby them almost as much as they do the actual legislators. David Bulova, a Virginia delegate, describes the role of staff in the legislative process: "Given the time constraints of the legislative process, many legislators don't fully understand the ramifications or ins and outs of the issues we deal with, and if you look at any complicated issue such as higher education or health care or environment and energy, you are going to find that there are fewer than ten people who have real expertise in those areas, and everyone else will rely upon their voices and the full-time staff who are focused on that area. We often rely on staff and the cabinet secretaries to make sure we aren't pushing in the wrong directions or barking up the wrong tree." Legislators have to balance competing demands on their time, so the legislative staff—along with lobbyists hired by the higher education sector—has necessarily taken on a larger role. One university leader described the influence of the staff this way: "They don't vote, but they inform and they opine, so they have influence."

Legislative skepticism   At a time when higher education is under great scrutiny for escalating costs, low efficiency, highly paid faculty and administrators, the lacking focus of the curriculum, and unclear learning outcomes, some legislators expressed a mixture of what Robert Berdahl described as "hostility and ignorance." Even those who support higher education expressed skepticism—often quite deep skepticism—about higher education overall, public higher education more generally, and the flagship university specifically.

Legislative skepticism could be viewed as part of a healthy questioning of all state spending, particularly during challenging economic times, and due diligence to be certain that the citizens' money is being used for the highest and most efficient purposes. The skepticism also revealed a belief that higher education, for too long, has been "fat, dumb, and happy" with state dollars, growing into what is now perceived as a bloated and inefficient enterprise. Finally, the growing skepticism expressed by so many legislators was manifested in conversations in which they revealed their belief that higher education is today seen as more of a private benefit to the individual student than a public good for the state and its citizens overall.

Perhaps because higher education has received such generous public funding historically, legislators are increasingly wary of how those tax dollars are being used and what outcomes the state is achieving as a result of the investment. The most common criticism expressed by legislators was about research and its role in the university, as well as the curriculum and its lack of focus and practical applicability. Representative Paul Stam of North Carolina, who was House majority leader when we spoke and is now speaker pro tempore, describes the view that some university research has little value to the state: "You can always have fun by dredging up some of the course descriptions. Some of them are a riot . . . [In one case], there were six senior faculty members who had one student each in the English department. You can imagine that in physics, where somebody is just doing research on a grant. But try to imagine that in English, where cutting-edge research on Middle English literature is fascinating but is not likely to lead to any improvements in our standard of living." Representative Stam reflects a common skepticism expressed by legislators across the country—namely, that research for the sake of research is not valuable to the state and comes at the cost of teaching more students, and scholarship in the humanities and social sciences is not valued. As higher education has come under scrutiny, the role and funding of research, to the extent that it is seen as being in conflict with teaching, is at the heart of much of the legislative skepticism.

Even legislators who support higher education and research had concerns about the focus of the research and the overall shifts in curriculum into areas that legislators did not see as being central to the state's needs. Ethnic, women's, and gender studies, for example, were cited several times by legislators as "unnecessary" or "disconnected" from more practical needs. Legislators such as John Chichester, former chairman of the Senate Finance Committee in Virginia, said that when state funding goes to those programs, it "tak[es] the zeal out of us to fund them." Chichester also described a belief, expressed by other legislators as well, that universities care more about research than undergraduate education: "Given their druthers, I think many colleges prefer graduate students to undergraduate students but—since that will never be the case—they do what they can to be accommodating. Many of the senior professors would prefer teaching three hours per semester and [doing] research the rest of the time. I have no quarrel with research whatsoever, so long as it is pertinent to our daily lives. As an example, it makes little sense to spend a year doing research for the sake of breeding longer ears on rabbits. That might be self-satisfying, but it does little to advance the public good." Legislators were equipped with endless stories of research that seemed to them to be less than valuable, but more importantly, Senator Chichester emphasizes how many legislators are interested primarily in practical research and lament that the focus of many research universities has shifted to the point that undergraduate teaching is no longer valued as highly. While this is certainly not true at community colleges, liberal arts colleges, and some comprehensive universities, there are many legislators that point to their flagship research university and to the diminishing focus on teaching.

Further skepticism from legislators was exemplified when they looked at how universities spent public dollars on areas they considered less than crucial. Delegate David Albo, who has been a critic of Virginia institutions for not using their funding to enroll more in-state students, also said that universities use their money for ends that are not in line with the state's goals: "I castigate the universities a great deal about not spending their money on educating in-state students, but I am sympathetic to what their problem is. They need money to create more slots [for enrollment]. However, they don't spend the money they have wisely. I've never seen their money going to the things I want them to do. Left to their own devices with lots of money, they would not fund more enrollment for in-state students. The money would get sucked up into niche studies like anthropology of *x* society or the literature of group *y*." Moving from block funding to performance-based funding, as described in chapter 4, is a clear progression across the states and was described by many legislators as a goal that is partially motivated by legislative skepticism about how state money is being used. Delegate Steve Landes, chairman of Virginia's House Education Committee, further described a lack of trust and confidence in higher education that leads to skepticism, because some legislators believe that higher education is not transparent and faculty and administrators are paid highly for very little productivity, relative to the rest of state government. The decreasing focus on undergraduate teaching is raised again as a concern:

> When you look at faculty and staff salaries, we feel like they are paid a heck of a lot, especially for faculty who aren't even doing that much regarding teaching students. You try to raise those questions and hold their feet to the fire and they push back, rather than giving us facts and figures; so there's not always a lot of transparency and trust in higher education. They hate people having information on who is being paid what, how much faculty are teaching, and they don't seem to like transparency. First and foremost, they should focus on educating our citizens. Faculty focus on research because they enjoy that more, and they often make more money on research-related projects and writing books. We're all for their academic freedom, but when you work in a state institution, there has to be some accountability to the state and its citizens. Legislators don't feel a lot of trust when questions are not answered, and details and answers are too hard to get from them.

Transparency or the lack thereof is a consistent issue raised by legislators wanting to know the facts and feeling as though universities are not always forthcoming with them.

Interestingly, several legislators pointed out a shift in the backgrounds of legislators, from the traditional lawyers to an increasing number of K–12 teachers. Privately, these legislators noted that the K–12 teachers spend eight hours in the classroom teaching, so they are often more suspicious of the low teaching loads and focus on research at universities. One legislator describes the skepticism about teaching loads in higher education as follows:

There is a big push among legislators to have more of these professors physi-
cally in the classroom instead of using the university to take a sabbatical to
research some obscure article. Some of them teach one class or two classes a
semester. It seems that as soon as college professors gain tenure, they just "re-
tire." Everything is under the guise of research, but let's face it—if you want
a laid-back job and you can read and write, a college professorship is great.

Many of us legislators are probably more skeptical of a lot of the folks who
are working in universities. Just think about it: if a professor taught a full load,
about half of what a high school teacher teaches—three classes, I mean—we
could cut millions, millions of dollars off what we give to colleges. And they
would save tons of money, allowing students to save in tuition.

While this colorful description of faculty research and productivity may
seem completely distorted to those in the academy, it is one reflection of how
legislators see scholarship and research as well as the less visible forms of teaching, such as advising students. Policy makers in many states see much of the
research coming from the universities as disconnected from public interests,
since each member of the faculty determines his or her own research agenda.

Even with the widespread and sometimes flagrant skepticism that legislators expressed about faculty teaching loads, salaries, curricular focus, and
economic efficiencies, a solid minority of legislators, particularly among the
most knowledgeable, still believed that the faculty were the lifeblood of the
university and that good research is part and parcel of good teaching. This
subset of legislators recognized that the preeminence that highly ranked research universities have achieved is largely because of the strength of their
faculty, and they wholly supported the direction the universities had taken to
bolster their research portfolio, particularly because they saw it as a benefit to
the state in terms of economic development and the pure discovery that can
lead to real breakthroughs. One legislator expressed the support I heard from
a few legislators for research and exploration, even in an era of dwindling
resources: "We need research for research's sake. I think that is a valuable
function that colleges and universities can fill because if we say, 'Well, your
research should only be for economic development,' we will miss something
big. If you have research for research's sake, you will stumble across some
sort of big breakthrough or major find that could later lead to a new drug or
a new cure for something, but it's never a guarantee." While this legislator's
support for pure discovery was strong, most expressed support for STEM
fields, rather than research and scholarship more broadly in the humanities

and social sciences. Some legislators in all three states believed higher educa-tion is a worthy investment, that the balance between teaching and research could be achieved, and that the public institutions were balancing it appro-priately. However, a deep and growing divide still exists between universities and their legislatures.

Autonomy as a foundation of privatization builds upon the two founda-tions beneath it and helps us to understand what factors affect an institution's relationship with the state, particularly the legislative branch. Autonomy also lays the groundwork for the fourth foundation—finance—which is the el-ement of privatization that is perhaps most often discussed. While we may have been focused intensely on the changes in finance, understanding uni-versity finance requires an understanding of the cumulative effects of the first three foundations.

Finance

You already know that state funding for higher education has declined in most states and now accounts for a much smaller portion of the operating budget; that fact has been documented throughout this book. This financial reality—confronting an institution that is competing for faculty, students, and prestige—is one motivating factor in privatization. However, although finance is the foundation of privatization most often discussed publicly, it builds upon the three previous foundations. These universities have a long history of public funding, so we can't look only at today's level of financial support with a blind eye toward more than two centuries of significant public funding. Understanding "how are we funded?" helps explain a harsh truth of privatization—but only after we grasp its previous foundations.

In each of the state chapters, we delved deeply into the finances for that state to understand total higher education appropriations as well as funding at the flagship institution. Figure 8.1 shows clearly the rise in tuition and de-crease in per-FTE-student appropriations at the three flagship institutions over a decade. While all three "bubbles" have risen and moved toward the higher tuition on the chart and lesser appropriations, it is notable how lit-tle UNC-CH has moved relative to the other two flagship institutions; UC Berkeley, in particular, has seen drastic change in a decade. Nonetheless, in all three cases, the push from the state and the pull from the federal govern-ment helped contribute to the changing financial reality at these three insti-tutions and elsewhere in the country.

FIGURE 8.1A   Public flagship universities, 2001 (in constant 2011 dollars)

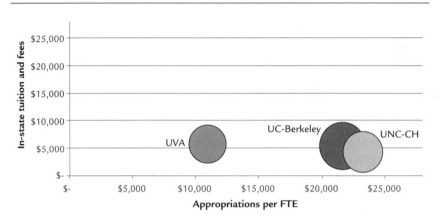

FIGURE 8.1B   Public flagship universities, 2011 (in constant 2011 dollars)

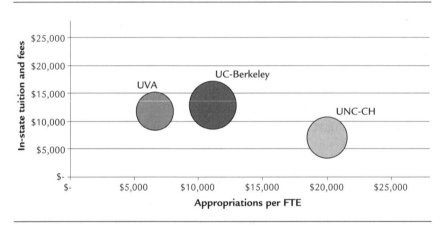

Source: IPEDS, 2012

Note: Appropriations per FTE were calculated using state appropriations divided by fall FTE enrollment. Inflation-adjusted totals were calculated using 2011 HECA. Bubble size reflects fall FTE enrollment.

Pushed by state finances   History aside for a moment, legislators and governors are facing very difficult decisions today—politics is, after all, about the here and now. State coffers are diminished, and future projections do not look as rosy as they did in previous decades. State funding for higher education will likely be stagnant in the years ahead because once state economies start growing again, many services will come ahead of higher education—either due to mandate or a shift in prioritization. So while many legislators lament the privatization of higher education, they know that their options are limited. The reality of politics is that a legislator does not want to be responsible for raising tuition at the state's public institutions in the years following one of the worst recessions in a century. The result is what legislators sometimes covertly and sometimes overtly described as a "wink and a nod." One legislator described for me the politics of reducing funding for higher education and then complaining about rising tuition: "It's almost like a wink and a nod of legislators knowing that they can't fund [higher education] at the level that's needed. So they'll make some statement about, 'This is deplorable. This is awful. We can't have tuition rise. It's bad. It hurts our families.' But at the same time, it's sort of, 'Oh well, we're gonna have to let that happen because we can't fund it, either.' So it is almost a little bit of a wink and a nod to the universities."

Other legislators used different analogies, but they described a similar phenomenon—a dance over the past twenty years between legislators and university leaders. University leaders described the need to pay "homage" whenever stable or increased funding does come in for the university and to bite their tongues when the criticism comes following an increase in tuition. The push by the state for greater privatization can be felt in each of these states; in an era of diminishing state revenues, further privatization may be a continuing trend.

Pulled by federal research funding   Beyond the push from the states toward privatization as a result of shifting state funding, legislators see a significant pull from the federal government and other national entities that fund research at top-tier research universities. Earlier in this chapter, legislative skepticism was discussed in regard to the role of research in the university, but there are also real concerns about what that means for the mission of public universities. In a time of economic uncertainty, legislators want their public institutions to focus on reducing costs and increasing productivity, which conflicts with having a research faculty focused on both teaching and research. North Carolina Senate President Pro Tempore Philip Berger describes the impact of research from the legislative perspective: "The expansion of research grants at universities . . . has created some concern amongst legislators about the mission—'Is it a teaching or research institution, or can you have both side by side?' That has created some tension and concern about what is the overall mission."

Federal research funding was a significant factor in the past fifty years at all top-ranked institutions in increasing research output and lowering teaching expectations for faculty. National rankings, such as those of *US News & World Report*, focus heavily on research, as do the faculty themselves when contemplating where they want to spend their careers. As a result, there has been a pull by the federal government and other research funding agencies toward privatization where public universities are seeking to raise their research profile. Legislators described this as the greatest tension they see at the universities, which, they say, are naturally being drawn away by the flow of external research funding from a focus on the state toward larger and broader issues that are national or global in scale. The "pull" of federal research dollars is significant, particularly when viewed in comparison to state appropriations. As noted in the state chapters, federal research funding surpassed state appropriations several years ago and now constitutes a much larger share of the overall operating budget at each flagship university. Federal research funding continues to grow today on a per-FTE-student basis, while appropriations continue to decline.

Robert Gates, the only secretary of defense to serve under two presidents of different political parties, has deep knowledge of higher education as the former president of Texas A&M University and current chancellor of William & Mary. Gates brings the legislators' concerns into perspective when he reflects on the role research plays in our national security as well as the basic educational experience:

> While the funding shortfalls at universities hit economically disadvantaged and middle class students hardest, they also affect the ability of universities to conduct basic research. What is discovered in research one day is taught in the classroom the next, and then employed as a tool of economic development, innovation, and, in some cases, national defense. The notion that teaching in universities serves students and research in universities does not—and that the two are at cross purposes instead of fundamentally linked, integrated into one another at the core—betrays on the part of its purveyors a profound

misunderstanding of how great universities get that way and stay that way and of the entire enterprise of higher education.[4]

Comparing wealth and spending   Virginia, North Carolina, and California—and their three flagship universities—can be compared on a number of measures relating to their autonomy, but it is the difference in state funding that is most dramatic. One important measure is a state's relative wealth and how much it spends on higher education in relation to that wealth. By comparing tax capacity in the states to understand the differences in wealth among them, and the per capita tax effort for higher education, we can see one measure of the differences in how each state prioritizes higher education.

Figure 8.2 shows the total taxable resources per capita for the three states, which is a measure of the relative fiscal capacity of the states. In other words, how much money do they have available to fund public priorities on a per capita basis, including higher education? We can see the gap in wealth among the three states by mapping the "tax capacity" that the states have available to fund public purposes, along with their effective tax rates. Figure 8.3, in contrast, shows how much the states actually spend of their total taxable resources on higher education. While Virginia is a wealthy state, relatively speaking, and has the most resources per capita ($58,967), it spends the least

FIGURE 8.2   Total taxable resources per capita and effective tax rate: Virginia, North Carolina, and California, 2010

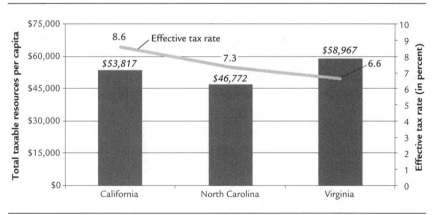

Source: SHEEO, 2013

Note: Population and tax revenues data from U.S. Census Bureau; total taxable resources per capita from U.S. Treasury Department.

FIGURE 8.3   Higher education support per capita: Virginia, North Carolina, and California, 2011

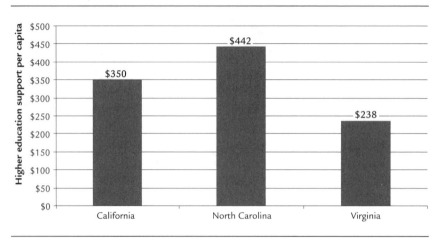

Source: SHEEO, 2013

Note: Higher education support = state and local tax and nontax support for public and independent higher education. Includes special-purpose appropriations for research/agricultural/medical. Population and personal income data from U.S. Census Bureau and Bureau of Economic Analysis; state and local tax revenue data from U.S. Census Bureau; lottery profit data from North American Association of State and Provincial Lotteries.

per capita on higher education at $238. North Carolina, the least wealthy of the three states with $46,772 per capita in total taxable resources, spends the most of the three states at $442 per capita (nearly double Virginia and almost $100 more than California). These measures are helpful in highlighting the support each state has for higher education overall, compared to available resources.

The more familiar measures are shown in figures 8.4 and 8.5, where appropriations are charted for each state. Figure 8.4 reveals the trends in all three states on a total dollar basis in terms of the investment in higher education over the past twenty-five years. In 1987, the three states had fairly similar appropriations per FTE student, with North Carolina and California spending almost the exact amount. Virginia has seen its appropriations cut in half, while California has only recently taken a nosedive, but North Carolina has remained strongly committed to its system of public higher education, even if it has declined slightly.

Looking specifically at the three flagship institutions in terms of the per-FTE-student funding, figure 8.5 shows the trends at these campuses, which

FIGURE 8.4 Total higher education appropriations per FTE student: Virginia, North Carolina, and California, 1987–2012 (in constant 2012 dollars)

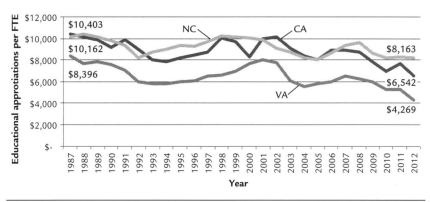

Source: SHEEO, 2013

Note: Constant 2012 dollars adjusted by SHEEO Higher Education Cost Adjustment (HECA). Educational appropriations include ARRA funds.

largely mirror the trends overall in the state—flat or declining. It is not surprising but worth noting that appropriations for each of these three flagship institutions are higher than the average overall in the respective states. Virginia comes up significantly short in this measure: California spends more than twice as much per student at UC Berkeley, and North Carolina spends over three times as much per student at UNC-CH as Virginia spends per student at UVA.

There can be no question that, in the past twenty-five years, each of these states has maintained a significant commitment to funding public higher education—but that funding was not as generous as the universities hoped for or believed they should receive (and probably could never have completely kept pace with the rise in cost and growth of the overall system of higher education). Using these inflation-adjusted numbers, we can see that, on a per student and a per capita basis, North Carolina held true to its constitutional mandate that higher education should be as close to "free" for the people of the state. In my interviews with state legislators, policy makers, and institutional leaders, all agreed that the level of historical support for the university was virtually unheard of across the fifty states.

Virginia, on the other hand, with its long history of low funding and relative institutional autonomy, has allowed individual institutions to pursue

FIGURE 8.5   State appropriations per FTE student, UVA, UNC-CH, and UC
Berkeley, 1987–2010 (in constant 2010 dollars)

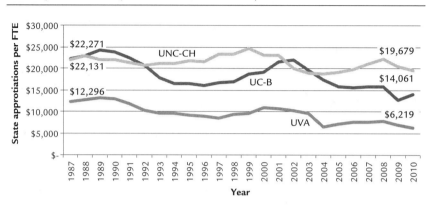

Source: Delta Cost Project dataset, 2012

Note: The fall FTE enrollment was used for FTE calculations. Constant 2010 dollars adjusted by
SHEEO Higher Education Cost Adjustment (HECA).

higher tuition and alternative revenues for so long that the recent declines in
state funding do not appear to faze institutional leaders the way the first cuts
did twenty years ago. This is where the foundations of privatization reveal
the importance of state context, vision, institutional autonomy, and legislative involvement. Though Virginia's current reality is starkly different from
North Carolina's and California's, it is in line with the state's long trajectory
of privatization.

California and UC Berkeley appear to be charting new territory and head-
ing in the direction Virginia has taken—financially, at least—in the past
twenty years. Significant declines in state appropriations have been met with
large increases (albeit on a very low starting base) and a doubling of out-of-
state students in the past five years to close the gap. Philanthropy is taking an
increasing role in the state and its flagship institution as well. What is fascinating to me as a researcher is listening to and comparing the outlook of legislators and administrators in the three states. In California, similar to North
Carolina, there is extreme optimism among almost all those interviewed that
once the state's finances are back in order and tax revenues are flowing, there
will be a massive investment again in higher education. Perhaps this is part
of the entrepreneurial spirit that has always characterized the state, but there
were relatively few who stated outright that the golden days won't return.

By contrast, most legislators and university leaders alike in Virginia openly stated that funding for higher education will never return to historic levels.

National and federal perspectives on privatization   The national economy has seen dramatic swings over the past seventy years. But, overall, it has been a prosperous period for higher education in this country. Following World War II, the GI Bill provided greater access to higher education, but it also encouraged more significant federal support for research funding at universities around the nation, including many public research universities, which were among the largest research engines at the time. Higher education has historically been the responsibility of the states, but the federal government drove funding for research and access, particularly after the war.

In writing this book, though I was searching primarily for the state legislative and executive branch perspectives on privatization, I also sought to understand the national and federal awareness and perceptions of privatization. I interviewed several leading individuals at national research, higher education, and governmental agencies and organizations, as well as a few members of Congress, capturing their perspectives about privatization at public universities; the role and influence of the federal government in driving and reacting to privatization; and the impacts, seen from the national level, on these universities and the public good. In short, the national and federal agencies that support and are most closely involved with higher education, particularly in research funding, have very little awareness of the forces, impacts, or effects of privatization at public universities. Similarly, these agencies do not differentiate clearly in their funding and involvement with universities based on whether they are public or private.

U.S. Representative Rush Holt is something of a rarity in Congress because he comes from higher education, having led a plasma physics laboratory at Princeton University before running for office. Representative Holt shared his perspective about privatization, as seen in Washington: "I think it [higher education] has even less attention than usual. Going back over the decades, it would be a rare member of Congress who gives much thought to the purpose of higher education, let alone the philosophical underpinnings and the structure of higher education. And I think there's even less of that now. So my guess is, most members of Congress would be oblivious to [privatization]. And I think the shift is real." While members of Congress may be unaware of what is happening in public higher education, they (like state legislators) are quick to point out the rise in tuition over time. It is not surprising, in some ways, that they are not fully informed about public higher education since it has largely been the province of the states. Sadly, however, the primary federal funding agencies may not be much better. The composition of leaders at the National Science Foundation (which is responsible for about 20 percent of all federally funded research at universities) are largely faculty, so they are aware of the shifts, but the National Institutes of Health (where 80 percent of its $30 billion budget goes to support research conducted at universities) are staffed by permanent scientists who are much less aware of the changes in the states.

I had the opportunity to interview Charles Vest about a year before he died in 2013 to talk about privatization from his perspective as president of the National Academy of Engineering and president emeritus of MIT. From his viewpoint in Washington, he offered a candid perspective on the federal role in research funding and the challenges faced today in competing for resources: "Most people in Washington haven't the foggiest idea what's happened to public higher education." Timothy Killeen, the National Science Foundation's assistant director for geosciences from 2008 to 2012 and now president of the SUNY Research Foundation, offered another perspective on the federal involvement in the privatization phenomenon at public research universities and the impacts his agency saw from the shortage of dollars at these universities. Killeen's words reflect a common belief—that while federal research funding contributed to the privatization phenomenon, it is now time for a new model: "I do think that there needs to be a new compact between science and society in general, into which would fit the public universities with their role. We need something to clarify the role in the public sector of these research universities where the balance has shifted from where it was to a new place."

Beyond research funding, however, the federal government may contribute to the privatization phenomenon with its significant support in underwriting students' tuition costs through federal financial aid programs, as discussed in chapter 4. One member of Congress I interviewed described the federal government as artificially propping up high tuition and tuition increases so that students can get low-interest loans; ultimately, this could lead to something similar to the housing and credit bubble that started the Great Recession. Eduardo Ochoa, president of California State University, Monterey Bay, sat for an interview with me when he was the assistant secretary for postsecondary education, the senior-most leader on issues of higher education in the U.S. Department of Education. He discussed the role of the federal government in public higher education and the shifting perception of how the federal government is involved: "What's happening now is that as the states are disinvesting in higher education, the federal government is stepping in, but in a sort of different mechanism. Instead of funding institutions of higher education directly, we [the federal government] have stepped up support for students. So essentially, we have a situation where the states cut back on support, the public universities raise tuition to partially compensate, and then we step in and provide students with Pell Grants and student loans so they can afford that tuition." Ochoa echoed the sentiments of many state legislators who are now more interested in performance-based funding for institutions or supporting students directly, rather than providing any form of block grants to be used at the broad discretion of institutions. He also highlights the feeling of some state legislators and many in Congress that they are caught on a treadmill, trying to keep up with funding shortfalls and financial needs in higher education.

Though many leaders at the national and federal level acknowledged some disconnect between Washington and the public universities across the country, most felt that privatization is an issue for the states because higher education was and is a responsibility of the states. Federal research funding has begun to decline, and there is little optimism among these leaders that it will return to historically high levels. Bills have been proposed in Congress that would reduce Pell Grant funding and limit the amount of debt college students can take on from the federal government. Many national leaders have concerns about the legislative leaders around the country who have little regard for the research and service missions in higher education; they see a need for broader awareness of the benefits research brings for the states as well as for the public good in the country as a whole. Harvey Fineberg, president of the Institute of Medicine of the National Academies, described the "unintended consequences" of a series of state and federal actions that have led to greater privatization in public higher education and how those changes will impact the public mission and service of the public good:

> The mission in most state schools was initially formulated to serve the educational needs of the residents of the state and to fulfill a mandate to be accessible to all within the state. There is a growing disparity between that original mission and the realities of support and financing for the university. As an institution gets more dollars from research rather than appropriations, it would naturally lead to a strategy focused on gaining needed financial support, which is where the federal government became a more significant force.

Every major university has always had the discovery of new knowledge as a part of its mission, so that was not a change in mission so much as a change in proportionality.

This tension between an original weight of mission focused on state residents and the realities of much more diverse sources of financial support naturally leads state-based institutions to reexamine their relationships to the legislatures, to the immediate community, to national institutions, and to the world at large. The proportionate sense of mission will naturally shift over time to reflect changing capacities and purposes of financial support.

Dr. Fineberg's perspective offers some insight into how the federal government has been one of the driving forces for privatization in public higher education—spurring the nationalization of these institutions. Knowing how the public mission is defined in the twenty-first century—and who is defining it—helps to understand the effects of privatization.

Politics and finance   Politics is one of the most decried yet least understood elements in discussions of privatization and finance in public higher education. Politics and public policy are, at the core, about the allocation of public funds, so politics is essential to an understanding of the fourth foundation of privatization—finance. All three flagship universities receive public funding and are creatures of the state. As such, they are subject to politics and are, in some ways, at the center of the current national debates about individual benefits versus public responsibilities. The shifting political winds in these and many other states are increasingly pointing toward greater accountability for diminished resources on a per-student basis and toward a more universal feeling that higher education is an individual responsibility.

Politics is an inevitable aspect of university leadership, and, historically, public university presidents have been very skilled at working closely with their state legislatures. Politics in higher education today is becoming increasingly contentious for universities; philosophies about how higher education should be supported and managed from a state perspective are evolving. Richard Riley, who served as U.S. secretary of education from 1993 to 2001 and governor of South Carolina from 1979 to 1987, discussed the increasing level of politics in higher education in the states and reminds us that higher education overall is in a tenuous position: "In the future, we will always have politics involved in funding for higher education and politics in setting the priorities of higher education. Tough economies put pressure on soft items such as higher education, unless you believe in the importance of it to the larger state and national goals, which I do, but not all politicians do."

In these states, the politics of higher education funding and policy involves more than state appropriations; today, the debates are more often tied to tuition and enrollment. Several legislators acknowledged that there is a severe disconnect between the level of state support and the public's expectations for the institution, even taking into account the historic support for operations and capital expenditures. John Edwards, a Virginia state senator, described the disconnect: "It's like the 'flat earth society.' It's not worth arguing with the people who are confident that higher education needs reform and doesn't need more revenue. Politics is more about mythology than reality." Truly, he encapsulates one of the great challenges for higher education: some people are convinced that higher education is inefficient, bloated, and disconnected from the primary mission of teaching, and you most likely can't change their minds very quickly.

Finally, tuition is perhaps the most visible and contentious sign of the changing finance of public universities. This element harkens back to the first three foundations of privatization; we must understand the historical roots of the university, who the institution is serving, and how the university is funded. As state support has declined, tuition has been the easiest tool at the system or institutional level to make up for the loss of state revenues.

Because higher education institutions are among the very few state agencies that can raise revenues outside of tax dollars, and they have significant market pricing power, legislators often choose to cut funding to higher education first because it is the least painful cut they can make. Several legislators concurred that it is easier to cut funding to higher education because it has an alternative source of revenue. Institutional leaders may be forced to focus intently on finance because it drives much of their on-campus decision making, but finance flows from the foundations of state context, vision and focus, and autonomy beneath it. It also influences the fifth foundation above it, which focuses on the students whom the institution serves.

Enrollment and Access

The fifth foundation of privatization is enrollment and access. Public universities were founded as places where the residents of the state would be able to get a good education at low cost, and they were avenues of access for millions of students in the nineteenth and twentieth centuries. This foundation of privatization builds upon the previous four foundations and tangibly encapsulates the focus of the institution and the connection to the history and mission. Understanding where an institution falls on the continuum helps to describe the cumulative impact of privatization built upon the first four foundations and embodied in the most direct form of service to the state: educating students. This foundation could be summarized with the question, "Who are our students?"

In each of these states, legislators openly raised their concerns about the relatively small number of in-state students who would be fortunate enough to attend the flagship university. The discussions most often focused on the cost of attendance and who should be responsible for paying it. While each of these three universities has generous financial aid policies for low-income students, legislators said—usually off the record—that middle-income students were the ones who concerned them the most, and that they were uneasy about using tuition from wealthier students to subsidize poorer ones. As private universities have grown their endowments and increased tuition to help subsidize students with lesser means, in some cases it has become cheaper to attend a high-priced private university than a lower-priced public university, because more financial aid is available. California Assemblyman Richard Gordon provided very thoughtful insight into the role of a public university in serving the middle class in America. He shared what I heard from several legislators:

> I think part of the great strength of America has always been that we've had a strong middle class. I think that's been an important part of who we are. For me, the public university is the university for the middle class. Poor kids who have the right skills and talents can attend private schools—they will be sought after with scholarships. Rich kids can attend private schools. Now, that's not to say that poor kids and rich kids can't attend a public university, and should. But it seems to me that it's those kids in the middle class who aren't poor enough to really qualify for some of the scholarships, even if they've got good educational attainment, and certainly whose families can't afford tuition at a private institution, need opportunities.
>
> So it seems to me that it's [public universities] that have been the place where we've provided the education for the middle class. And I think that's what is potentially at risk as you increase tuition, increase fees, and make it more difficult for folks to participate in a public institution.

Middle class students were mentioned quite frequently in interviews because they tend to be the ones who most frequently complained to legislators about being squeezed—not needy enough to get financial aid but not wealthy enough to pay the full cost of tuition. Enrollment and access strike at the core of the balance between the state's interests in ensuring access and affordability for the best and brightest students, regardless of financial ability, and the political reality of the need to fund ever-increasing costs for higher education.

In-state and out-of-state enrollment, mixed with politics   UC Berkeley, UVA, and UNC-CH each have a financial model predicated on strong market positioning, which allows each institution to feel confident that it will have solid enrollment (usually ten times as many applicants as those admitted). As we've seen, enrollments have risen modestly over the past two decades, and the in-state/out-of-state enrollment mix at the three institutions has remained largely steady through that time (with the exception of UC Berkeley, which has seen a doubling of its out-of-state students in the last five years, from 10 to 19 percent—still less than UVA and roughly equal to UNC-CH). Figure 8.6 shows the slow but steady rise in FTE student enrollment at the three institutions.

What is perhaps most notable about the enrollment at these three flagships is how small the student body sizes are, relative to the overall enrollment in the respective states and to the need for educating far more students in the

FIGURE 8.6   Total fall FTE student enrollment: UC Berkeley, UNC-CH, and UVA, 1986–2012

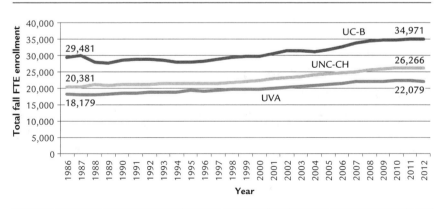

Source: Merged dataset with IPEDS and Delta Cost Project, 2013

Note: DCP data was used until fall 2000, when IPEDS began reporting the variable.

nation. We have to keep institutions like these in perspective when we think about the broader system of higher education in the country. The United States has been outpaced internationally; while it ranks ninth in the world in the proportion of young adults enrolled in college, it has fallen to sixteenth in the world in the share of certificates and degrees awarded to adults ages twenty-five to thirty-four. President Obama set a goal that by 2020 America would once again have the highest proportion of college graduates in the world. That goal, if feasible, will likely be achieved at the access-based institutions, such as community colleges and comprehensive universities where the growth potential is the greatest. As evidenced in figure 8.6, flagship universities such as these will not be able to (and may not feel the need to) meet the growth needed in the college population. So, while much of the case study discussion has focused on these flagships, it is important to remember their place in the larger educational system aimed at achieving greater rates of participation in higher education.[5]

Public universities most often face criticism from legislators and governors over the cost of tuition and the high number of out-of-state students on campus. Today, out-of-state students often pay more than 100 percent of the cost of their education, so few will argue that they are an added burden on the state's revenues. However, because these public universities are enmeshed in a political environment, they face criticism over the mix of in-state and out-of-state students, or whether they are increasing in-state enrollments quickly enough. Politics is always local, and several legislators focused on the need to increase enrollment for their constituents; I heard numerous stories from legislators about the student with a 4.0 GPA and perfect SAT score who was denied admission to the flagship university. Legislators consistently said that they wanted to exert control but did not have adequate funding to do so, resulting in the perceived irrationality of making demands without offering alternative solutions. This issue, perhaps more than any other, is at the nexus of politics and privatization.

As an example, about one-third of UVA students enrolled at the undergraduate level come from states other than Virginia. In almost every legislative session of recent years, a bill has been introduced in the House of Delegates to cap out-of-state enrollment at UVA and other public universities, but it never advances beyond committee because legislators acknowledge that the state does not have the resources to make up for the lost tuition from out-of-state students. David Albo is one of the Virginia legislators who has proposed an out-of-state enrollment cap often in recent years, and he describes Virginia higher education politics related to enrollment in his own colorful way:

> The universities are increasing tuition and not increasing in-state slots, but we are not funding at the same level; so the universities are mad, and the general assembly members are mad. From our perspective, these guys are spending money like drunken sailors, far beyond the rate of population and inflation, and we can't figure out where the money has gone. We need to get more kids from my district into these schools so they can get a good job. Frankly, I don't care about fancy research or famous professors if my kids can't get into the school.
>
> Over the years, I have given them lots of options. Once I proposed a phase-in of increasing in-state enrollment by 2 percent per year until they get to 75 percent in-state, but they didn't want to do it. So then I proposed that everyone who is in-state gets four years of in-state tuition and after that, the student would pay out-of-state tuition. The idea here would be to get the students through in four years, thus opening up space for new in-state slots. They didn't want to do that. Then I proposed to raise out-of-state tuition and use the extra money for new in-state slots, and they didn't like that. Since they shot down every one of my ideas, eventually we figured out that they just want to do what they want to do. So I told the schools, "I don't care if you don't want to do it, just do it. Guess what, you're not the boss of the school, my constituents are the boss, and they are saying, 'Open up more in-state slots.'" So open up some more slots!
>
> In the end, the bills don't go anywhere because it's hard to get a bill through when the universities have lobbyists convincing all the legislators they need the money, and the average citizen is not down in the general assembly to fight back.

Though legislators spoke publicly about the need for reform and accountability, many said privately that this was mostly for show. Virginia Senator Thomas Norment describes the political nature of higher education: "It's posturing, but you do have a couple of knuckleheads that do not understand that when you don't fund higher education, which is the state's responsibility, it pressures the tuition. They don't understand that the only way to keep the business or the economic engine of higher ed running on the campus is you've got to bring in more out-of-state students because they are paying for 100 percent of the cost of their education plus something toward capital. They don't get that, so some of it's demagoguery, and some of it is just not knowing." While the enrollment mix was a frequent topic of conversation in

Virginia, it was rarely raised or discussed in California or North Carolina, where, historically at least, the universities have been filled with more than 80 percent in-state students. Whether that conversation will shift in the years ahead as the universities press toward greater national and international student bodies remains to be seen. Former California State Senator Joe Simitian is one of the rare legislators who believes that the cap on out-of-state students hurts the university and the state's economic prospects overall:

> This debate about students coming from other states, and in some cases other countries, has created some political tension here in California. I have a slightly different take on this, which is entirely apart from the economic implications that drive those kinds of debates. I think California would be smart to attract the best and brightest from other states and from other countries. That is what has made California prosperous and successful during its first one hundred fifty years and I hope it will continue to be a model for us in the next one hundred fifty years.
>
> Part of what makes the system remarkable is the fact that your youngster will have the opportunity to learn with some of the finest young minds from around the nation and the world. And part of what helps us grow the economy long-term, big picture, and thereby generate the revenue necessary to support these institutions is the fact that top talent comes to California. California is full of people that used to be from somewhere else, and that's not a modern phenomenon.

As the fifth foundation of privatization, enrollment and access help us to understand how the cumulative effects of privatization, manifested in the previous four foundations, are reflected in the student body—one of the most visible representations of how an institution is serving the people of the state and meeting its needs. Legislators often criticized the flagship institutions for being too selective, too expensive, and too focused on educating the elite, but also expressed gratitude for having such tremendous institutions to serve the best and brightest students from their state. In the context of glonacal, state boundaries will likely become less meaningful in the years ahead as globalization changes the way we think about place and location in terms of higher education.

Leadership

The first five foundations of privatization in this model highlight the cumulative effects of changes, over time and in differing ways, as universities and their states dance with one another in reaction to market forces, politics, and ambition. At the top of this model sits the institutional leadership—not because presidents and chancellors are the most central figures in privatization, but instead because they must interpret the foundations. As the model indicates, the institutional leadership often serves as a bridge between the state and the institution. Put another way, the institutional leadership serves as an interpreter between the public interest and the institutional interest.

In this book, I have focused heavily on gaining the perspectives of state and federal policy makers. However, the data—both from policy makers and institutional leaders—revealed the need for a bridge to maintain the tether between the state's interests and the institution's interests. Legislators often criticized university presidents for crying poverty while "Taj Mahal–like" structures are built on campus with state dollars; meanwhile, leaders of other state agencies look on with contempt and frustration. Even so, legislators understand that universities are different and should be different, because the value most of them (and the public they represent) place on higher education is greater than that of the DMV, for example. In exchange for their understanding, though, legislators wanted university presidents to at least halt their criticism of state government and try to understand that resources are scarce.

The tension between legislators' political and financial realities and the wants and needs of university leaders helps create the rationale for the universities to push for privatization. Some of this tension has always been present in public higher education, but it is growing sharper in many states. The true question, however, is how the divide has impacted legislators' beliefs about a public university's mission and focus on the public good.

As a foundation of privatization, leadership must bridge the gap between the university, which pursues and disseminates knowledge, and the state, which seeks to educate the state's citizens and to bolster economic and human capital for the benefit of all. Though the past two decades saw leaders of public institutions take a less coordinated and, in some cases, combative approach to legislatures that they saw as indifferent or antagonistic to higher education, many institutional leaders today are taking a much more nuanced and collaborative approach with the governor, legislature, and the state systems of higher education.

The sixth foundation of privatization serves in many ways as the final layer through which an institution views its role in the larger public agenda rather than focusing solely on institutional ambitions. The institutional leader must interpret the changes that the state is experiencing (declining tax revenues, new work force needs, less money for families to pay higher tuition) and balance that with how they affect the institution. Faculty—some of whom can appear disconnected from these external realities—must hear from the university leadership about the public agenda and the public interests.

To the extent that university leaders were more focused on the public agenda in the past (as many legislators suggested), former presidents and long-serving legislators lamented the loss of the role of the institutional leader as the chief spokesperson for the public agenda. Many of these individuals pointed to the decades before the 1990s, when appropriations were much higher and it was easier for institutional leaders to look beyond their own campuses and speak to issues of civil rights, civic education, and the broadest goals of education. Today, these lions of an earlier time readily admit that the financial realities rule the day, and so institutional leaders must spend their time focusing on meeting the direct financial needs of their own institutions with legislators and donors.

Impacts on the Public Good: Outcomes of Privatization

After examining the six foundations of privatization and examples from the three case studies, we turn now to answer a question that has been central to this book. What is the impact on the public good when an institution, rather than the state or university system, makes decisions about policies and practices such as funding changes (including tuition and financial aid), program approval, capital project planning, and student enrollments? This question, raised quite frequently by higher education policy experts, strikes at the core of privatization and at understanding the true impacts of the changes in public higher education over the past twenty years. Many states are at a crossroads in regard to their system of public higher education, and to answer this question effectively, we must understand how legislators, in particular, perceive the changes in the relationship between the university and the state and the resulting impact on the public good.

While a growing divide and deep skepticism permeate legislators' perceptions of public higher education in general, they agree nearly unanimously that public higher education serves invaluable public purposes and that their state's institutions have not moved significantly away from their mission of serving the public good. They expressed a great deal of anxiety and fear that these institutions *could* move away from their mission of serving their states and serving the public good. Most of the legislators, governors, legislative staff, and university leaders I interviewed believe that today—more than ever—the country's public colleges and universities are, in fact, fulfilling that mission. David Bulova, a Virginia legislator, said, "I haven't seen any diminution of the mission. I suspect it's in the back of every legislator's mind, but I don't think we've seen those changes yet in any kind of way that signaled a shift in serving the public good." Laura Fornash, who was then Virginia's secretary of education, agrees that her state's public universities have continued to serve important public purposes and to balance the state's needs with the institutional interests: "I think they do balance their public mission with institutional interests very nicely. They're growing the number of students that they're taking. Yes, they're going to take more out-of-state [students], but that's going to help offset the cost to in-state students. They're being innovative with new degree programs and expanding STEM majors where institutionally appropriate to help address work force shortages. I think they are striking that balance."

On the surface, privatization often appears to be in direct conflict with the historic public mission of public universities—but largely because of a belief that privatization, by definition, is bad for the public good (remember the state senator who scolded me in the introduction about what he believed I meant when I asked about privatization?). When managed with an eye toward clarifying public policy objectives and creating clear expectations for what constitutes an institution's responsibility for the public good, however, privatization need not represent a departure from public mission.

Perception, however, is a mighty thing in the public arena. So, for public universities, the perception of a diminished connection to the state and to the business of the people can be incredibly damaging, impacting the legislative will to support the institutions. It was evident that, deep down, most legislators wanted to see their public institutions continue to flourish with increased funding (or at least increased autonomy to achieve that funding). Legislators—many of whom seemingly love to hate universities, if we judge by their public statements alone—express deep admiration and fondness for their flagship universities and the broader system of higher education when you have a deeper conversation with them. Many shared stories of how, when they travel the country or the world, they are reminded of just how great their universities are, because legislators from other states or leaders from other countries say, "I would trade anything to have your university."

Though it is significant that most legislators do not see any measurable shift away from serving the public good as a result of privatization, those who follow higher education most closely—state policy analysts, national think tanks, former leaders of institutions, and centers studying higher education—have seen noticeable, if not seismic, shifts in the commitment to the public good by many public universities. Former university president Gene Nichol, who is now director of the UNC Law School's Center on Poverty, Work & Opportunity, believes that legislators don't understand what is happening, albeit slowly, to the public institutions: "[Many of these public universities] have gone too far down the path of privatization and, contrary to what lawmakers may believe, it has had a detrimental impact on the institutions and their focus on serving the public interest. It has been silently done by university administrators, and you can't find them talking about how they have done it. Legislators are not informed enough to know or see that it is happening." Policy analysts point to hard statistics—rising tuition and low proportions of Pell recipients. Institutional leaders, however, say they must balance public mission with the goal of seeing their institutions not only survive, but grow and thrive.

Is what is happening to public higher education the result of a simple lack of state resources to continue to fund public universities at the historical levels of the second half of the twentieth century? Or does it indicate a lack of political will to continue to support public higher education because it is coming to be viewed as more of a private benefit than a public good? My research indicates that the issues are much more complicated, comprising resources and politics, certainly, but also the historical commitment to the state and the public agenda, tuition, access and transfer opportunities, economic development, and efficiencies at the institutional level—including faculty and the curriculum.

Legislators from both parties overwhelmingly spoke about the challenges as resource-based—an increasing number of fixed costs, such as Medicaid, coupled with a diminishing tax base. University leaders seem to believe that a lack of resources is combined with a lack of political leadership and a changing political landscape that does not place the same value on public higher education. Gordon Davies, former director of the State Council for Higher Education in Virginia, offered a third option: "I am not sure that the problem can be stated as either lack of resources or lack of will. Another possibility is a lack of a clear sense of direction—or confusion. It is what marks our nation's political life in general, and that of other nations as well. We know the world has changed, but we don't know what to do about it. Basing actions on ideologies is never a good idea, but today's ideologies are too incoherent to base anything on. Confusion results, with no clear sense of direction."

Perhaps the effects of privatization are only just beginning to force a new conversation about public higher education, one that is focused less on revenues and autonomy and more on how public colleges and universities can continue to serve an important role in our states and in the country. Such a conversation would constitute a redefinition of what it means to be a public university—with new sources of revenue and certain freedoms from state bureaucracy, but also with a heightened sense of public mission. This new model breaks the notion of the "iron triangle"—where cost, quality, and access are locked in a zero sum game—and posits that public higher education can and should be both well funded and high quality and, above all else, focused on a public mission that is tied closely to the fundamental needs and public policy objectives of the state.[6]

CHAPTER NINE

The New Public-Private Model

Education is here placed among the articles of public care, not that it would be proposed to take its ordinary branches out of the hands of private enterprise, which manages so much better all the concerns to which it is equal; but a public institution can alone supply those sciences which, though rarely called for, are yet necessary to complete the circle, all the parts of which contribute to the improvement of the country, and some of them to its preservation.

—Thomas Jefferson[1]

COLLEGES AND UNIVERSITIES are powerful engines of creativity and innovation. Throughout the first three centuries of higher education in the United States, they have served to examine our society and help to improve it, educate our citizens toward a goal of civic engagement and greater quality of life, and spur the creation and development of new inventions, procedures, and technologies that have forever changed our world. Now, however, it is time for these engines to turn that creativity and entrepreneurism inward and reimagine higher education for the twenty-first century. Public colleges and universities, in particular, must begin to imagine new ways of structuring their relationship with the nation, the state, the citizens, the students, and the faculty. Henry David Thoreau once famously noted, "As in geology, so in social institutions, we may discover the causes of all past changes in the present invariable order of society."[2]

267

How public colleges and universities—and all of higher education more broadly—will change and adapt is dependent on many factors, but the six foundations of privatization discussed in this book will serve as barometers for change. Technology will undoubtedly continue to shape the very notion of teaching and learning as we have known it for thousands of years—that of teacher and student, face to face. What constitutes a degree, a credential, or some other form of certification that someone has learned something will evolve, as will the specific disciplines and "interdisciplines" in the academy. Tenure and the role of faculty in the academy will certainly evolve in this century—perhaps slowly at first, but no doubt more rapidly as new conceptions of employment evolve.

But before I venture too far into futuristic thinking and creep into the predictions of what the university will be in twenty-five or one hundred years, I want to focus on what this future model of higher education will require from public colleges and universities. What I conceive of as the public-private model for higher education is largely with us already as a result of privatization, as I have discussed throughout this book. What remains to be seen is how far a particular institution or state moves on that continuum of higher education—between the stark black and white of private and public are thousands of shades of gray.

One of my academic mentors, Robert Zemsky, has an uncanny knack for capturing complex ideas in memorable images. He served on the Secretary of Education's Commission on the Future of Higher Education, charged by Margaret Spellings to deliver a comprehensive national strategy on higher education. Zemsky later recalled the charge as being focused on what he called the "Four Horsemen of Academic Reform."[3] These four horsemen, surely not as scary as the apocalypse, are access, affordability, accountability, and quality. Any discussion about reforming higher education, the future of colleges and universities, or a new public-private model must address these horsemen.

Throughout my interviews with legislative and federal leaders, access, affordability, accountability, and quality were discussed either directly or just beneath the surface, but, as is true with much of the discussion around privatization, the words have very little clear meaning to these elected officials. What defines quality, and how much do students need? Affordable for whom, and how much debt is acceptable? Is higher education affordable if we think about the cost as being amortized over one's lifetime earning potential? Access, sure, we want students to have access, but to which institutions?

Accountability—now that is something legislators understand clearly, but what accountability do the states have to the institutions? The four horsemen seem elusive when you probe more deeply, yet state and federal leaders expect institutions of higher education to tackle these issues immediately.

Regardless of the solutions to the broader issues facing all of higher education, public institutions and their states must imagine a new compact that is truly a public-private model. As we have seen throughout this book, the federal and state tills are not as full as they once were, so new financial arrangements will be required. But beyond money, the challenges facing public higher education are immense because there is an inherent accountability to the state, a mission that requires access and affordability, and a goal of achieving the highest quality possible, however that is defined.

My examination of three public universities and their changing relationships with their states illuminates the challenges in the years ahead as state funding is stretched and the need for more degrees grows exponentially. In a time of diminishing state resources, how can states maintain and even strengthen their relationship with their public institutions to ensure that they focus on important public purposes and meeting the state's needs? And how can a public university, generously funded by the state for centuries, achieve its full potential in an academic marketplace where it must compete with better-funded private universities for faculty, staff, students, funding, and prestige, or with for-profit institutions that employ a more efficient business model? The case studies illustrate both promise and pitfalls as universities and states seek to balance institutional aspirations with important public policy objectives as they work toward the public-private model.

The Future of Public-Private

Tom Friedman, the New York Times columnist, made a prediction in late 2012 that sums up well the challenges and opportunities ahead for the public-private partnership. His prediction was focused on the need to turn around the drastic loss of middle class jobs, which have been severely impacted by technology and globalization. In answering this challenge, Friedman suggested that we "will require a new level of political imagination—a combination of educational reforms and unprecedented collaboration between business, schools, universities and government to change how workers are trained and empowered to keep learning."[4] The connections between industry, education, and government are at the core of public higher education today—and for the future—and the partnership will have to be about more than just money.

One university president told me that the primary reason we need to rethink the model of public higher education entirely is that public expectations have continued to rise while public funding has steadily diminished. This is accurate, yet it only scratches the surface of a very deep relationship. The actual environment of higher education funding and public policy at the state and national levels has additional, complex dimensions. Public expectations will likely remain high, particularly as higher education becomes more important to the economic viability of states and of the nation overall. Institutions will be expected to increase degree production, slow the rise of costs, and assist the state with economic development—perhaps in more cost-efficient ways.

Though the lofty vision of universities as ivory towers, pursuing knowledge and ideas wherever they lead with little regard for cost, can be an important aspiration, these institutions must also focus intensely on the current needs of the state. Today, in the minds of legislators, jobs are public purpose number one for higher education. Anthony Carnevale, director of Georgetown University's Center on Education and the Workforce, elaborates on state legislators' perspective in this regard:

> What you are hearing from legislators is an unhappy conclusion that they don't know what to do about the shortage of funding for higher education, given that they don't have much money. This is going on all over the place and nobody who is pro-education feels good about this. With money short, you've got to decide what's the purpose here. And in the end, my own bias is that it's jobs. In the United States, if you can't get a person a job, they're sunk. So if there is a public purpose today, it's jobs. The other public purposes are perfectly viable. But they don't mean much without the first one unless this society changes very substantially. The mission of higher education is to allow people to live fully in their time, but in market economies you can't live fully in your time if you are forced to live under a bridge.

Carnevale and Friedman provide stark reminders that one of higher education's most important public purposes today is economic and work force development, which is central to higher education's case for increased funding and relevance to the public good.

Successful public colleges and universities in the years ahead will have to make the case with legislators and governors that they are a worthy investment of public dollars, that they are connected to and focused on the needs and people of the state, and that a great public university brings many benefits to the state broadly—beyond just the benefits that accrue to the graduates themselves. The social value of higher education, as discussed in chapter 3, exceeds the value to the individual, and more legislators need to understand this. Further, these successful universities must develop new and alternative revenue sources that give them greater financial stability and flexibility, while still preserving the accessibility and public mission that differentiate them from private peers.

The growing disconnect between the leadership of universities and the body politic in the states is astonishing. University leaders, seeking to strengthen and bolster the long history of public higher education, are inclined to make incremental changes to the structure of the institutions, which have moved little in centuries (one noted higher education critic has taken this to the extreme and made the bold assertion that "With the possible exception of prostitution, teaching is the only profession that has seen absolutely no productivity advance in the twenty-four hundred years since Socrates taught the youth of Athens").[5] Legislators, reacting to the fiscal crisis of the moment and to constituents who are demanding new ways of thinking, see the world in very different and starkly economic terms today.

Universities Are from Mars, Politicians Are from Venus

The divide between public universities and the public (particularly as represented by state leaders) can and should be closed through a more intentional and focused discussion about how and where the university can meet the needs of the state and still serve the public good. University leaders, when they request state funding, should closely tie their requests to the needs of the state—access, economic development, and additional research and degrees in high-need fields. Too many university leaders in my interviews appeared to be ready to give up on future state funding rather than continue to make the case for steady or even increased funding. Legislators, for their part, remain hopeful that they will be able to increase funding in the future when the economy rebounds, but they need a more willing partner than they have found in universities.

Some of the skepticism that legislators expressed about public higher education in general can be attributed to political posturing that may play well back home with constituents. The deeper significance of their skepticism, however, is that it points to a large and growing divide between state legislators and public university leaders about the role, purpose, and function of public higher education.

The long-held belief that higher education is a public good—worthy of generous funding and of benefit to all in the population—has given way to a perception among many legislators that it is a private good that should be funded in new ways and refocused on economic development and career-based disciplines. Legislators do not see the universities as being as closely tied to the needs of the state. If left unaddressed, this divide will continue to grow, leading to further diminished funding and greater conflict between legislators and university leaders. College and university leaders may have to bridge the gap, finding new ways to connect with and assist legislators in meeting state goals and priorities. As noted in the sixth foundation of privatization—leadership—college and university presidents have to serve as the bridge between the state and the campus, always focusing on how the campus is serving the broader goals beyond institutional interests but also bringing harsh realities back to the campus.

The divide between the perceptions of state legislators and those of university leaders is notable, primarily in the outlook for funding from the state. Many legislators pointed to the long history of public support for the flagship university over two centuries as evidence of a commitment to supporting public higher education. Yet legislators described a feeling that university leaders were "ungrateful" and had an attitude of "what have you done for us lately?" in regard to funding. An interesting exchange with one state policy maker revealed the core of how both legislators and many state-level bureaucrats feel when university leaders complain about state funding. "We had a former legislator who would basically say, 'the universities are never grateful when you do something—they forget. They have long arms and short memories.' That perception has always made it a battle for us to try to figure out how can we get higher education to become more of a priority. For a bunch of smart people, they [university leaders] sometimes can do stupid things. You know, everything is not a catastrophe unless you listen to a college president."

Legislators report hearing a consistent refrain—"the university needs more money." In the midst of a severe economic recession, legislators feel as though the university is completely disconnected from the realities of the state. Former Senator John Chichester of Virginia described a "seemingly unquenchable thirst for more dollars where there is never enough to satisfy the university," at a time when funds are limited and priorities are shifting. Anthony Carnevale speaks to this growing disconnect between university leaders and legislators:

> The higher education system is not cooperative. The state doesn't have any money. Legislators are saying, "I keep hearing from my constituents that they don't want to pay what you're asking them to pay, and you won't do anything

about it. So you put me in a tough position. I keep trying to help you, and you just screw me all the time. Because no matter what I do, it's not enough. You have no sympathy for my problem—we just don't have any money in the state coffers, and you're just obstinate."

It's more emotional than it is rational. I've been around legislators long enough to know they're like everybody else; they want their world to work, and higher education is something that doesn't work for them these days.

In order to address the perennial issues of access, affordability, accountability, and quality, public higher education will have to adapt to meet the needs legislators are expressing, or explain more effectively how they are already doing so. "Long arms and short memories" is not the kind of descriptor most college presidents want as the impression of their institution—which speaks again to recognition of the state context and history.

Communicating and Lobbying: Making the Case

In many states, an uncertain economic future is coloring the conversation about higher education. Nonetheless, countless legislators and other state leaders urged the universities to more clearly articulate their needs, as well as the impacts of diminishing state support. Legislators who are most supportive of the universities understand the real damage caused by cuts in state funding and believe that universities can do a better job making the case to the legislature and to the public. Gerald Baliles, former governor of Virginia, urges universities to reshape their message about the important public purposes that higher education serves:

> I think there is a message that has to be shared that is, increasingly, higher education is this country's number one asset; it is increasingly the engine that drives the American economy. Given the uncertainties in the world in which we live, the more certain we should be of higher education's role in our future.
>
> During the Cold War period, for example, the country's greatest concern was national security, and we built a preeminent military force. Today, our best protection is a well-educated citizenry. The message of the value of higher education has to be clear and concise and compelling, and we should restate the case for higher education to make the connections between investments and returns. Those connections need to be clearly described, and they're not.

Governor Baliles went on to say that, "while higher education needs to stress the value of higher education in this time of change, it also needs to be clear that higher education itself needs to change." Clearly, in this new public-private model, everyone will have to do their part to evolve and change the relationship between public institutions and the state.

Legislators encouraged university leaders to visit them in their home districts and to communicate the relevance of the university's impact both on the state and their district. Though not always obvious, the university's impact can be felt in ways large and small across the state, and lobbying in legislators' home districts meant more to them than a visit in the state capitol. James P. Massie III, a Virginia legislator, said, "I don't think the university has lost our trust. When you think about the volume of stuff that we have coming at us, I think if they would just do a better job of communicating with us and a better job of proving to us that their existing cost structures are where they should be, it would help. Proving to us that they are generating a student who is getting his great education at a great price. Remember, you need to put yourself in our shoes and then communicate with us. I think they have some compelling arguments; they just need to do a better job of communicating."

Many state legislators expressed a feeling of being "disrespected" by university leaders—either because they didn't feel adequately lobbied or because their requests for information or change fell on deaf ears, without an attempt to address their concerns. University leaders should remember that state legislators want to know and understand what is happening at the university as they ponder future funding and public policy. On a pragmatic level, legislators have egos and need them to be occasionally (read: quite frequently) stroked.

Teresa Sullivan, president of UVA, sees continuously making the case to the legislature as an important role for her and for every public university president:

> No legislature can bind the next legislature; that is the most important thing for a public university president to keep in mind. If there ever was a compact, it never bound the next legislature. I am in the same position Thomas Jefferson was, back in 1825. I have to make the case in every legislative session, and I am willing to keep doing that. But, I am also determined to make sure that they see the value they get by investing in us—that they are getting something for that money that they send us, even if it is not as much as we would like to have. And I can make sure that we are as accountable as possible for that money, so that they know that they are getting the value out of their investment in us.

Certainly, university leaders could do a better job communicating with and lobbying state legislators. While I am certain many of the presidents feel they are already communicating effectively, the number of legislators who asked for greater transparency and deeper understanding of the value of higher education shows that they want to better comprehend the university, its impact, and the effects of state funding and how additional investment could connect to the state's goals. In the words of John Bennett, former secretary of finance in Virginia, "something has to be done to demystify higher education to the public and to the policy makers, or higher education is just going to continue to get what it's gotten in the last twenty years, which does not make for a bright future."

Blurred Lines Between Public and Private

The findings of this research make abundantly clear that the old distinctions between public and private universities are beginning to blur. Sources of funding—tuition, research, and philanthropy—are becoming more similar at public and private institutions as state funding shrinks in the mix of revenues at these universities. The great private universities are increasingly focusing on access and financial aid, helping low- or middle-income students to attend the institutions. These private universities recognize the value of diversity for the university, but they are also attempting to recruit and retain the very best students and faculty.

The way that public universities and states perceive the public mission, however, continues to differentiate these universities. Harvey Fineberg, president of the Institute of Medicine of the National Academies, describes the historic and current distinctions between public and private and how the two have become more similar:

> The old distinctions between public and private have been largely outgrown. The early private universities in America often grew out of a desire to provide for an educated ministry in the new world. Centuries later, the land-grant universities had a distinct mission in serving educational needs in agriculture, science, and engineering. Now both types of institutions have broad educational missions. Historical differences are sharper than any contemporary differences among the great public and private universities today.
>
> My own guess is that this trend toward similarity in scope and mission is likely to continue because the forces are very powerful. The fiscal difficulties of every state and the nation as a whole, the growing importance of research, the pressures and attractions of globalization, the desired diversity of student populations and excellence in faculty all drive toward harmonization across public and private institutions. Over time, schools will be described as public or private more in terms of historical origin rather than future trajectory.

Fineberg accurately describes one way of conceiving of the public-private model, but the history of a state will continue to require the coupling of mission and revenue for institutions to survive and thrive in the years ahead.

Perhaps because the trend of decreasing state funding began earlier in Virginia, UVA has become a national model for the kind of public-private partnership that may be required if other great public institutions are to weather the storm of diminishing state appropriations. UVA began private fundraising in earnest much earlier than many of its public peers and, as a result, has built an endowment on par with that of many private research universities. It recently completed a $3 billion fundraising campaign—a feat that very few public or private universities have accomplished. Some leaders at UVA describe their institution as the "first privately financed public university," a description that could speak to the future of public-private partnerships in a new type of public university.

Each of these case studies also presents challenges for achieving a sustainable public-private partnership, most notably in making state funding reliable and stable from year to year, allowing for predictable planning. The roller-coaster cycles of funding do not allow university leaders to make the kinds of strategic investments that are required to adapt to the changing needs of the university and the state. Many states now face economic uncertainty, which makes future funding hard to forecast. The autonomy granted in some states has positioned the universities to secure greater external funding and achieve efficiencies that should provide some cushion against the ups and downs of state funding.

Creativity and Innovation Required

Having worked for many years at Georgetown University, I had become quite accustomed to seeing our faculty on the evening news, talking about current topics as the experts they were. These faculty were teaching students in a traditional classroom, while online education was something left to others. If Bill Gates himself had told me in the early part of 2012 that it would later be called the "Year of the MOOC," with the likes of Harvard, Stanford, Princeton, Michigan, and UC Berkeley signing up to offer their course content online for free, I would have thought he was losing brain cells.[6] After all, our students were spending tens of thousands of dollars for that content. But, by December 2012, Georgetown had partnered with one of the leading MOOC providers, EdX, and was preparing to offer its course content online. At academic institutions that traditionally change at a speed that can only be measured by geologists, that was lightning speed. MOOCs, for those who don't yet have the word firmly in their vocabulary, are massive open on-line courses.

I had worked with and spent countless hours over a decade with George-town's then provost, Jim O'Donnell, and he had told me stories about a class on the life of St. Augustine he taught online in 1994 while at the University of Pennsylvania where, seemingly overnight, he had signed up five hundred virtual students. I had worked with Jim long enough to catch his passion for ancient civilizations, but I never really believed that many people would be interested enough to take a course online. Then, in late 2011, Peter Norvig of Google and Sebastian Thrun of Stanford offered a MOOC—Introduction to Artificial Intelligence—and one hundred sixty thousand people signed up for the course. All of a sudden, Jim O'Donnell's enrollment in his St. Augus-tine course seemed much more believable to me. While only twenty-three thousand of the one hundred sixty thousand completed the course, that is still more students than most faculty will teach in a lifetime. Further, none of the students paid a penny for the course.

While I am not one of those predicting that MOOCs will mean the end of higher education as we know it, I do think technology has the potential to assist in the evolution of public (and private) higher education. After all, cor-respondence courses by mail and radio earlier in the twentieth century didn't put universities out of business, but it did force them to reimagine the cur-riculum, the delivery of that curriculum, and elements of the business model. Fifteen years ago, famed business guru Peter Drucker made the bold state-ment that the traditional university would vanish in the next twenty years, but there are now more than four thousand institutions of higher education, with more added each year.[7] Rather, my research has brought me to the point where I can see that public institutions need to experiment with technol-ogy as one option of tackling the four horsemen; governors, legislators, and boards are increasingly demanding it.

Public colleges and universities will have to both put some of their own course content online but also begin to determine how to accept courses stu-dents have taken online from other content providers (both universities and new entities) or measure competencies rather than just seat time. For exam-ple, while California's Master Plan was enormous in terms of its magnitude and reach in its day, the evidence points to the need for much greater creativ-ity in the twenty-first century to create what Mark Yudof and others have de-scribed as a "hybrid" university.[8]

A recent report argued that the Master Plan has actually worked to restrict access for many students, especially students of color, due to its rigid academic requirements. The authors of the report proposed a new arrangement to increase enrollment, which involves much greater collaboration between community colleges and universities to create new kinds of hybrid institutions. Examples of such hybrid models include "university centers" and two-year university branch campuses. Under the university center model, four-year universities would offer upper-division coursework at community college campuses, enabling "place-bound" students to complete their baccalaureate degree program there. Under the two-year university branch model, some community colleges would be converted, in effect, into lower-division satellites of public universities, thereby expanding capacity at the four-year level and eliminating the need for the traditional transfer process. What these and other hybrid models have in common is that they help bridge the divide between two-year and four-year institutions, enabling more students to enter baccalaureate programs directly from high school and progress seamlessly to their degrees.[9]

MOOCs have emerged as one vehicle for easing the strain on available seats at public colleges and universities by providing more content virtually. California Senate President Pro Tempore Darrell Steinberg spoke about a bill moving through the legislature that would require all three sectors of California's system of higher education to accept MOOCs for course credit, just as they now accept Advanced Placement credit. Steinberg says, "We want to be the first state in the nation to make this promise: no college student in California will be denied the right to move through their education because they couldn't get a seat in the course they needed."[10]

More faculty are "flipping" their courses by putting online some of the content they usually cover in lectures and then spending the time in class engaging in more robust discussions and exercises. While there are those who worry about the "dumbing down" created by students sitting in their room watching a professor on the computer, flipping actually has the potential to strengthen the in-class experience. As many technology proponents have quipped, sitting in the back of a five-hundred-student lecture hall is even less interactive and engaging than a MOOC, and it's hard to argue that a course taught by the world's foremost expert in a subject online is not as valuable as the same course taught by an instructor straight out of graduate school.[11]

As is often the case, the public-private partnerships involved in the use of technology will ultimately have to address a profit—several of the MOOC providers are for-profit entities—because the academic content is still the core of what is being offered, and that is not free or even cheap to produce. Additional concerns include the intellectual property and who owns it—the professor, the university, the online provider?—and who profits from the distribution of the content (at whatever point there is a profit). Nonetheless, technology will necessarily be a critical component going forward in the reimagining of public higher education, particularly in the goal of addressing access, affordability, accountability, and quality.

Changing the Paradigm

While technology and its introduction in a massive way to higher education may seem jarring to some, legislators and policy makers are pushing for other ways of getting more students to a degree in less time at lower cost with the same quality. They are asking questions related to the "seat time" required for a degree, for instance, and whether institutions can move toward a more focused, three-year model of a bachelor's degree. The $10,000 degree, discussed in depth in chapter 4, is not just about reducing the cost to the student for a degree, it's also focused on finding new ways to deliver the education. Time and again I heard legislators asking for more creativity from universities—in essence, asking higher education to change the paradigm and adapt to the changing world, as other industries have had to do.

The curriculum, for example, is something that has long been the domain of the faculty but has been described recently as suffering from the "tragedy of the commons."[12] This is a reference to the story of the community-owned pasture (or commons) that is at capacity. If any farmer adds more animals to graze, the whole pasture will begin to decline and eventually all will suffer; individuals act in their own interests, rather than the interests of the public good. Over time, students have demanded more courses and faculty have created new disciplines and courses as the frontiers of knowledge expand, resulting in a tremendous growth in the curriculum. One national report from 1985 declared, "We have reached a point at which we are more confident of the length of a college education than its content and purpose."[13] The growth and variety of courses offered today allows faculty to teach courses related to their own interests and research, which make them very intellectually rich courses, but it is an expensive outcome, and as legislators look for innovation in higher education, the curriculum is one area they are questioning.

Can faculty teach on Fridays? Is the traditional fifteen-week course the only way to deliver a higher education? Should the academic calendar still revolve around the agrarian cycle of harvesting and planting crops? Can the campus be utilized fully twelve months per year, with faculty teaching during the summer months as well? These questions were asked of me by state legislators trying to imagine new ways of delivering the same high-quality public higher education with greater efficiency and productivity.

The expansion of the curriculum has led to the need for a much larger work force to teach the expanded classes, along with increased costs. Ironically, the larger number of adjunct faculty teaching at public universities today is in part the direct result of the growth of the curriculum. Some of these are academics who were unable to find tenure-track positions, but others are faculty who have chosen to pursue the teaching-only route rather than the teaching and research route required of faculty at research universities. The changing paradigm will require integrating these faculty within the university with a role in governance, a more meaningful wage, and a status higher than the academic equivalent of the day laborer.

Let me be clear: I am not advocating that tenure should be eliminated immediately or that teacher-scholars should be replaced solely with teachers, but I have met with enough legislators to know they are weary of the traditional argument that "higher education is different than everyone else." New innovations and ways of thinking about higher education and faculty governance—particularly public universities—will be required in the new public-private model. In late 2013, for example, the assembly speaker in Wisconsin positioned the legislature's involvement in changing faculty governance as a question of "when, not if."[14] If public institutions do not lead the change and innovation themselves, it will not be long before legislators and governing boards direct the change instead. My sense is that those inside the academy will be much happier with the outcome if they devise the solutions, rather than having solutions dictated for them. Former Secretary of Defense Robert Gates makes the point even more precisely: "If public colleges and universities don't reform themselves to contain costs, improve access, and increase graduation rates, federal and state governments will step in. That can only be bad news because, like the dinosaur, government has a heavy foot, a small brain, and no fine motor skills."[15]

Some Hope for Tuition

While I did find staunch opposition to any alteration of the focus on educating in-state students, there was much greater flexibility expressed by legislators on the issue of tuition. Publicly, many will speak out against any increases in tuition, but when pressed in private, they acknowledge that tuition is low relative to the value received and they would rather stand firm on the enrollment than tuition. Coupling tuition increases with greater financial aid could actually result in both higher net revenues for the institution and lower costs for middle class students. I was pleasantly surprised on this account, as such a change in tuition flexibility would require a changing of the paradigm on the state's side. It is increasingly apparent to these legislators that tuition will need to rise closer to market rates in order to maintain the in-state enrollment they desire.

Unique Solutions Involving the Feds

Though most of the cases examined in this book involve altering the relationship between the state and the institution, there is also a need to discuss transformations that would maintain the public nature of an institution but expand its reach beyond the state boundaries. Throughout my research for this book, I was struck at how public higher education has come to be largely defined as a state-based entity, whereas almost everything else in our lives is borderless—national or global in nature. We seamlessly travel between states and countries, order and deliver goods across state boundaries, and consume content online without regard for where it was produced. Public higher education is one of the remaining vestiges of the time when state borders mattered more.

The federal government's support for institutions today tends to focus on financial aid for students and direct research investment; rarely is there general unrestricted support for individual public institutions. Recently, there have been several public calls for a more overt national strategy for higher education and, in particular, more direct federal funding for a select number of public research universities' operating expenses and students, to create a new model of national public universities.[16]

One interesting privatization proposal would supply matching gifts to a select number of public universities that would receive both federal and state funding on a matching basis with private philanthropy and would enroll students from across borders, with all paying the same tuition. This model would most likely work in favor of only the most highly selective public universities, and, because out-of-state residents would have equal access to state-owned institutions, state leaders would likely decry the lack of access for state residents (when I mentioned this idea to legislators, most said "no" without thinking more than a second). The model disregards the universities' historic state-based mission and state funding, but a private-public/federal-state relationship is worth further exploration.[17]

Overall, the case studies examined in this book highlight several elements that public universities need to succeed in today's market-based system, where greater accountability and lower appropriations are the norm. Given more flexibility, universities can be far more entrepreneurial and strategic, achieving greater resources that will allow them to thrive despite the fluctuations of the economic cycle. The decentralized system of higher education served the United States well in the past, as the variation among institutions allowed the nation to grow and develop a diverse system of institutions to serve various needs and interests. Now, however, although students are increasingly viewed as consumers, the federal government will need to continue to invest in higher education and assist in the development of a national strategy.

Currently, state governments have been unable or disinclined to pursue a broader national strategy and, although President Obama has recognized the college attainment problem on a national scale and made it a priority, he must use federal resources to lead the development of a federal-state partnership that will in fact put coordinated policies in place. The Affordable Care Act (aka Obamacare) has taken much more of his administration's time, attention, and funding than higher education.

The federal government could better spend public dollars by encouraging and facilitating fundraising for the university on behalf of private corporations and foundations. For example, the government could pioneer a federal matching program that would raise major philanthropic contributions in support of public higher education. Given government support for business-university linkages, the federal government could also encourage philanthropy and ensure state aid by making federal matching funds depend on the state governments' maintenance of financial support.[18]

If institutions are to change and evolve to meet the four horsemen described earlier, then states will also have to make some changes, perhaps reconsidering the state-federal partnership in public higher education. Certainly, the public-private partnership that higher education is today is dependent on both the federal and state government, so the feds will undoubtedly need to remain involved in developing new strategies going forward.

The Public Consensus for Higher Education: Time for a Renewed Conversation

There are plenty of predictions about what technology, demographics, market forces, diminishing state support, and the other forces of privatization discussed in this book will mean for higher education, but what is remarkable is that nothing has yet settled to the point where anyone is in a position to imagine the twenty-first century version of the California Master Plan, which is what the states and the nation truly need. This book can help in framing the conversation about the new public-private model in the years ahead.

In each state, interviewees suggested in various ways that the new public-private model requires five key elements: increased private support in the form of philanthropy and alternative business revenues; increased efficiency and cost reduction; stable, even if diminished, funding from the state; sufficient autonomy to achieve these elements; and a continued public mission that emphasizes achieving state goals such as access, economic development, and increased degree attainment. These five elements are essential to the future for public higher education and will require each stakeholder—state and federal governments (public support and autonomy); students (higher tuition, particularly for those who can afford to pay); faculty and staff (increased efficiency and productivity); and alumni, corporations, and foundations (philanthropy)—to do more or change in meaningful ways. In other words, everyone has to do their part.

Though new models for public higher education will differ from state to state, Virginia, North Carolina, and California present three interesting examples of great public universities facing an uncertain future. These states have taken bold steps toward a new approach that involves increased autonomy, although with strings attached to maintain the connection to the state. The universities have passionate and committed leaders who are seeking to preserve national treasures—institutions created by the people and for the people to educate and serve the interests of the state and the nation.

But many institutional leaders and veteran legislators believe that the public consensus that supported higher education at significant levels has all but disappeared. One former president described the situation as bleak: "The public consensus that existed for so long is now gone." Other university and legislative leaders described the same perplexing feeling that higher education was no longer seen as a public good for the benefit of all in the state. My interviews with legislators and other state officials offer some evidence for despair, because higher education does not appear to be at the zenith of its popularity. Changes in political leadership are reshaping priorities, and fewer legislators are focused on higher education.

Still, all is not as bleak as it might appear. Even though legislators do not expect new funding anytime soon, most of them believe that the universities are critically important to the state, that they are tremendous assets in which there is universal pride, and that they continue to serve important public purposes that are tremendously valuable to the state and its people. This demonstrates significant support on which to build and should be central to any discussion linking public purposes with public funding. The first step toward the new public-private partnership is a strong belief in the state that the university is still serving important public purposes—central to and in service of the public good. My research suggests that the country needs a spirited public dialogue, at both the state and federal levels, about the role of higher education. Such a dialogue could reestablish some consensus and trust as the country looks to an uncertain future and as institutions—particularly public colleges and universities—seek to fulfill their mission in the years ahead.

When institutions are examined along the multiple continua in my new model of privatization, it becomes increasingly clear that the six foundations present an opportunity for institutional leaders to engage more fully with the state's leaders about the public agenda and how to fulfill it. It is not realistic for an institution to walk away from the state or for the state to abandon an institution. As the model suggests, there is too much history, connection, and interdependency for one to survive or thrive without the other. A new and renewed conversation—focused on all the elements of privatization, not just autonomy, finance, and enrollment—would allow us to return to the core public purposes that were envisioned when the public universities were founded.

Looking Forward

Each state has a very different approach to higher education. But after deep examination of the legislative, gubernatorial, and national perspectives, it appears that even with the dramatic shifts in public funding over the past twenty years and pressures and ambitions to achieve a more national and global portfolio, public higher education has maintained a focus on serving the public good and these universities are still widely viewed as public goods, albeit at different levels and in different ways in each state. The most dramatic differences are at the level of public policy in the states.

As universities, legislators, and policy makers in other states look to Virginia, North Carolina, and California for evidence of how privatization affects an institution, the state, and the public good, these case studies can suggest how best to achieve a mutually beneficial relationship between the institution and the state. Legislators and governors expressed an inherent and deep desire to see public higher education thrive, and all three states have seen attempts at developing strong public policy for higher education—with funding often being the lone limitation. State legislators want to find the "win-win" scenario whereby the state and the institution can prosper and achieve the state's objectives.

History serves as one guide for the current environment. The United States appears to be in another cycle of aversion to investment in public goods. There have been periods of great investment such as the Civil War and post–Civil War era (e.g., the Morrill Act and the Homestead Act), the early twentieth century leading up to the 1920s, and the post–World War II era through the 1970s, with the GI Bill and the massive state and federal investments in public higher education. Interspersed between those eras of strong public investment have been periods of individualism and aversion to public funding, similar to what we see across the United States today. But over the long term, public support for public goods such as higher education is likely to rebound. Former Virginia Governor Gerald Baliles recognized the cyclical nature of public focus and funding, but also spoke with me about much larger concerns, namely how our actions today will affect future generations: "There are 'ups and downs' in funding and reputations and progress, and I suspect and hope that we are back on the upward swing, and I hope that is achievable in the near future. My enduring concern is whether we have the vision in higher education and the vision in public life to govern our nation and its vital institutions. Higher education is the surest path to a much better society, and I worry sometimes about the damage that is being done to future generations by our failure to recognize the need."

Since the earliest days of our republic, education has been considered synonymous with democracy, and we have been a people focused on the larger public good. We will often disagree about the best way to use public dollars and what defines the public good, but a vigorous dialogue about the public purposes of higher education can help build consensus and strengthen the bonds among institutional leaders, state and federal leaders, and the public at large. The challenges facing public colleges and universities are complex, but all stakeholders must work together to achieve a new, mutually beneficial model of privatization—the public-private partnership—where both the aspirations of the institution and its service to the public good can shine.

NOTES

Introduction

1. David Breneman, *An Essay on College Costs* (Washington, DC: US Department of Education, Office of Educational Research and Improvement, 2001), 16; Phillip Altbach, Liz Reisbert, and Laura Rumbley, *Trends in Global Higher Education* (Boston: Center for International Higher Education, 2009), 68; Bruce Johnstone, "The Fiscal Future of Higher Education: Austerity, Opportunity and Accessibility" (Pullias lecture, University of Southern California, Los Angeles, CA, September 15, 2003).

2. John Immerwahr, *Meeting the Competition: College and University Presidents, Faculty and State Legislators View the New Competitive Academic Arena* (Providence, RI: The Futures Project, 2002), 2–13.

3. Gordon Davies, *Twenty Years of Higher Education in Virginia* (Charlottesville: State Council for Higher Education in Virginia, 1997), 2.

4. The state senator's true name has been changed to conceal the identity.

5. Dr. Martin resigned upon accepting the presidency of Amherst College and was not actually fired by the University of Wisconsin–Madison, but she was believed to be under significant pressure because of her dealings directly with the governor to secure greater autonomy for the flagship Madison campus, which is discussed in chapter 4.

6. Brian Clemow, "Privatization and the Public Good," *Labor Law Journal* 43, no. 6 (1992): 344–349; Peter Eckel, *Bridging Troubled Waters: Competition, Cooperation, and the Public Good in Independent and Public Higher Education* (Washington, DC: American Council on Education/The Futures Project, 2005), 6–8; Robert Zemsky, Gregory R. Wegner, and William F. Massy, *Remaking the American University: Market Smart and Mission Centered* (New Brunswick, NJ: Rutgers University Press, 2005), 4–10.

7. Breneman, *College Costs*, 13–21; Eckel, *Bridging Troubled Waters*, 7–13.

8. Altbach, Reisbert, and Rumbley, *Trends*, 1–37; Johnstone, "Fiscal Future"; Kevin Kinser et al., *The Global Growth of Private Higher Education* (Hoboken, NJ: Jossey-Bass, 2010), 36; Irungu Munene, "Privatizing the Public: Marketization as a Strategy in Public University Transformation," *Research in Post-Compulsory Education* 13, no. 1 (2008): 1–17; Per Nyborg, "Higher Education as a Public Good and a Public Responsibility," *Higher Education in Europe* 28, no. 3 (2003): 355–360; Carlo Salerno, "Privatizing the Public University," in *Privatizing the Public University: Perspectives from Across the Academy*, ed. Peter Eckel and Christopher Morphew (Baltimore: Johns Hopkins Press, 2009), 160–180; Gareth Williams, "The Many Faces of Privatization," *Higher Education Management* 8, no. 3 (1996): 39–57.

9. James Duderstadt, *The View from the Helm: Leading the American University During an Era of Change* (Ann Arbor, MI: University of Michigan Press, 2007), 34, 145.

Chapter 1

1. Gordon Davies, *Twenty Years of Higher Education in Virginia* (Charlottesville: State Council for Higher Education in Virginia, 1997), 2.

2. These conversations go back many years, and one great report from forty years ago asked these same questions: Carnegie Commission on Higher Education, *Higher Education: Who Pays? Who Benefits? Who Should Pay?* (San Francisco: Carnegie Commission on Higher Education, 1973).

3. Richard Vedder, *Going Broke by Degree: Why College Costs Too Much* (Washington, DC: AEI Publishers, 2004), 3.

4. Sebastian Thrun, interview with *Wired* magazine, May 1, 2012.

5. David Longanecker, "A Tale of Two Pities: The Story of Public Higher Education Finance," *Change* 38, no. 1 (2006): 23–24. Title of section used with permission from David Longanecker.

6. Karin Fischer, "Crisis of Confidence Threatens Colleges: Rising Costs Test 335 Families' Faith, While 1 in 3 Presidents See Academe on Wrong Road," *Chronicle Of Higher Education*, May 15, 2011; John Immerwahr, Jean Johnson, and Paul Gasbarra, *The Iron Triangle: College Presidents Talk About Costs, Access, and Quality* (San Jose, CA: National Center for Public Policy and Higher Education and Public Agenda, 2008), 5–7; John Immerwahr et al., *Squeeze Play 2010: Continued Public Anxiety on Cost, Harsher Judgments on How Colleges Are Run* (San Jose, CA: National Center for Public Policy and Higher Education and Public Agenda, 2010), 2–10; Paul Taylor et al., *Is College Worth It? College Presidents, Public Access Value, Quality and Mission of Higher Education* (Washington, DC: Pew Research Center, 2011), 58; David J. Weerts, *If We Only Told Our Story Better . . . Re-envisioning State–University Relations Through the Lens of Public Engagement* (Madison: Wisconsin Center for the Advancement of Postsecondary Education, University of Wisconsin, 2011), 2–5.

7. Importantly, the claim made by presidents and chancellors does not account for the fact that overall institutional budgets have risen dramatically (especially the research function at research universities), making the state's appropriations appear to be a much smaller contribution to university budgets. In reality, state appropriations have always been focused on the undergraduate educational components, not the many and varied functions at colleges and universities that have grown dramatically, including, but not limited to, graduate education and the research function as well as auxiliary enterprises.

8. Graham Spanier, *Press Conference in Response to Governor Corbett's Budget Proposal*, Pennsylvania State University, March 9, 2011.

9. David Bloom, Matthew Hartley, and Henry Rosovsky, "Beyond Private Gain: The Public Benefits of Higher Education," in *International Handbook of Higher Education,* ed. James Forest and Phillip Altbach (Dordrecht, The Netherlands: Springer, 2006), 293–308; Peter Eckel, *Bridging Troubled Waters: Competition, Cooperation, and the Public Good in Independent and Public Higher Education* (Washington, DC: American Council on Education/The Futures Project, 2005), 2–3; Ronald Ehrenberg, "The Perfect Storm and the Privatization of Public Higher Education," *Change* 38, no. 1 (2006): 50–51; David Longanecker, "State Governance and the Public Good," in *Higher Education for the Public Good: Emerging Voice from a National Movement,* ed. Adrianna Kezar, Tony Chambers, and John Burkhardt (San Francisco: Jossey-Bass, 2005), 57–70; Christopher Newfield, *Unmaking the Public University: The Forty-Year Assault on the Middle Class* (Cambridge, MA: Harvard University Press, 2008), 3–11; William Sullivan, "The University as Citizen: Institutional Identity and Social Responsibility," in *Philanthropy, Volunteerism & Fundraising in Higher Education*, ed. Andrea Walton and Marybeth Gasman (Washington, DC: Association for the Study of Higher Education, 2008),

166–176; William Zumeta et al., *Financing American Higher Education in the Era of Globalization* (Cambridge, MA: Harvard Education Press, 2012), 10–12.

10. Frank Newman and Laura Couturier, "Rhetoric, Reality and Risks," *American Academic* 1, no. 1 (2004): 61–75. Further, the notion of higher education as a public good may seem romantic in retrospect, but it is important to remember that at the beginning of the twentieth century, less than 1 percent of high school graduates went on to college. So while higher education was a public good, it was one that impacted directly very few citizens. The historic legacy of higher education as a public good was confronted by real tensions in the twentieth century with the massification of higher education.

11. Vedder, *Going Broke*, 129.

12. Milton Friedman, *Capitalism and Freedom: A Leading Economist's View of the Proper Role of Competitive Capitalism* (Chicago: University of Chicago Press, 1962), 99. Friedman went on to discuss his view that governmental support for higher education was less important, but necessary nonetheless to "train youngsters for citizenship and community leadership" (p. 99). He argued for something closer to a voucher system, however, rather than support for institutions, and this is discussed more in chapter 4.

13. Aims C. McGuinness Jr., "Autonomy and Accountability: Who Controls Academe?" in *American Higher Education in the Twenty-first Century: Social, Political, and Economic Challenges,* ed. Phillip Altbach, Robert Berdahl, and Patricia Gumport (Baltimore: Johns Hopkins University Press, 1999), 184–185.

14. These institutions were private from a legal standpoint, but many of them were still founded for very public purposes.

15. Integrated Postsecondary Education Data System ("Enrollment Figures in U.S. Postsecondary Institutions"), accessed December 23, 2013, http//nces.ed.gov/ipeds/.

16. A term originally used by Richard Moll in his 1985 book *The Public Ivys: A Guide to America's Best Public Undergraduate Colleges and Universities* (Viking). The original eight public ivies listed in his book were: the College of William & Mary (Williamsburg, Virginia), Miami University (Oxford, Ohio), the University of California (six campuses as of 1985), the University of Michigan (Ann Arbor), the University of North Carolina at Chapel Hill, the University of Texas at Austin, the University of Vermont (Burlington), and the University of Virginia (Charlottesville).

17. James Duderstadt, "A Master Plan for Higher Education in the Midwest: A Roadmap to the Future of the Nation's Heartland," in *Heartland Papers* 3 (2011): 33–39; Peter McPherson, Howard Gobstein, and David Shulenburger, *Ensuring Public Research Universities Remain Vital* (Washington, DC: Association of Public and Land Grant Universities, 2010), 8.

18. State Higher Education Executive Officers. *FY 2012, State Higher Education Finance* (New York: State Higher Education Executive Officers, 2013).

19. Fischer, "Crisis"; John Immerwahr, *Meeting the Competition: College and University Presidents, Faculty and State Legislators View the New Competitive Academic Arena* (Providence, RI: The Futures Project, 2002), 17–23; Immerwahr, Johnson, and Gasbarra, *The Iron Triangle*, 5–7; Immerwahr et al., *Squeeze Play 2010*, 2; Taylor et al., *Is College Worth It?*, 60.

20. Newfield, *Unmaking the Public University*, 272.

21. Virginia State Government. *The Governor's Blue Ribbon Commission on Higher Education* (Richmond: Office of the Governor, 2000), 98.

22. Margery Foster, *Out of Smalle Beginnings: An Economic History of Harvard College in the Puritan Period* (Cambridge, MA: Harvard University Press, 1962), 1–259, quoted in Andrew Delbanco, *College: What It Was, Is, and Should Be* (Princeton, NJ: Princeton University Press, 2012), 1–248.

23. Mark Yudof, "Higher Tuitions: Harbinger of a Hybrid University?" *Change* 34, no. 2 (2002): 16–20; Vedder, *Going Broke*, xxiv. James Duderstadt has suggested that the notion of "state" universities is outdated because these institutions are increasingly "national" and the funding comes nationally, as do students and faculty. See also: Mark Fogel and Elizabeth Malson-Huddle, *Precipice or Crossroads: Where America's Great Public Universities Stand and Where They Are Going Midway Through Their Second Century* (Albany: State University of New York Press, 2012).

24. Clark Kerr, *The Uses of the University* (Cambridge, MA: Harvard University Press, 1963), 1–12.

25. Charles McCarthy, *The Wisconsin Idea* (New York: Macmillan, 1912). 23.

26. Martin Trow, *Problems in the Transition from Elite to Mass Higher Education* (Berkeley, CA Carnegie Commission on Higher Education, 1973), 8; Newfield, *Unmaking the Public University*, 10.

27. Robert Berdahl, *Statewide Coordination of Higher Education* (Washington, DC: American Council on Education, 1971), 4.

28. Ibid., 5.

29. James Perkins, *The University in Transition* (Princeton, NJ: Princeton University Press, 1966), 88.

30. One of the few models for privatization is Bruce Johnstone's "Continuum of Privatization," in which he argues that there are virtually no purely public or private institutions, and so viewing privatization as a continuum helps to account for the many shades of gray between public and private. The model, however, did not account for any weighting of importance of the dimensions and did not account for an ordering of dimensions. Bruce Johnstone, "Privatization in and of Higher Education" (unpublished report, Project for Research on Private Higher Education, SUNY Buffalo, Buffalo, NY, 2002).

31. Roger Geiger, "Expert and Elite: The Incongruous Missions of Public Research Universities," in *Future of the American Public Research University,* ed. Roger Geiger, Carol Colbeck, Roger Williams, and Christian Anderson (Rotterdam, The Netherlands: Sense, 2007), 15–33.

32. James Duderstadt, *The View from the Helm: Leading the American University During an Era of Change* (Ann Arbor: University of Michigan Press, 2007), 14.

33. Immerwahr, Johnson, and Gasbarra, *The Iron Triangle*, 3; Robert Zemsky et al., "Seeing Straight Through a Muddle," *Policy Perspectives* 1, no. 1 (1988): 2.

34. Geiger, "Expert and Elite," 28.

35. Longanecker, "A Tale of Two Pities," 24–25.

Chapter 2

1. George Washington, "First Annual Message to Congress," January 8, 1790.

2. David Bloom, Matthew Hartley, and Henry Rosovsky, "Beyond Private Gain: The Public Benefits of Higher Education," in *International Handbook of Higher Education,* ed. James Forest and Phillip Altbach (Dordrecht, The Netherlands: Springer, 2006), 293–308; Peter Eckel, *Bridging Troubled Waters: Competition, Cooperation, and the Public Good in Independent and Public Higher Education* (Washington, DC: American Council on Education/The Futures Project, 2005), 2–3; Ronald Ehrenberg, "The Perfect Storm and the Privatization of Public Higher Education," *Change* 38, no. 1 (2006): 50–51; Longanecker, "State Governance and the Public Good," 57–70; Christopher Newfield, *Unmaking the Public University: The Forty-Year Assault on the Middle Class* (Cambridge, MA: Harvard University Press, 2008), 3–6; William Sullivan, "The University as Citizen: Institutional Identity and Social Responsibility," in *Philanthropy, Volunteerism & Fundraising in Higher Education*, ed. Andrea Walton and

Marybeth Gasman (Washington, DC: Association for the Study of Higher Education, 2008), 166–176; William Zumeta et al., *Financing American Higher Education in the Era of Globalization* (Cambridge, MA: Harvard Education Press, 2012), 10–12.

3. Samuel Adams, letter to James Warren, Boston, 1779.

4. Newfield, *Unmaking the Public University*, 3–7; Frank Newman and Laura Couturier, "Rhetoric, Reality and Risks," *American Academic* 1, no. 1 (2004): 61–75.

5. Zumeta et al., *Financing American Higher Education*, 34–78; Richard Richardson, Kathy Bracco, Patrick Callan, and Joni Finney, *Designing State Higher Education Systems for a New Century* (Phoenix, AR: Oryx Press, 1999), 1–95.

6. Steven Rosenzweig, *The Political University: Policy, Politics, and Presidential Leadership in the American Research University* (Baltimore: Johns Hopkins University Press, 1998), 20–108; Burton Clark, *The Higher Education System: Academic Organization in Cross-National Perspective* (Berkeley: University of California Press, 1983), 17–147; Aims C. McGuinness Jr., "Autonomy and Accountability: Who Controls Academe?" in *American Higher Education in the Twenty-First Century: Social, Political, and Economic Challenges,* ed. Phillip Altbach, Robert Berdahl, and Patricia Gumport (Baltimore: Johns Hopkins University Press, 1999), 184–185; William Zumeta, "What Does It Mean to Be Accountable? Dimensions and Implications of Higher Education's Public Accountability," *Review of Higher Education* 35, no. 1 (2011): 131–148.

7. Zumeta et al., *Financing American Higher Education*, 1–25.

8. U.S. Department of Education, National Center for Education Statistics, "Table 402," accessed December 17, 2013, http://nces.ed.gov/programs/digest/d12/tables/dt12_402.asp.

9. James Duderstadt, *The View from the Helm: Leading the American University During an Era of Change* (Ann Arbor, MI: University of Michigan Press, 2007), 317; James Duderstadt, "A Master Plan for Higher Education in the Midwest: A Roadmap to the Future of the Nation's Heartland," in *Heartland Papers* 3 (2011): 21–29; Michael Redding, "Autonomy Policy in U.S. Public Higher Education: A Comparative Case Study of Oregon and Virginia," (dissertation, University of Pennsylvania, 2009), 1–25; Frank Newman, Laura Couturier, and Jamie Scurry, *The Future of Higher Education: Rhetoric, Reality and the Risks of the Market* (San Francisco: Jossey-Bass, 2004), 134.

10. Duderstadt, "Master Plan," 21–29; Michael McLendon, James Hearn, and Christine Mokher, "Partisans, Professionals, and Power: The Role of Political Factors in State Higher Education Funding," *Journal of Higher Education* 80, no. 6 (2009); 700–707; David J. Weerts and Justin Ronca, "Examining Differences in State Support for Higher Education: A Comparative Study of State Appropriations for Research I Universities," *Journal of Higher Education* 77, no. 6 (2006); 939–940; David J. Weerts, "Funding the Flagships: Governance, Politics and Identity in State Support for Public Research Universities" (paper presented at the Annual Meeting of the American Educational Research Association, San Diego, CA, April 2009); David J. Weerts, "Can Community Engagement Leverage State Appropriations for Higher Education?" (paper presented at the Annual Meeting of the Association for the Study of Higher Education, Indianapolis, IN, November 2010); David J. Weerts, *If We Only Told Our Story Better . . . Re-envisioning State–University Relations Through the Lens of Public Engagement* (Madison: Wisconsin Center for the Advancement of Postsecondary Education, University of Wisconsin, 2011), 4–8.

11. James Fairweather, "U.S. Higher Education: Contemporary Challenges and Policy Options," in *Structuring Mass Higher Education: The Role of Elite Institutions*, ed. David Palfreyman and Ted Tapper (New York: Routledge, 2009) 13–34; Edward St. John and Ontario Wooden, "Privatization and Federal Funding for Higher Education," in *Privatization and Public Universities*, ed. Douglas Priest and Edward St. John (Bloomington: Indiana University Press,

2006), 38–64; Nannerl Keohane, *Higher Ground: Ethics and Leadership in the Modern University* (Durham, NC: Duke University Press, 2006), 121–123; John R. Thelin, *The History of American Higher Education* (Baltimore: Johns Hopkins University Press, 2004), 41–110; Martin Trow, "Federalism in American Higher Education," in *Higher Learning in America: 1980–2000*, ed. Arthur Levine (Baltimore: Johns Hopkins University Press, 1993), 39–66.

12. Trow, "Federalism," 39–66; Fairweather, "U.S. Higher Education," 16–25; Keohane, *Higher Ground*, 122.

13. Trow, "Federalism," 39–67; Thelin, *History of American Higher Education*, 41–110; Donald Heller, "Financing Public Research Universities in the United States: The Role of Students and Their Families," in *The Future of the American Public Research University*, ed. Roger Geiger, Carol Colbeck, Roger Williams, and Christian Anderson (Rotterdam, The Netherlands: Sense, 2007), 35–53.

14. Heller, "Financing Public Research Universities," 35–53; Fairweather, "U.S. Higher Education," 35; Trow, "Federalism," 39–67.

15. Roger Geiger, "The Ten Generations of American Higher Education," in *American Higher Education in the Twenty-First Century: Social, Political, and Economic Challenges,* ed. Phillip Altbach, Robert Berdahl, and Patricia Gumport (Baltimore: Johns Hopkins University Press, 1999), 38–70; James Fairweather, "U.S. Higher Education: Contemporary Challenges and Policy Options," in *Structuring Mass Higher Education: The Role of Elite Institutions,* ed. David Palfreyman and Ted Tapper (New York: Routledge, 2009), 13–34.

16. National Center for Education Statistics, "State Education Data Profiles, 2010–2011," accessed January 2, 2014, http//nces.ed.gov/programs/stateprofiles.

17. Coy Cross, *Justin Smith Morrill: Father of the Land-Grant Colleges* (East Lansing: Michigan State University Press, 1999), 83.

18. Thelin, *History of American Higher Education*, 74–110; Keohane, *Higher Ground*, 4; Fairweather, "U.S. Higher Education," 1–35; Cross, *Justin Smith Morrill*, 78–83; Trow, "Federalism," 39–67; Phillip Altbach, "Patterns of Higher Education Development," in *American Higher Education in the Twenty-First Century: Social, Political, and Economic Challenges,* ed. Phillip Altbach, Robert Berdahl, and Patricia Gumport (Baltimore: Johns Hopkins University Press, 1999), 15–37; Geiger, "The Ten Generations," 38–70.

19. Cross, *Justin Smith Morrill*, 78–83; Zumeta et al., *Financing American Higher Education*, 56–67.

20. Clifton Conrad and David J. Weerts, "Federal Involvement in Higher Education Desegregation: An Unfinished Agenda," in *Public Funding of Higher Education: Changing Contexts and New Rationales*, ed. Edward St. John and Michael Parsons (Baltimore: Johns Hopkins University Press, 2004), 61; Fairweather, "U.S. Higher Education," 1–35; Keohane, *Higher Ground*, 4–5; Cross, *Justin Smith Morrill*, 86–89.

21. Association of Public and Land-Grant Universities. *Annual Report 2012* (Washington, DC: Association of Public Land-Grant Universities,2013).

22. Heller, "Financing Public Research Universities," 35–53; Trow, "Federalism," 39–67; Altbach, "Patterns of Higher Education Development," 15–37; Clark Kerr, *The Uses of the University* (Cambridge, MA: Harvard University Press, 1963), 35–39.

23. Altbach, "Patterns of Higher Education Development," 15–37; Kemal Gürüz, *Higher Education and International Student Mobility in the Global Knowledge Economy* (Albany: State University of New York Press, 2008), 149–169; Keohane, *Higher Ground*, 126.

24. Thelin, *History of American Higher Education*, 100.

25. Heller, "Financing Public Research Universities," 35–53; Thelin, *History of American Higher Education*, 74–110; William R. King, "The Contemporary University," in *The University in*

the Global Age, ed. William R. King (Basingstoke, UK: Creative Print & Design, 2004), 1–26; Trow, "Federalism," 39–67.

26. Thelin, *History of American Higher Education,* 262; Christopher Loss, *Between Citizens and State: The Politics of American Higher Education in the 20th Century* (Princeton, NJ: Princeton University Press, 2012), 12–113.

27. Ibid., 58–70.

28. David Wolfe, "The Role of Universities in Regional Development and Cluster Formation," in *Creating Knowledge, Strengthening Nations: The Changing Role of Higher Education,* ed. Glen Jones, Patricia McCarney, and Michael Skolnik (Toronto: University of Toronto Press Incorporated, 2005), 167–194; Thelin, *History of American Higher Education,* 205–315.

29. Thelin, *History of American Higher Education,* 205–315.

30. Loss, *Between Citizens and State,* 91–210; Thelin, *History of American Higher Education,* 262; Trow, "Federalism," 58–59; Zumeta et al., *Financing American Higher Education in the Era of Globalization,* 1–35; Gürüz, *Higher Education and International Student Mobility,* 71–168.

31. Fairweather, "U.S. Higher Education," 13–35; Thelin, *History of American Higher Education,* 223–273; James Duderstadt and Farris Womack, *The Future of the Public University in America: Beyond the Crossroads* (Baltimore: Johns Hopkins University Press, 2003), 54; Keohane, *Higher Ground,* 129.

32. Thomas Husen, "The Idea of the University: Changing Roles, Current Crisis, and Future Challenges," in *Higher Education in an International Perspective: Critical Issues,* ed. Phillip Altbach and Zaghloul Morsy (New York: Garland Publishing Inc., 1996), 90–110; Duderstadt and Womack, *The Future of the Public University in America,* 53; Thelin, *History of American Higher Education,* 260–317.

33. Zumeta et al., *Financing American Higher Education in the Era of Globalization,* 80–87; Harry S. Truman, *President's Commission on Higher Education* (report requested by the president of the United States, Washington DC, 1947).

34. Heller, "Financing Public Research Universities," 35–53.

35. Thelin, *History of American Higher Education,* 205–317.

36. Heller, "Financing Public Research Universities," 35–53; Thelin, *History of American Higher Education,* 273.

37. Loss, *Between Citizens and State,* 140.

38. Zumeta et al., *Financing American Higher Education in the Era of Globalization,* 100–103; Thelin, *History of American Higher Education,* 260–317; Loss, *Between Citizens and State,* 72–174.

39. Paul Courant, James Duderstadt, and Edie Goldenberg, "Needed: A National Strategy to Preserve Public Research Universities," *Chronicle of Higher Education,* January 3, 2010, http://chronicle.com/article/A-Plan-to-Save-Americas/63358/.

40. Zumeta et al., *Financing American Higher Education in the Era of Globalization,* 5–34; Conrad and Weerts, "Federal Involvement," 61–64.

41. Zumeta et al., *Financing American Higher Education in the Era of Globalization;* 201; Heller, "Financing Public Research Universities," 35–53.

42. Kerr, *Uses of the University,* 106.

43. Peter Manicas, "Higher Education at the Brink," in *The University in Transformation: Global Perspectives on the Futures of the University,* ed. Sohail Inayatullah and Jennifer Gidley (Westport, CT: Bergin & Garvey, 2000), 31–40; Thelin, *History of American Higher Education,* 260–317; Arthur Cohen and Florence Brawer, *The American Community College* (San Francisco: Jossey-Bass, 2008), 320-321; U.S. Department of Education, National Center for

Education Statistics, "Table 196," accessed December 20, 2013, http://nces.ed.gov/programs/digest/d11/tables/dt11_196.asp.

44. Kerr, *Uses of the University*, 1.

45. Thelin, *History of American Higher Education*, 317–363; Bruce Johnstone, "Higher Education in the United States in the Year 2000," in *Higher Education in an International Perspective: Critical Issues,* ed. Phillip Altbach and Zaghloul Morsy (New York: Garland Publishing Inc., 1996), 180; Manicas, "Higher Education at the Brink," 31–40.

46. Deane Neubauer, "Will the Future Include US?" in *The University in Transformation: Global Perspectives on the Futures of the University,* ed. Sohail Inayatullah and Jennifer Gidley (Westport, CT: Bergin & Garvey, 2000), 41–54; Patrick Callan, *California Higher Education, The Master Plan, and the Erosion of College Opportunity* (San Jose, CA: National Center for Public Policy and Higher Education, 2009). 3–20.

47. St. John and Wooden, "Privatization and Federal Funding for Higher Education," 38–64; Neubauer, "Will the Future Include US?" 41–54; Callan, *California Higher Education*, 3–20.

48. Thelin, *History of American Higher Education*, 317–380.

49. Geiger, "The Ten Generations," 38–70; David Breneman and Joni Finney, "The Changing Landscape: Higher Education Finance in the 1990s," in *Public and Private Financing of Higher Education,* ed. Patrick Callan and Joni Finney (Phoenix, AR: The Oryx Press, 1997), 74–77; David Breneman and H. Lane Kneedler. "Negotiating a New Relationship with the State: The Virginia Experience" (paper presented at the TIAA-CREF Institute Conference, New York, NY, May 2005); Joni Finney and Patrick Kelly, "Affordability: Obtaining and Making Sense of Information About How Students Families and States Pay for Higher Education," *Change* 36, no. 4 (2004): 54–59; Roger Geiger, *Knowledge and Money: Research Universities and the Paradox of the Marketplace* (Stanford, CA: Stanford University Press, 2004), 232–275; Harold Hovey, *State Spending for Higher Education in the Next Decade: The 336 Battle to Sustain Current Support* (Washington, DC: The National Center for Public Policy in Higher Education, 1999), 1–69; Taylor et al., *Is College Worth It?*, 10; Zumeta et al., *Financing American Higher Education in the Era of Globalization*, 59.

50. John Cheslock and Harry Gianneschi, "Replacing State Appropriations with Alternative Revenue Sources: The Case of Voluntary Support," *Journal of Higher Education* 79, no. 2 (2008): 209–210; Zumeta et al., *Financing American Higher Education in the Era of Globalization*, 3–23; Altbach, Reisbert, and Rumbley, "Trends in Global Higher Education," 65–83; Bruce Johnstone, "Financing the American Public Research University: Lessons from an International Perspective," in *The Future of the American Public Research University,* ed. Roger Geiger, Carol Colbeck, Roger Williams, and Christian Anderson (Rotterdam, The Netherlands: Sense, 2007), 55–69; Kevin Kinser et al., *The Global Growth of Private Higher Education* (Hoboken, NJ: Jossey-Bass, 2010), 36; Irungu Munene, "Privatizing the Public: Marketization as a Strategy in Public University Transformation," *Research in Post-Compulsory Education* 13, no. 1 (2008): 1–17; Per Nyborg, "Higher Education as a Public Good and a Public Responsibility," *Higher Education in Europe* 28, no. 3 (2003): 355–360; Carlo Salerno, "Privatizing the Public University," in *Privatizing the Public University: Perspectives from Across the Academy,* ed. Peter Eckel and Christopher Morphew (Baltimore: Johns Hopkins Press, 2009), 160–180; Gareth Williams, "The Many Faces of Privatization," *Higher Education Management* 8, no. 3 (1996): 39–57.

51. King, "The Contemporary University," 1–26; St. John and Wooden, "Privatization and Federal Funding for Higher Education," 38–64; Charles Clotfelter, Ronald Ehrenberg, Malcom Getz, and John Siegfried, *Economic Challenges in Higher Education* (Chicago: University of Chicago Press, 1991), 13.

52. Callan, *California Higher Education*, 3–19.

53. Eric Kelderman, "State Spending on Higher Education Edges Down, as Deficits Loom," *Chronicle of Higher Education*, January 24, 2011; Scott Jaschik, "The Sinking States," *Inside Higher Ed*, January 24, 2011; Dennis Jones and Jane Wellman, "Breaking Bad Habits: Navigating the Financial Crisis," *Change* 43, no. 3 (2010): 8; Robert Archibald and David Feldman, *Why Does College Cost So Much?* (Oxford, UK: Oxford University Press, 2011), 235–252; Duderstadt and Womack, *The Future of the Public University in America*, 79; Ehrenberg, "The Perfect Storm," 50–51; John Hawkins, "Higher Education Transformation: Some Trends in California and Asia," *Policy Futures in Education* 6, no. 5 (2008): 532–544; Peter McPherson, Howard J. Gobstein, and David E. Shulenburger, *Forging a Foundation for the Future: Keeping Public Research Universities Strong* (Washington, DC: Association of Public and Land Grant Universities, 2010b), 23–24; Arthur Zusman, "Issues Facing Higher Education in the Twenty-First Century," in *American Higher Education in the TwentyFirst Century: Social, Political, and Economic Challenges,* ed. Phillip Altbach, Robert Berdahl, and Patricia Gumport (Baltimore: Johns Hopkins University Press, 1999), 109–148.

54. U.S. Department of Education, National Center for Education Statistics (Table 349, average cost of undergraduate tuition, accessed December 20, 2012), http://nces.ed.gov/programs/digest/d11/tables/dt11_349.asp.

55. Duderstadt and Womack, *The Future of the Public University in America*, 79–85.

56. John Immerwahr et al., *Squeeze Play 2010: Continued Public Anxiety on Cost, Harsher Judgments on How Colleges Are Run* (San Jose, CA: National Center for Public Policy and Higher Education and Public Agenda, 2010), 2–17.

57. Bloom, Hartley, and Rosovsky, "Beyond Private Gain," 293–208; George Dennison, "Privatization: An Unheralded Trend in Public Higher Education," *Innovative Higher Education* 28, no. 1 (2003): 7–20; Duderstadt and Womack, *The Future of the Public University in America*, 80–83; Duderstadt, "A Master Plan," 69; Ehrenberg, "The Perfect Storm," 50–51; Geiger, *Knowledge and Money*, 1–12; Joanne Jacobs, "The Colorado Voucher System: Will It Help or Hurt Public Higher Education?" *Change* 38 no. 1 (2006): 54–59; David Kirp and Patrick Roberts, "Mr. Jefferson's University Breaks Up," *Public Interest* 148 (2002): 70–84; David Leslie and Robert Berdahl, "The Politics of Restructuring Higher Education in Virginia: A Case Study," *Review of Higher Education* 31, no. 3 (2008): 309–328; Katrina Meyer, "Privatizing Public Higher Education: Beliefs That Fuel the Conversation," *Planning for Higher Education* 34, no. 3 (2006), 34–44; Per Nyborg, "Higher Education as a Public Good and a Public Responsibility," *Higher Education in Europe* 28, no. 3 (2003): 355–360; Laura Perna, "The Private Benefits of Higher Education: An Examination of the Earnings Premium," *Research in Higher Education* 44, no. 4 (2003): 451–472; Sullivan, "The University as Citizen," 166–176; Taylor et al., *Is College Worth It?*, 2–13.

58. Zumeta et al., *Financing American Higher Education in the Era of Globalization*, 1–23; Keohane, *Higher Ground*, 129; Duderstadt and Womack, *The Future of the Public University in America*, 39; Trow, "Federalism," 59–61; Geiger, *Knowledge and Money*, 38–70.

59. Duderstadt and Womack, *The Future of the Public University in America*, 39; Zumeta et al., *Financing American Higher Education in the Era of Globalization*, 23–56; Loss, *Between Citizens and State*, 212–226.

60. Trow, "Federalism," 62; Geiger, *Knowledge and Money*, 38–70; Callan, *California Higher Education*, 3–20; Duderstadt and Womack, *The Future of the Public University in America*, 39–41.

61. Callan, *California Higher Education*, 3–20; Duderstadt and Womack, *The Future of the Public University in America*, 38–41; St. John and Wooden, "Privatization and Federal Funding," 38–64.

62. St. John and Wooden, "Privatization and Federal Funding," 38–64.

63. Sara Goldrick-Rab, "The Real College Barrier for the Working Poor," *Inside Higher Ed*, December 10, 2013, http://www.insidehighered.com/views/2013/12/10/federal-aid-needy-students-inadequate-essay#ixzz2pFVmoeAE.

64. St. John and Wooden, "Privatization and Federal Funding," 38–64.

65. Michael Gordon, "The Economy and Higher Education," in *Higher Learning in America: 1980–2000*, ed. Arthur Levine (Baltimore: Johns Hopkins University Press, 1993), 20–36; U.S. Department of Education, National Center for Education Statistics, "Table 395," accessed December 20, 2013, http://nces.ed.gov/programs/digest/d12/tables/dt12_395.asp; Fairweather, "U.S. Higher Education," 1–35; Blake Ellis, "Average Student Loan Debt: $29,400," *CNN Money*, December 5, 2013.

66. St. John and Wooden, "Privatization and Federal Funding," 50; U.S. Department of Education, National Center for Education Statistics (Table 395).

67. St. John and Wooden, "Privatization and Federal Funding," 38–64.

68. Duderstadt and Womack, *The Future of the Public University in America*, 39.

69. St. John and Wooden, "Privatization and Federal Funding," 38–64; US Department of Education, National Center for Education Statistics (Table 419).

70. Ibid; U.S. Department of Education, *The Budget for Fiscal Year 2014* (Washington, DC: U.S. DOE, 2014).

71. Duderstadt and Womack, *The Future of the Public University in America*, 79.

72. Ibid, 10; Derek Bok, *Universities in the Marketplace: The Commercialization of Higher Education* (Princeton, NJ: Princeton University Press, 2003), 1; Robert Birgeneau, Seth Garz, and Frank Yeary, *Knowledge Made in America: A Private-Public Funding Model for Leading Public Research Universities* (Berkeley: University of California, 2012), 1–5; U.S. Department of Commerce, *The Competitiveness and Innovative Capacity of the US* (Washington, DC: National Economic Council, 2012); Duderstadt and Womack, *The Future of the Public University in America*, 1.

73. Elizabeth Garnsey, "The Entrepreneurial University: The Idea and Its Critics," in *How Universities Promote Economic Growth*, ed. Shahid Yusuf and Kaoru Nabeshima (Washington DC: The International Bank for Reconstruction and Development/The World Bank, 2007), 227–238; Bok, *Universities in the Marketplace*, 58–64; U.S. Department of Commerce, *Competitiveness and Innovative Capacity*; Glen Jones, Patricia McCarney, and Michael Skolnik, "Introduction," in *Creating Knowledge, Strengthening Nations: The Changing Role of Higher Education*, ed. Glen Jones, Patricia McCarney, and Michael Skolnik (Toronto: University of Toronto Press Incorporated, 2005), 3–18.

74. Bok, *Universities in the Marketplace*, 58–64; Jones, McCarney, and Skolnik, "Introduction," 3–18.

75. Garnsey, "The Entrepreneurial University," 227–238; U.S. Department of Commerce, *Competitiveness and Innovative Capacity*; Wolfe, "Role of Universities," 167–194.

76. Janice Newson, "Constructing the 'Post-Industrial University': Institutional Budgeting and University-Corporate Linkages," in *The Funding of Higher Education: International Perspectives*, ed. Phillip Altbach and Bruce Johnstone (New York: Garland Publishing Inc, 1993), 285–303; Wolfe, "Role of Universities," 167–194; U.S. Department of Commerce, *Competitiveness and Innovative Capacity* (Washington, DC, 2005).

77. Ibid.

78. Altbach, "Patterns of Higher Education Development," 15–37; William Massy, "Financing Research," in *Financing Higher Education in a Global Economy*, ed. Richard Anderson and Joel Meyerson (New York: Macmillan Publishing Company, 1990), 41–56.

79. Massy, "Financing Research," 41–56; National Research Council, Engineering Research and America's Future: Meeting the Challenges of a Global Economy (Washington, DC: The National Academies Press, 2005); Wolfe, "Role of Universities," 167–194; Altbach, "Patterns of Higher Education Development," 15–37.

80. James Duderstadt, "The Changing Nature of Research and the Future of the University," in Reinventing the Research University, ed. Luc Weber and James Duderstadt (London: Economica, 2004), 73–87.

81. Bok, Universities in the Marketplace, 197; U.S. Department of Commerce, Competitiveness and Innovative Capacity.

82. Richard Anderson, "The Economy and Higher Education," in Financing Higher Education in a Global Economy, ed. Richard Anderson and Joel Meyerson (New York: Macmillan Publishing Company, 1990), 13–40.

83. Jandhyala Tilak, "The Privatization of Higher Education," in Higher Education in an International Perspective: Critical Issues, ed. Phillip Altbach and Zaghloul Morsy (New York: Garland Publishers, 1996), 59–71; Liz Reisberg and Laura Rumbley, "ETHIOPIA: The Dilemmas of Higher Education Expansion," International Higher Education 58, no. 1 (2010), 23–24; King, "The Contemporary University," 1–26.

84. Ernest Boyer, "Introduction," in The Funding of Higher Education: International Perspectives, ed. Phillip Altbach and Bruce Johnstone (New York: Garland Publishing Inc., 1993), xv; King, "The Contemporary University," 1–26.

85. King, "The Contemporary University," 1–26; Tilak, "The Privatization of Higher Education," 59–71; Simon Marginson, "Dynamics of East Asian Higher Education," in The Globalization of Higher Education, ed. Christine Ennew and David Greenaway (Hampshire, UK: Palgrave Macmillan, 2012), 40–53; Boyer, "Introduction," 1–26; Gürüz, Higher Education and International Student Mobility, 71–168..

86. Garnsey, "The Entrepreneurial University," 227–238.

87. Birgeneau, Garz, and Yeary, Knowledge Made in America, 1–5; Marginson, "Dynamics of East Asian Higher Education," 40–53; Altbach, "Patterns of Higher Education Development," 15–37; Gürüz, Higher Education and International Student Mobility, 71–168.

88. Bruce Johnstone, "The Costs of Higher Education: Worldwide Issues and Trends for the 1990s," in The Funding of Higher Education: International Perspectives, ed. Phillip Altbach and Bruce Johnstone (New York: Garland Publishing Inc, 1993), 3–24.

89. Tilak, "The Privatization of Higher Education," 59–71; Richard Hartnett, "Higher Education Funding in Open Door China," in The Funding of Higher Education: International Perspectives, ed. Phillip Altbach and Bruce Johnstone (New York: Garland Publishing Inc, 1993), 127–150; Marginson, "Dynamics of East Asian Higher Education," 40–53; Birgeneau, Garz, and Yeary, Knowledge Made in America, 1–5; Garnsey, "The Entrepreneurial University," 227–238; Jasvir Singh, "Higher Education and Development: The Experience of Four Newly Industrializing Countries in Asia," in Higher Education in an International Perspective: Critical Issues, ed. Phillip Altbach and Zaghloul Morsy (New York: Garland Publishers, 1996), 142–156.

90. Johnstone, "The Costs of Higher Education: Worldwide Issues and Trends for the 1990s," 3–24; Robert Birgeneau and Frank Yeary, "Rescuing our Public Universities," Washington Post, September 27, 2009.

91. Singh, "Higher Education and Development," 142–156

92. Marginson, "Dynamics of East Asian Higher Education," 40–53.

93. Garnsey, "The Entrepreneurial University," 227–238; Courant, Duderstadt, and Goldenberg, "Needed."

94. U.S. Department of Education, Integrated Postsecondary Education Data System. "Post-secondary Revenues by Source," accessed December 20, 2012, http://nces.ed.gov/datalab/tableslibrary/viewtable.aspx?tableid=4576.

95. U.S. Department of Commerce, *Competitiveness and Innovative Capacity*; National Research Council, Engineering Research and America's Future: Meeting the Challenges of a Global Economy (Washington, DC: The National Academies Press, 2005).

Chapter 3

1. W. E. B. Du Bois, "The Field and Function of the Negro College," in *The Education of Black People: Ten Critiques, 1906–1960*, ed. Herbert Aptheker (New York: Monthly Review Press, 1973), 84.

2. Andrew Carnegie, "Wealth," *North American Review*, 184 (1889): 653–654.

3. Organization for Economic Co-operation and Development, *United States: Education at a Glance 2013*. Paris: Organization for Economic Co-operation and Development, 2013.

4. Ibid.

5. Sandy Baum, Jennifer Ma, and Kathleen Payea, *Trends in Public Higher Education: Enrollment, Prices, Student Aid, Revenues, and Expenditures* (New York: The College Board, 2012), 4.

6. The College Board, *Trends in College Pricing 2012* (New York: The College Board, 2012).

7. Brian Pusser, "The Role of Public Spheres," *Governance and the Public Good*, ed. William G. Tierney (Albany: State University of New York Press, 2006), 14.

8. Elchanan Cohn and Terry G. Geske, *The Economics of Education* (Oxford, UK: Pergamon, 1990), 1–430; Michael Grossman, "Education and Non-market Outcomes," in *Handbook of the Economics of Higher Education*, ed. Eric Hanushek and Finis Welch (Amsterdam, The Netherlands: North Holland, 2006), 576–633; Mark Berger and Paul Leigh, "The Effect of Alcohol Abuse on Wages," *Applied Economics* 20 (1989): 1343–1351; Neri Lando, "The Inter-action Between Health and Education," *Social Security Bulletin* (1975): 16–22.

9. Robert Goheen, *The Human Nature of a University* (Princeton, NJ: Princeton University Press, 1969), 9.

10. David Bloom, Matthew Hartley, and Henry Rosovsky, "Beyond Private Gain: The Public Benefits of Higher Education," in *International Handbook of Higher Education,* ed. James Forest and Phillip Altbach (Dordrecht, The Netherlands: Springer, 2006), 293–308; George Dennison, "Privatization: An Unheralded Trend in Public Higher Education," *Innovation in Higher Education* 28, no. 1 (2003): 7–20; James Duderstadt and Farris Womack, *The Future of the Public University in America: Beyond the Crossroads* (Baltimore: Johns Hopkins University Press, 2003), 75; James Duderstadt, "A Master Plan for Higher Education in the Midwest: A Roadmap to the Future of the Nation's Heartland," in *Heartland Papers* 3 (2011): 16; Ronald Ehrenberg, "The Perfect Storm and the Privatization of Public Higher Education," *Change* 38, no. 1 (2006): 46–53; Roger Geiger, *Knowledge and Money: Research Universities and the Paradox of the Marketplace* (Stanford, CA: Stanford University Press, 2004), 180–232; Joanne Jacobs, "The Colorado Voucher System: Will It Help or Hurt Public Higher Education?" *Change* 38 no. 1 (2006): 54–59; David Kirp and Patrick Roberts, "Mr. Jefferson's University Breaks Up," *Public Interest* 148 (2002): 70–84; David Leslie and Robert Berdahl, "The Politics of Restructuring Higher Education in Virginia: A Case Study," *Review of Higher Education* 31, no. 3 (2008): 309–328; Katrina Meyer, "Privatizing Public Higher Education: Beliefs That Fuel the Conversation," *Planning for Higher Education* 34, no. 3 (2006): 34–44; Per Ny-borg, "Higher Education as a Public Good and a Public Responsibility," *Higher Education in Europe* 28, no. 3 (2003): 355–360; Laura Perna, "The Private Benefits of Higher Education: An Examination of the Earnings Premium," *Research in Higher Education* 44, no. 4 (2003):

451–471; William Sullivan, "The University as Citizen: Institutional Identity and Social Responsibility," in *Philanthropy, Volunteerism & Fundraising in Higher Education*, ed. Andrea Walton and Marybeth Gasman (Washington, DC: Association for the Study of Higher Education, 2008), 166–176; Taylor et al., *Is College Worth It?* 2–13.

11. Jorge Klor de Alva and Mark Schneider, *Who Wins? Who Pays? The Economic Returns and Costs of a Bachelor's Degree* (Washington, DC: American Institutes for Research, 2011), 11–12.

12. Bloom, Hartley, and Rosovsky, "Beyond Private Gain," 295.

13. de Alva and Schneider, *Who Wins*, 11–12; Institute for Higher Education Policy, *The Investment Payoff: A 50-State Analysis of the Public and Private Benefits of Higher Education,* Washington, DC: Institute for Higher Education Policy, 2005; Longanecker, "State Governance and the Public Good," 57–70; Robert Zemsky, Gregory R. Wegner, and Maria Iannozzi, "A Perspective on Privatization," in *Public and Private Financing of Higher Education*, ed. Patrick Callan and Joni Finney (Phoenix, AR: Oryx Press, 1997b), 74–77; Sandy Baum and Michael McPherson, "Is Education a Public Good or a Private Good?," *The Chronicle of Higher Education*, January 19, 2011; David Dill, "Higher Education Markets and Public Policy," *Higher Education Policy* 10 no. 3/4 (1997): 167–185; John Donahue, *The Privatization Decision: Public Ends, Private Means* (New York: Basic Books, 1989), 18–20; Klaus Hufner, "Higher Education as a Public Good: Means and Forms of Provision," *Higher Education in Europe* 28 no. 3 (2003): 339–347; Neal Johnson, *Balancing Act: Public Higher Education in Transition* (Washington, DC: State Governance Action Annual Report, Association of Governing Boards of Universities and Colleges, 2004), 4–5; Judith Ramaley, "Service and Outreach: The Public Universities Opportunities and Obligations," in *The Future of the American Public Research University*, ed. Roger Geiger, Carol Colbeck, Roger Williams, and Christian Anderson (Rotterdam, The Netherlands: Sense, 2007), 145–161.

14. Robert Zemsky, Gregory R. Wegner, and William F. Massy, *Remaking the American University: Market Smart and Mission Centered* (New Brunswick, NJ: Rutgers University Press, 2005), 10.

15. Katherine Lyall and Kathleen Sell, "The De Facto Privatization of American Public Higher Education," *Change* 38, no. 1 (2006): 12.

16. Gary Becker, *Human Capital: A Theoretical and Empirical Analysis with Special Reference to Education, Second Ed.* (Chicago: University of Chicago Press, 1993), 4–13; David Olaniyan and Tim Okemakinde, "Human Capital Theory: Implications for Educational Development," *European Journal of Scientific Research* 24, no. 2 (2008): 157–62.

17. For two good books in this area, see: Ann Mullen, *Degrees of Inequality: Culture, Class, and Gender in American Higher Education* (Baltimore: John Hopkins University Press, 2010), 1–225; Daniel Golden, *The Price of Admission: How America's Ruling Class Buys Its Way into the Elite Colleges, and Who Gets Left Outside the Gates* (New York: Three Rivers Press, 2007), 1–309.

18. Daron Acemoglu, "Lecture Notes for Graduate Labor Economics" (lecture, Massachusetts Institute of Technology, Cambridge, MA, 2005).

19. Olaniyan and Okemakinde, "Human Capital Theory," 157–162.

20. Richard Vedder, *Going Broke by Degree: Why College Costs Too Much* (Washington, DC: AEI Publishers, 2004), 89–149.

21. Val Burris, "The Social and Political Consequences of Overeducation," *American Sociological Review* 48, no.4 (1983): 454–467.

22. Olaniyan and Okemakinde, "Human Capital Theory," 157–162.

23. Soloman Polachek and Stanley Siebert, *The Economics of Earnings* (Cambridge, MA: Cambridge University Press, 1993), 43; Solomon Polachek, *Earnings Over the Lifecycle: The Mincer*

Earnings Function and Its Applications Discussion paper 3181 (Bonn, Germany: The Institute for the Study of Labor, 2007), 1–111; Jacob Mincer, *Schooling, Experience, and Earnings* (New York: National Bureau of Economic Research, Inc., 1974), 1–167.

24. U.S. Department of Treasury and U.S. Department of Education, *The Economics of Higher Education* (Washington, DC, 2012).

25. See, for example, Phillip Oreopoulos and Kjell Salvanes, "Priceless, the Nonpecuniary Benefits of Schooling," *Journal of Economic Perspectives* 25, no. 1 (2011): 159–184.

26. Cohn and Geske, *Economics of Education*, 1–430.

27. Robert Archibald and David H. Feldman, *Why Does College Cost So Much?* (New York: Oxford University Press, 2011), 41.

28. Walter McMahon, *Higher Learning, Greater Good: The Private and Social Benefits of Higher Education* (Baltimore, MD: Johns Hopkins University Press, 2009), 1–383.

29. Robert Haveman and Barbara Wolfe, "Schooling and Economic Well-Being: The Role of Nonmarket Effects," *Journal of Human Resources* 19, no. 3 (1984): 377–407.

30. McMahon, *Higher Learning, Greater Good*, 118–256.

31. Cohn and Geske, *Economics of Education*, 1–430.

32. McMahon, *Higher Learning, Greater Good*, 126–166.

33. Ibid., 165.

34. Ibid., 156–169.

35. Ibid., 163.

36. Jonathan Gruber, *Public Finance and Public Policy* (New York: Worth, 2011), 293–365.

37. McMahon, *Higher Learning, Greater Good*, 118–121.

38. Ibid., 44.

39. Archibald and Feldman, *Why Does College Cost So Much*, 259.

40. Robert Toutkoushian, "An Economist's Perspective on the Privatization of Public Higher Education," in *Privatizing the Public University: Perspectives from Across the Academy*, ed. Christopher Morphew and Peter Eckel (Baltimore: Johns Hopkins University Press, 2009), 72.

41. Larry R. Faulkner, "The Changing Relationship Between Higher Education and the States" (the 2005 Robert H. Atwell Distinguished Lecture, delivered at the 87th Annual Meeting of the American Council on Education, Washington, DC, 2005).

42. Brian Pusser, "Governance and the Public Good," 13.

43. Cass R. Sunstein, *The Second Bill of Rights: FDR's Unfinished Revolution—and Why We Need It More Than Ever* (New York: Basic, 2006), 186.

44. U.S. Department of Education, National Center of Educational Statistics (Civic Participation by Educational Status, 2012).

45. Inge Kaul, Isabelle Grunberg, and Marc Stern, *Global Public Goods: International Cooperation in the 21st Century* (New York: United Nations Development Programme, 1999), 1–20.

46. Gruber, *Public Finance and Public Policy*, 121–319.

47. Ibid., 121–319.

48. McMahon, *Higher Learning, Greater Good*, 181–256.

49. Ibid.

50. Task Force on Higher Education and Society, "Higher Education in Developing Countries, Peril and Promise: Higher Education and the Public Interest," http://www.tfhe.net/report/Chapter2.htm.

51. McMahon, *Higher Learning, Greater Good*, 181–256.

52. George Psacharopoulos and Harry Anthony Patrinos, "Returns to Investment in Education: A Further Update," *Education Economics* 12, no. 2 (2004): 11–34.

53. Robert Solow, "A Contribution to the Theory of Economic Growth," *Quarterly Journal of Economics* 70, no 1 (1956): 65–94.

54. McMahon, *Higher Learning, Greater Good*, 182.

55. Ibid., 99.

56. Ibid., 225.

57. Larry Leslie and Paul Brinkman, *The Economic Value of Higher Education* (New York: American Council on Education, 1988), 86–103.

58. "Freedom in the World 2012, "Freedom House Index of Political Rights," http://www.huffingtonpost.com/2012/01/23/freedom-house-2012-index_n_1214573.html.

59. Larry Diamond, "Economic Development and Democracy," *American Behavioral Scientist* 35 (1992): 450–99; Christopher Clague, Suzanne Gleason, and Stephen Knack, *Determinants of Lasting Democracy in Poor Countries* (Munich, Germany: Annals of the American Academy of Political and Social Science 1.573, 2001), 16–41; McMahon, *Higher Learning, Greater Good*, 200.

60. McMahon, *Higher Learning, Greater Good*, 200–225.

61. Ibid., 211.

62. Glenn Blomquist et al., "Estimating the Social Value of Higher Education: Willingness to Pay for Community and Technical Colleges Discussion Paper 4086," (Bonn, Germany: The Institute for the Study of Labor, 2009), 8.

63. John F. Helliwell, "Well-Being, Social Capital, and Public Policy: What's New?," *The Economic Journal* 116, no. 510 (2006): 34–45.

64. Gruber, *Public Finance and Public Policy*, 293–365.

65. Ibid., 293–365.

Chapter 4

Some portions of this chapter were written by Christopher A. Bradie and Angelo J. Letizia and used with their permission.

1. Robert Zemsky and William F. Massy, "The Other Side of the Mountain," *Policy Perspectives* 3, no. 2 (1991): 1A–8A.

2. Derek Bok, *Universities in the Marketplace: The Commercialization of Higher Education* (Princeton, NJ: Princeton University Press, 2003), 100.

3. John Patrick Diggins, *Ronald Reagan: Fate, Freedom, and the Making of History* (New York: Norton Publishing, 2007), 326–327; David Harvey, *A Brief History of Neoliberalism* (New York: Oxford Press, 2005), 1–50.

4. Office of Budget and Management, *Enhancing Governmental Productivity Through Competition: A New Way of Doing Business Within the Government to Provide Quality Government at the Least Cost* (Washington, DC: Office of Budget and Management, 1988); Pascale Joassart-Marcell and Juliet Musso, "Municipal Service Provision Choices Within a Metropolitan Area," *Urban Affairs Review* 40 no. 4 (2005), 492–519; Richard Wornthrop, "Privatizing Government Services," *Congressional Quarterly Researcher* 6, (1996): 697–720.

5. Wornthrop, "Privatizing Government Services," 697–720.

6. Walter Brock, *The Privatization of Roads and Highways: Human and Economic Factors* (Auburn, AL: Ludwig Von Mises Institute, 2009), 1–46.

7. Ellen Schweppe, "Legacy of a Landmark: ISTEA After 10 years," *Public Roads* 65, no. 3 (2001), http://www.fhwa.dot.gov/publications/publicroads/01novdec/legacy.cfm.

8. Naomi Klein, *The Shock Doctrine: The Rise of Disaster Capitalism* (New York: Henry Holt and Company, 2007), 409–486.

9. Suzanne Simons, *Master of War: Blackwater USA's Erik Prince and the Business of War* (New York: HarperCollins Publishers, 2009), 7–26.

10. David Shapiro, *Banking on Bondage: Private Prisons and Mass Incarceration* (New York: American Civil Liberties Union Report, 2011), 10–13.

11. Vicky Pelaez, "The Prison Industry in the United States: Big Business or a New Form of Slavery?" *Global Research* 10 (2008), http://www.globalresearch.ca/the-prison-industry-in-the-united-states-big-business-or-a-new-form-of-slavery/8289; Kevin Mathews, "For-Profit Prisons: Eight Statistics That Show the Problems," *Truthout*, December 27, 2013, http://truth-out.org/news/item/20880-for-profit-prisons-eight-statistics-that-show-the-problems.

12. Richard Bartem and Sherry Manning, "Outsourcing in Higher Education: A Business Officer and Business Partner Discuss a Controversial Management Strategy," *Change* 33, no. 1 (2001): 42–47; Jean Marie Angelo, "Is Outsourcing Right for You?" *University Business* 31 (2005): 41–44.

13. Tessa Kaganoff, *Collaboration, Technology, and Outsourcing Initiatives in Higher Education: A Literature Review* (Santa Monica, CA: RAND Corporation, 1998), 14.

14. Richard Palm, "Partnering Through Outsourcing," *New Directions for Student Services* 96 (2001): 5–6.

15. Larry Moneta and William Dillon, "Strategies for Effective Outsourcing," *New Directions for Student Services* 96 (2001): 31–49.

16. Ibid., 33–35.

17. Christopher Bradie, *More Than Just One Breath: Exploring How Three Universities Decided Whether to Outsource Their Campus Bookstores* (dissertation, University of Pennsylvania, 2012), 17; Ronald Phipps and Jamie Merisotis, *Is Outsourcing Part of the Solution to the Higher Education Cost Dilemma: A Preliminary Examination* (Washington, DC: Institute for Higher Education Policy, 2005), 8; Joe Agron, "A Matter of Choice," *American School and University* 72, no. 1 (1999): 8.

18. Robert Zemsky and William F. Massy, "Cost Containment: Committing to a New Economic Reality," *Change* 22, no. 1 (1990): 19–21.

19. Kenneth Ender and Kathleen Mooney, "From Outsourcing to Alliances: Strategies for Sharing Leadership and Exploiting Resources at Metropolitan Universities," *Metropolitan Universities: An International Forum* 5, no. 3 (1994): 51–60.

20. John Pulley, "Whose Bookstore Is It, Anyway?" *Chronicle of Higher Education*, February 4, 2000, http://chronicle.com/article/Whose-Bookstore-Is-It/24007.

21. David Milstone, "Outsourcing Services in Higher Education: Consider the Campus Climate," *The Bulletin: Association of College Unions International* 78, no. 2 (2010): 1–9.

22. Carrie Kerekes, "Privatize It: Outsourcing and Privatization in Higher Education," in *Doing More with Less: Making Colleges Work Better*, ed. Joshua Hall (London, UK: Springer, 2010), 235–248.

23. Agron, "A Matter of Choice," 8; Bradie, *More Than Just One Breath*, 4–18; Kerekes, "Privatize It," 235–248; Milstone, "Outsourcing Services," 1–9.

24. Amy Milshtein, "Are You In or Out?" *College Planning & Management* 13, no. 11 (2010): 24.

25. Larry Dietz and Vicky Triponey, *Serving Students at Metropolitan Universities: The Unique Opportunities and Challenges* (San Francisco: Jossey-Bass Inc., 1997), 35; Joye Mercer, "Contracting Out: Colleges Turn to Private Vendors for Campus Services," *Chronicle of Higher Education*, July 7, 1995, http://chronicle.com/article/Colleges-Turn-to-Private/83835/; Kimberly VanHorn-Grassmeyer and Ken Stoner, "Adventures in Outsourcing," *New Directions in Student Services* 96, no.13 (2001): 13–29; Phipps and Merisotis, *Is Outsourcing Part of the Solution*, 8; Kerekes, "Privatize It," 235–248.

26. Richard Wertz, "Big Business on Campus: Examining the Bottom Line," *Educational Record* 78, no. 1 (1997): 18–24; Bartem and Manning, "Outsourcing in Higher Education," 45; Angelo, "Is Outsourcing Right for You?" 31.

27. This section is adapted and reprinted with permission from Christopher Bradie, 2012.

28. University of Pennsylvania, "Outsourcing the Bookstore: A Barnes & Noble Superstore," *Almanac*, April 30, 1996, http://www.upenn.edu/almanac/v42/n30/super.html.
29. Richard Pérez-Peña, "Ohio State Gets $483 Million Dollar Bid for Parking Lease," *New York Times*, June 4, 2012, www.nytimes.com/2012/06/05/us/ohio-state-gets-483-million-bid-for-parking-lease.html; Jeff McCallister, "Parking Deal, One Year Later," *onCampus: Ohio State's Faculty and Staff News Source*, December 28, 2013, http://oncampus.osu.edu/parking-deal-one-year-later/.
30. Derek Bok, *Universities in the Marketplace*, 44; David Kirp and Patrick Roberts, *Shakespeare, Einstein, and the Bottom Line: The Marketing of Higher Education* (Cambridge, MA: Harvard University Press, 2002), 132–136; Katherine Lyall and Kathleen Sell, "The De Facto Privatization of American Public Higher Education," *Change* 38, no. 1 (2006): 6–13.
31. Steven Jaschik, "Giving Up State Funds," *Inside Higher Ed*, September 7, 2010.
32. "Will UC March Down the Path of Privatization?" *Sacramento Bee*, July 6, 2013, http://blogs.sacbee.com/capitol-alert-insider-edition/2013/06/editorial-will-uc-march-down-path-of-privatization.html.
33. "Plan Gives St. Mary's College More Autonomy, Less Funding," *Baltimore Sun*, March 7, 1992, http://articles.baltimoresun.com/1992-03-07/news/1992067047_1_senate-committees-environmental-affairs-committee-administrative-law-committee.
34. Robert Berdahl and Terrance MacTaggart, "Charter Colleges: Evolution of a Plan," *Connection* 15, no.1 (2000): 37–40; Robert Berdahl and Jeanne Contardo, "The Quasi-Privatization of a Public Honors College," *Planning for Higher Education* 34, no. 4 (2006): 35–48; Peter Blake, "Restructuring Relationships in Virginia: The Changing Compact Between Higher Education and the State," *Change* 38, no. 1 (2006): 26–33.
35. Sharif Durhams, "UW–Madison Chancellor Says Plan to Split from UW System Unlikely," *Milwaukee-Wisconsin Journal-Sentinel*, May 27, 2011, http://www.jsonline.com/news/education/122730424.html.
36. Doug Lederman, "Flexibility—But For (and From) Whom?" *Inside Higher Ed*, February 28, 2011; Tamar Lewin, "Public Universities Seek More Autonomy as Financing from State Shrinks," *New York Times*, March 2, 2011, http://www.nytimes.com/2011/03/03/education/03colleges.html; Jack Stripling, "Flagships Just Want to Be Left Alone," *Chronicle of Higher Education*, March 13, 2011, https://chronicle.com/article/Flagships-Just-Want-to-Be/126696/; Jane Wellman and Charles Reed, "Mend, Don't End, State Systems," *Inside Higher Ed*, March 28, 2011; Goldie Blumenstyk, "U of Oregon's $1.6 Billion Proposal: An Endowment Instead of Appropriations," *Chronicle of Higher Education,* May 12, 2010, https://chronicle.com/article/U-of-Oregons-16-Billion/65498/; Doug Lederman, "Agreement in Oregon (for Now)," *Inside Higher Ed*, April 1, 2011.
37. Michael Redding, "Autonomy Policy in U.S. Public Higher Education: A Comparative Case Study of Oregon and Virginia" (doctoral dissertation, University of Pennsylvania, 2009), 47–98.
38. Ibid., 72.
39. Craig Calhoun, "The Public Good as a Social and Cultural Project," in *Private Action and the Public Good,* ed. Walter Powell and Elizabeth Clemens (New Haven, CT: Yale University Press, 1998), 3–20; Jane Mansbridge, "On the Contested Nature of the Public Good," in *Private Action and the Public Good,* ed. Walter Powell and Elizabeth Clemens (New Haven, CT: Yale University Press, 1998), 20–36.
40. Marian Wang, "Breaking Away: Top Public Universities Push for 'Autonomy' from States," *Huffington Post*, October 13, 2013.
41. University of Oregon, "President Gottfredson Testifies Before Legislators," April 4, 2012, http://uoregon.edu/president-gottfredson-testifies-legislators.

42. Relating to the Establishment of Institutional Boards for Public Universities in the Oregon University System; Declaring an Emergency, OR, Rev. Stat. Ann. SB 270 (passed August 14, 2013).

43. Kevin Kiley, "What Will $10,000 Get Me?," *Chronicle Higher Ed*, May 9, 2012; Steve Kolowich, "The $10,000 Question," *Chronicle Higher Ed*, February 14, 2011; Meredith Moriak, "UTPB Introduces $10K Science Degrees," *Midland Reporter-Telegram*, May 2, 2012.

44. Ben Jongbloed and Jos Koelman, *Vouchers for Higher Education?* (Hong Kong: Center Higher Education Policy Studies, 2000), 1–39.

45. Henry Levin, "Educational Vouchers: Effectiveness, Choice, and Costs," *Journal of Policy Analysis and Management* 17, no. 3 (1998): 373–392.

46. Henry Levin and Cyrus Driver, "Costs of an Educational Voucher System," *Education Economics* 5 (1997): 265–283.

47. Courtney McSwain, *Window of Opportunity: Targeting Federal Grant Aid to Students with the Lowest Incomes* (Washington, DC: Institute of Higher Education, 2008), 1–2.

48. Henry Giroux and Christopher Robbins, *The Giroux Reader* (New York: Paradigm Publishers, 2006), 230.

49. Richard Peet, *Unholy Trinity: The IMF, World Bank, and WTO* (New York: Zed Books, 2009), 1–26; Angelo Letizia, "Battle for the Enlightenment: Neoliberalism, Critical Theory, and the Role of Circumvential Education in Fostering a New Phase of the Enlightenment," *Journal for Critical Education Policy Studies* 11, no. 3 (2013): 172–175.

50. Shelia Slaughter and Gary Rhoades, *Academic Capitalism and the New Economy: Markets, State, and Higher Education* (Baltimore: Johns Hopkins University Press, 2004), 1–20.

51. Johan Overtvelt, *The Chicago School: How the University of Chicago Assembled the Thinkers Who Revolutionized Economics and Business* (Evanston, IL: Agate Publishing, 2007), 1–24; Harvey, *Brief History of Neoliberalism*, 75.

52. James Jacobs, "The Colorado Voucher System: Will It Help or Hurt Public Higher Education?" *Change* 38, no. 1(2005): 55–59.

53. Jacobs, "Colorado Voucher System," 55–59; Brian Prescott, "Is Colorado's Voucher System Worth Vouching For?" *Change* 38, no. 1 (2010): 20–26.

54. Dean Dad, "Thoughts on Vouchers," *Inside Higher Ed*, May 11, 2012.

55. Prescott, "Colorado's Voucher System," 20–26.

56. Slaughter and Rhoades, *Academic Capitalism*, 1–20; Robert Rhodes and Carlos Torres, *University, State, and Market: The Political Economy of Globalization in the Americas* (Palo Alto, CA: University of Stanford Press, 2006), 3–38.

57. Joseph Burke, "The Many Faces of Accountability," in *Achieving Accountability in Higher Education*, ed. Joseph Burke (San Francisco: Jossey-Bass, 2005), 1–24; William Zumeta, "What Does It Mean to Be Accountable? Dimensions and Implications of Higher Education's Public Accountability," *Review of Higher Education* 35, no. 1 (2011): 131–148; King Alexander, "The Changing Face of Accountability: Monitoring and Assessing Institutional Performance in Higher Education," *Journal of Higher Education* 71, no. 4 (2000): 411–431; Jane Wellman, "Rethinking State Governance of Higher Education," in *Governance and the Public Good*, ed. William Tierney (Albany, NY: SUNY Press, 2006), 51–67.

58. Kysie Miao, *Performance-Based Funding of Higher Education: A Detailed Look at Best Practices in 6 States* (New York: Center for American Progress, 2012), 1–2.

59. Slaughter and Rhoades, *Academic Capitalism*, 1–20.

60. Doug Lederman, "The Skinny on Sports Spending," *Inside Higher Ed*, December 4, 2013, http://www.insidehighered.com/news/2013/12/04/new-database-allows-users-compare-sports-and-academic-spending#ixzz2osbt9NKm.

61. Gerda Lerner, "Corporatizing Higher Education," *The History Teacher* 41, (2008): 219–227.

62. Robert Rhoads and Carlos Torres, *University, State, and Market: The Political Economy of Globalization in the Americas* (Palo Alto: Stanford University Press, 2006), 1–18.

63. Jennifer Washburn, *University Inc.: The Corporate Corruption of Higher Education* (New York: Basic Books, 2005), 73–102.

64. Government Accountability Office, *Performance and Accountability Report* (Washington, DC: Government Accountability Office, 2008); Higher Education Opportunity Act of 2008, Public Law 115-310, 2008.

65. Mary Jo Maydew, "Assessing Non-Instructional Costs and Productivity," *New Directions for Institutional Research* 19, (1992): 49.

66. Ender and Mooney, "From Outsourcing to Alliances," 51–60; Richard Wertz, *Outsourcing and Privatization of Campus Services: An Overview and Guide for College and University Administrators* (Charlottesville, VA: National Association of College Auxiliary Services, 2003), 5; Kerekes, "Privatize It," 235–238.

67. Olin Adams et al., "A Comparison of Outsourcing in Higher Education, 1998–99 and 2003–04," *Journal of Educational Research & Policy Studies* 4, no. 2 (2004): 98.

68. David L. Kirp, "Higher Ed Inc.: Avoiding the Perils of Outsourcing," *Chronicle of Higher Education*, March 15, 2002, http://chronicle.com/article/Higher-Ed-Inc-Avoiding-the/7711.

69. Henry Giroux, "Neoliberalism, Corporate Culture, and the Promise of Higher Education: The University as a Democratic Public Sphere," *Harvard Educational Review* 72, no. 4 (2002): 446.

70. David L. Kirp, *Shakespeare, Einstein, and the Bottom Line: The Marketing of Higher Education* (Cambridge, MA: Harvard University Press, 2003), 113; Milstone, "Outsourcing Services," 1–9; Zemsky and Massy, "The Other Side of the Mountain," 1A–8A.

Chapter 5

1. Thomas Jefferson's letter to Joseph Priestly, 1800, excerpted from Julian Boyd et al., *The Papers of Thomas Jefferson* (Princeton, NJ: Princeton University Press, 1950).

2. State Council for Higher Education in Virginia, *Making Connections: Matching Virginia Higher Education's Strategies with the Commonwealth's Needs.* Richmond: Commission on the Future of Higher Education, 1989, 35.

3. Virginia State Government, *The Governor's Blue Ribbon Commission on Higher Education* (Richmond: Office of the Governor, 2000), 98; Dumas Malone, *Jefferson and His Time: The Sage of Monticello* (Boston: Little Brown and Company).

4. State Council for Higher Education in Virginia, *Making Connections*, 23, 27–28.

5. Ibid., 2–3.

6. Virginia State Government, *Governor's Blue Ribbon Commission*, 48.

7. Gordon Davies, *Twenty Years of Higher Education in Virginia* (Charlottesville, VA: State Council for Higher Education in Virginia, 1997), 2.

8. State Council for Higher Education in Virginia, *Making Connections*, 30.

9. Ibid., 1.

10. Governor's Commission on Higher Education Reform, Innovation and Investment, "Preparing for the Top Jobs of the 21st Century" (report), December 20, 2010.

11. Ibid., 14; Virginia General Assembly, *Budget for 2010–2012 Biennium* (Richmond: Virginia Department of Planning and Budget, 2012).

12. Governor's Commission on Higher Education Reform, Innovation and Investment, "Preparing for the Top Jobs," 57.

13. Ibid., 13.

14. University of Virginia, "Six Year Graduation Rates," http://avillage.web.virginia.edu/iaas/instreports/studat/hist/gradrates/rate6_by_gender.htm.

15. University of Virginia, "Research by the Numbers," http://www.virginia.edu/vpr.

16. David Leslie and Robert Berdahl, "The Politics of Restructuring Higher Education in Virginia: A Case Study," *Review of Higher Education* 31, no. 3 (2008): 315.

17. Virginia General Assembly, *Budget for 2010–2012 Biennium*.

18. Governor's Commission on Higher Education Reform, Innovation and Investment, "Preparing for the Top Jobs," 19.

19. Virginia General Assembly, *Two-Year Review of Initial Higher Education Management Agreements* (Richmond: Joint Legislative Audit and Review Commission, 2008), 70.

Chapter 6

1. North Carolina state constitution, article 9, sections 8–9.

2. Holden Thorpe, "Inauguration Speech" (University of North Carolina, Chapel Hill, NC, October 12, 2008).

3. William Powell, Encyclopedia of North Carolina (Chapel Hill: University of North Carolina Press, 2006), 4; North Carolina state constitution of 1776, article XLI, 15 (as printed in Powell).

4. Ibid., 4.

5. Annette Cox and Jason Tomberlin, *The Carolina Story: A Virtual Museum of University History* (Chapel Hill: University of North Carolina at Chapel Hill; Center for the Study of the American South, 2007).

6. Numan V. Bartley, *The New South, 1945–1980: The Story of the South's Modernization* (Baton Rouge: Louisiana State University Press, 1995).

7. University of North Carolina System, "About Our System," http://www.northcarolina.edu/?q=content/about-our-system.

8. University of North Carolina System, "Our Mission," http://www.northcarolina.edu/?q=about-our-system/our-mission.

9. Delta Cost Project, "University of Virginia, UNC–Chapel Hill, and UC Berkeley Funding per Student Comparison" (table), accessed April 9, 2014.

10. *US News and World Report*, "Best Colleges," http://colleges.usnews.rankingsandreviews.com/best-colleges; *Kiplinger*, "Best Values in Public Colleges, 2014," http://portal.kiplinger.com/article/college/T014-C000-S002-best-values-in-public-colleges-2014.html; *Peterson's*, "College Bound," http://www.petersons.com/.

11. Mary Ruth, "General Assembly Establishes University Cancer Research Fund at UNC," *UNC Cancer Care*, October 12, 2011, http://unclineberger.org/news/2011-news/general-assembly-establishes-ucrf.

12. Joe Lapchick, "Dean Smith and a Civil Rights Legacy," ESPN, May 17, 2011, http://sports.espn.go.com/espn/commentary/news/story?page=lapchick/110517; Carolyn R. Mahoney, "The Institutions in African American and American Life," in *Precipice or Crossroads*, ed. Daniel Fogel and Elizabeth Malsom-Huddle (Albany, NY: SUNY Press, 2012), 17–50; D. G. Martin, "William C. Friday, University of North Carolina Leader, Dies at 92," *New York Times*, October 13, 2012, http://www.nytimes.com/2012/10/14/education/william-c-friday-university-of-north-carolina-president-dies-at-92.html?_r=0.

13. Maximillian Longley, *Speaker Ban Law* (Chapel Hill: North Carolina History Project, 2014).

14. Michael Walden, *Economic Benefits in North Carolina of the University of North Carolina Campuses* (Raleigh: North Carolina State University, 2009), 1–2, https://www.northcarolina.edu/sites/default/files/documents/unc_economic_impact_-_walden.pdf; Rick Weddle, Elizabeth Rooks, and Tina Valdeconas, "Research Triangle Park: Evolution and Renaissance" (paper

presented at the International Association of Science Parks World Conference, Helsinki, Finland, June 2006).

15. North Carolina Community College System, "Get the Facts," http://www.nccommunitycolleges.edu/.

16. James Johnson, Jr., *Implications for Our State and the University of North Carolina: North Carolina's Higher Education Demographic Challenges* (Chapel Hill: University of North Carolina at Chapel Hill, Kenan-Flagler Business School, 2007), 3.

17. Rep. Paul Stam, personal conversation with author, August 23, 2011.

18. Kevin Kiley, "Another Liberal Arts Critic," *Inside Higher Ed*, January 30, 2013, http://www.insidehighered.com/news/2013/01/30/north-carolina-governor-joins-chorus-republicans-critical-liberal-arts.

19. University of North Carolina, *2013–15 Budget Priorities of the Board of Governors: The University of North Carolina* (Chapel Hill: University of North Carolina, 2013).

20. Michael Vollmer, "Tuition Bill Statement" (memo), University of North Carolina, June 27, 2013.

21. http://www.citizensforhighered.org/.

22. Frank Porter Graham, "Inauguration Speech" (speech, University of North Carolina, Chapel Hill, NC, November 11, 1931).

23. University of North Carolina Tomorrow Commission, "Final Report" (December 2007), 2, http://old.northcarolina.edu/nctomorrow/reports/commission/Final_Report.pdf.

24. Thorpe, "Inauguration Speech."

Chapter 7

1. Thomas Jefferson's letter to George Wythe in 1786, from The Works of Thomas Jefferson, Federal Edition, vol. 5 (New York: G.P. Putnam's Sons, 1904–1905).

2. Clark Kerr, *The Uses of the University* (Cambridge, MA: Harvard University Press, 1963), 36.

3. John A. Douglass, *The California Idea and American Higher Education: 1850–1960 Master Plan* (Stanford, CA: Stanford Press, 2000); Patrick Callan, *California Higher Education, The Master Plan, and the Erosion of College Opportunity* (San Jose, CA: National Center for Public Policy and Higher Education, 2009).

4. John A. Douglass, *From Chaos to Order and Back? A Revisionist Reflection on the California Master Plan for Higher Education @50 and Thoughts About Its Future* (Berkeley, CA: Center for Studies in Higher Education 7.10, 2010), 14.

5. Carnegie Foundation for the Advancement of Teaching, Commission of Seven, *State Higher Education in California* (Sacramento, CA: California State Printing Office, 1932).

6. Clark Kerr, *The Gold and Blue: Academic Triumphs* (Berkeley: University of California Press, 2001), 71–89.

7. Douglass, *The California Idea,* 170–223.

8. Steven Brint and John Karabel, *The Diverted Dream: Community Colleges and the Promise of Educational Opportunity in America, 1900–1985* (New York: Oxford University Press, 1989), 1–20.

9. John Patrick Diggins, *Ronald Reagan: Fate, Freedom, and the Making of History* (New York: W. W. Norton and Company, 2007), 301.

10. Anthony Fischel, "Did *Serrano* Cause Proposition 13?" *National Tax Journal* 42, no. 4 (1989): 470.

11. Ibid., 471.

12. Arthur O'Sullivan, *Property Taxes and Tax Revolts: The Legacy of Proposition 13* (New York: Cambridge University Press, 1995), 45–48; Terri Sexton, Steven Sheffrin, and Arthur O'Sullivan, "Proposition 13: Unintended Effects and Feasible Reforms," *National Tax Journal* 52, no. 1 (1999): 100; Diggins, *Ronald Reagan,* 245.

13. Chuck Spence, *Proposition 98 & California Community Colleges: A History of Broken Promises* (San Pablo, CA: Contra Costa College, 2002), 5–12; Anthony Davis, "The Importance of Workforce Training in Community Colleges: A Case Study on the Discourse and Best Practices During Financial Difficulty" (dissertation, California State University, 2013), 20.
14. "Official Voter Information Guide, Prop. 36 Pros and Cons," *Official Voter Information Guide of California Website*, http://www.smartvoter.org/2012/11/06/ca/state/prop/36/; Frank Stoltze, "New Battle Over 3 Strikes Law Looms," *California Public Radio Website*, December 16, 2011, http://www.scpr.org/news/2011/12/16/30368/new-battle-over-three-strikes-looms/.
15. Anand Prema, *Winners and Losers: Corrections and Higher Education in California* (Los Altos: California Common Sense, 2012), 1.
16. Paul Zingg, "Any Direction Home for California's Master Plan," *Liberal Education* (Summer 2010): 60–64.
17. Roger Geiger, "The Rise and Fall of Useful Knowledge: Higher Education for Science, Agriculture & the Mechanics Arts, 1850–1875," *History of Higher Education Annual* 18, (1998): 58; John Thelin, *A History of American Higher Education* (Baltimore: Johns Hopkins Press, 2004).
18. University of California, Office of the President, "Master Plan," University of California, Office of the President, accessed January 3, 2014, http://www.ucop.edu/academic-personnel/programs-and-initiatives/faculty-resources-advancement/faculty-handbook-sections/master-plan.html.
19. Christopher Newfield, *Unmaking the Public University: The Forty-Year Assault on the Middle Class* (Cambridge, MA: Harvard University Press, 2008), 120.
20. Levin, 57; Douglass, *From Chaos to Order and Back?*, 14.

Chapter 8

1. Robert Gates, "Charter Day Remarks" (speech, The College of William & Mary, Williamsburg, VA, February 8, 2013).
2. Bruce Johnstone, "Privatization in and of Higher Education" (unpublished report, Project for Research on Private Higher Education, SUNY Buffalo, Buffalo, NY, 2002).
3. Simon Marginson and Gary Rhoades, "Beyond Nation States, Markets, and Systems of Higher Education: A Glonacal Agency Heuristic," *Higher Education* 43, no. 3 (2002): 289.
4. Gates, "Charter Day Remarks."
5. In addition to the Obama 2020 Challenge, the Lumina Foundation has set a similar goal to be reached by 2025 and is tracking the progress in the states. You can see state and district-level data on college achievement at http://www.luminafoundation.org/stronger_nation/report/.
6. John Immerwahr, Jean Johnson, and Paul Gasbarra, "The Iron Triangle: College Presidents Talk About Costs, Access, and Quality" (San Jose, CA: National Center for Public Policy and Higher Education and Public Agenda, 2008), 10.

Chapter 9

1. Thomas Jefferson's Sixth Annual Message to Congress, 1806.
2. Henry David Thoreau, "A Week on the Concord and Merrimack Rivers" in *The Writings of Henry David Thoreau, vol. 1* (New York: Houghton Mifflin, 1906), 132–133.
3. Robert Zemsky, *Making Reform Work: The Case for Transforming American Higher Education* (Piscataway, NJ: Rutgers University Press, 2009), 107–125.
4. Thomas Friedman, "Hope and Change Part Two," *New York Times*, November 7, 2012, http://www.nytimes.com/2012/11/07/opinion/friedman-hope-and-change-part-two.html?ref=thomaslfriedman&_r=0.

5. Richard Vedder, *Going Broke by Degree: Why College Costs Too Much* (Washington, DC: AEI Publishers, 2004), 52.

6. Laura Pappano, "The Year of the MOOC," *New York Times*, November 2, 2012, http://www.nytimes.com/2012/11/04/education/edlife/massive-open-online-courses-are-multiplying-at-a-rapid-pace.html?pagewanted=all&_r=0.

7. Simon Marginson, "Making Space in Higher Education," in *Global Creation: Space, Mobility and Synchrony in the Age of the Knowledge Economy*, ed. Simon Marginson, Peter Murphy, and Michael Peters (New York: Peter Lang, 2010), 181.

8. Mark Yudof, "Higher Tuitions: Harbinger of a Hybrid University?" *Change* 34, no. 2 (2002): 16.

9. Saul Geiser and Richard C. Atkinson, *Beyond the Master Plan: The Case for Restructuring Baccalaureate Education in California* (Los Angeles: The Civil Rights Project, 2010).

10. Tamar Lewin, "California Bill Seeks Campus Credit for Online Study," *New York Times*, March 12, 2013, http://www.nytimes.com/2013/03/13/education/california-bill-would-force-colleges-to-honor-online-classeshtml?pagewanted=all.

11. For further reading about MOOCs, technology, and how the future of higher education is changing and will continue to do so, I recommend Jeffrey J. Selingo, *College (Un)bound: The Future of Higher Education and What It Means for Students* (New York: New Harvest, 2013) and Salman Khan, *The One World School House: Education Reimagined* (London: Hodder & Stoughton, 2012). The Khan Academy, in particular, is a remarkable example of how technology has completely changed how students learn math and other subjects (see http://www.khanacademy.org to explore).

12. Robert Zemsky and Joni Finney, "Changing the Subject: Costs Graduation Rates and the Importance of Re-thinking the Undergraduate Curriculum," *National Crosstalk*, May 2010, http://www.highereducation.org/crosstalk/ct0510/voices0510-zemfin.shtml.

13. Association of American Colleges (AAC). *Integrity in the College Curriculum: A Report to the Academic Community.* Washington, DC: Association of American Colleges, 1985.

14. Colleen Flaherty, "Wisconsin Faculty Object to the Idea that Shared Governance Should Change," *Inside Higher Ed*, September 9, 2013, http://www.insidehighered.com/news/2013/09/09/wisconsin-faculty-object-idea-shared-governance-should-change.

15. Robert Gates, "Charter Day Remarks" (speech, The College of William & Mary, Williamsburg, VA, February 8, 2013).

16. Robert Birgeneau, Seth Garz, and Frank Yeary, *Knowledge Made in America: A Private-Public Funding Model for Leading Public Research Universities* (Berkeley: University of California, 2012), 1–5; Paul Courant, James Duderstadt, and Edie Goldenberg, "Needed: A National Strategy to Preserve Public Research Universities," *Chronicle of Higher Education*, January 3, 2010, http://chronicle.com/article/A-Plan-to-Save-Americas/63358/.; James Duderstadt, "A Master Plan for Higher Education in the Midwest: A Roadmap to the Future of the Nation's Heartland," in *Heartland Papers* 3 (2011): 21–29; Mark Yudof, *Exploring a New Role for the Federal Government in Higher Education* (Oakland: University of California, 2009), 1–10.

17. Birgeneau, Garz and Yeary, *Knowledge Made in America*, 1–5; Yudof, *Exploring a New Role*, 1–10.

18. Neal Johnson, *Balancing Act: Public Higher Education in Transition* (Washington, DC: State Governance Action Annual Report, Association of Governing Boards of Universities and Colleges, 2004), 1–39; Birgeneau, Garz, and Yeary, *Knowledge Made in America*, 1–5.

ACKNOWLEDGMENTS

This book was inspired by a deep desire to understand more clearly and to share how public colleges and universities are balancing institutional interests with the larger public good in an era of diminishing public support. As a product of one private and two public research universities, I have seen firsthand the impact that these institutions can have on an individual, the local community, a state, the nation, and the wider world. My hope is that this book will help spur the conversation between the higher education and policy-making communities, as well as inform the public more broadly about why and how higher education is evolving.

Through my research for this book, I learned three important lessons about public higher education and would like to acknowledge some of those who helped teach these lessons. First, the public agenda—a broader perspective on what higher education can and should be achieving—is paramount in any discussion of the future of public higher education. Joni E. Finney taught me many important lessons along this journey that opened my eyes to how the public agenda often trumps an individual institution's ambitions. Second, good research—seeking truth and knowledge about a topic as important as public higher education—should not be taken lightly, and we achieve it only by persistently asking deep questions, rigorously challenging hypotheses, and relentlessly focusing on avoiding biases and the status quo. Robert M. Zemsky taught me, in a way that only he can, the methods, meaning, importance, and value of good research. Third, there are a number of world-class public universities, and these institutions are worth fighting for because they are national treasures. They cannot be allowed to wither and must be treated with the same care and attention that we devote to other national landmarks. These special places are the people's universities. James J. Duderstadt reminded me that we must stand up for these great public universities, and he remains a wise voice of leadership in higher education.

I would like to thank and acknowledge the many colleagues, first at Georgetown University and then at the College of William & Mary, who supported me throughout the research and writing of this book. Georgetown's then Provost James J. O'Donnell—a true scholar and my frequent business travel partner—served as a reader of several drafts and offered helpful feedback and encouragement along the way as a sage voice about all things academia. W. Taylor Reveley III, president of William & Mary, was supportive and encouraging in helping me get this book completed, even as I was just beginning a new administrative role. Our frequent, priceless conversations about the evolution of public universities helped shape my understanding of the role of politics and the public in higher education.

During the course of the research and writing of this book, several higher education leaders and policy experts were generous in reading portions of the manuscript and providing critical feedback, offering insight about a state or an institution, or generally helped me dig more deeply into the issues. Patrick Callan, David Breneman, Gordon Davies, David Feldman, Robert Archibald, Timothy Sullivan, and Matthew Hartley were each in their own way part of shaping this book.

There were several extremely talented students who worked with me as research assistants. Jason Ilieve and Priyanka Bagrodia signed up for the seminar I taught at Georgetown's School of Foreign Service and were part of the earliest incarnations of this book as I tested portions of it in class; both helped enormously with the research. Janak "Arjun" Upadhyay was a tremendous contributor to my own economic understanding and in finding new ways of explaining the value of higher education. At William & Mary, Kelly Hench assisted with editing and tracking down data, and Angelo Letizia was a great asset in the later stages of the book's development. Among many other things, Angelo helped develop my own understanding of the topic of performance-based funding.

Several talented editors assisted with this book. Louise Lambert Kale tackled several chapters in an early stage, and later Jonathan Wallace clarified some of my own thinking after I'd stared at the pages for far too long. My wife, Karen, spent many late nights and early mornings reading and editing every single page. Any remaining mistakes in this manuscript are my own.

Christopher Bradie, an exceptionally talented scholar, helped significantly with the topics of outsourcing and contracting. He was always a terrific sounding board and was truly helpful at bringing concepts in formation into clearer focus. Jeremy Martin is a master of data and a first-rate researcher who helped to quantify the qualitative research with the development and refinement of many of the charts and tables in the book. Karen Ferguson kept me organized during the most intense period of research and travel and helped design the model of "foundations of privatization" after making sense of my sketches.

Douglas Clayton, executive director at Harvard Education Press, was an early and enthusiastic supporter of this book and saw its potential as part of the national conversation about the future of public higher education. I am appreciative of his help, along with that of his many colleagues at Harvard.

Finally, those most deserving of acknowledgment are my friends and family, who encouraged and supported me from the earliest points when I expressed a deep interest in issues of higher education public policy. This book is the product of many conversations with many people over the years, and I am grateful to all of them. My parents—Carol and Charles—and grandparents, in particular, sacrificed greatly to send me to college and believed that higher education was critical to formation and success. For that, I shall always be thankful. My mother-in-law, Kathleen, has helped and supported me throughout this adventure.

My wife, Karen, was the motivation for my pursuing this research, as well as the reason I was able to undertake this effort. She fully and lovingly cared for our two boys while I was away so many early mornings and late nights. I will always be grateful to her for the many sacrifices she made and for her example to me of what is most important in life. Our two sweet boys, who inspired, motivated, cheered, and loved me throughout this journey, always made me smile. William, so full of wonder and love, and Harrison, a blessing of smiles and laughter who joined us in the middle of this adventure, give my life new meaning each day, and they give me great hope and excitement for the future. Karen—my best friend, my loving wife, and my adventure partner—has always given so much of herself for our family and me. She, above anyone else in this world, has given me the greatest gifts for a lifetime and deserves equal credit for this book.

ABOUT THE AUTHOR

MATTHEW T. LAMBERT is the Vice President for University Advancement at The College of William & Mary, where he also teaches undergraduate and graduate students in public policy and education. Prior to working at William & Mary, he managed multiple areas of university advancement at Georgetown University, where he also taught in the Walsh School of Foreign Service.

Dr. Lambert received his bachelor's degree from William & Mary, his master's degree from The Ohio State University, and his doctorate from the University of Pennsylvania. His research interests center on the changing landscape of American higher education, where new models of public and private support will shape educational institutions in the century ahead. He lives in Williamsburg, Virginia, with his wife and two sons.

INDEX

public higher education (*continued*)
  economic value of (*see* economic
    value of higher education)
  enrollment numbers, 14
  erosion in society's valuation of edu-
    cation as a public good, 77
  essential challenge in, 7
  history of being viewed as a public
    good, 13–14
  interplay between enrollment, fund-
    ing, and tuition, 14–15
  layered elements in the privatization
    discussions, 18–19
  legislators' belief that institutions
    are serving the public good,
    262–264
  missions of, 24
  national appropriations for, 11, 12
  need for a public dialogue on public
    policy, 7–8
  notion of public goods and, 78,
    79–80, 106
  public interest defined, 19–20
  relationship with the state, 14, 15–16
  research role of public universities,
    15
  shift in the commitment to the public
    good by public universities,
    264
  shift in the view of who benefits from
    higher education, 44, 45–46,
    59–60, 61
  social compact between citizens and
    public universities, 27–28,
    30–31, 77
  societal and individual benefits,
    62–63
  state context and, 19, 20, 21–23 (*see
    also individual states*)
  tension between institutional priori-
    ties and public purposes, 24–26
public-private model
  challenge of sustaining a belief in the
    public purpose, 283–284
  challenges and opportunities ahead,
    269–270, 284–285
  consequences from expansion of the
    curriculum, 279–280
  current public purpose of higher
    education, 270–271
  diminishing distinctions between
    public and private institutions,
    275–276
  disconnect between university leaders
    and state politicians, 271–273
  factors influencing changes, 268
  federal philanthropic matching pro-
    gram potential, 282
  "flipping" courses, 278
  hybrid model of university centers,
    278
  key elements, 283
  legacy of higher education, 267
  main focus areas in reform of higher
    education, 268–269
  national public universities model,
    55, 281
  need for non-traditional thinking,
    280
  need for universities to communicate
    the value of higher education,
    273–275
  room for creativity and innovation,
    276–279
  technology's increasing role, 277–278
  views of tuition levels, 280–281
public-private partnerships. *See also*
    finance and higher education
  accountability as framed by policy
    makers, 117–118
  co-branding partnerships examples,
    101–102
  collaborative outsourcing examples,
    102
  complete outsourcing examples, 101,
    102
  cost reduction challenge in some
    states, 107–109